"Practical, focused, specific, detailed. It doesn't get any better than this! If you are looking for a case study in supporting and leveraging communities of practice for business success, this is it. Saint-Onge and Wallace have created an indispensable guide for increasing knowledge sharing and learning across the organization."

> —**Verna Allee**, author, *The Knowledge Evolution* and *The Future of Knowledge*

"Clarica Life Insurance is one of the most admired knowledge enterprises in the world. Here is the inside scoop on how Clarica is creating business value by sharing knowledge through its online communities. Hubert Saint-Onge, Canada's best known KM strategist, and Deb Wallace, community builder par excellence, have written an engaging practitioner's guide on how to develop communities of practice as forums for learning and knowledge sharing."

> —**Chun Wei Choo, Ph.D.**, Associate Professor, Faculty of Information Studies, University of Toronto; co-author, *Strategic Management of Intellectual Capital and Organizational Knowledge*, author, *The Knowing Organization*

"This book is so valuable because it is intellectually stimulating, and at the same time, it's chock full of practical advice. Through their success at Clarica, Hubert Saint-Onge and Deb Wallace have risen above all of the chatter about collaboration and have given us a best-of-breed primer for people who want to get results from communities of practice."

> —**Diane Hessan**, President & CEO of Communispace Corporation; author, *Customer-Centered Growth: 5 Strategies for Building Competitive Advantage*

"With a wealth of practical experience to augment their insightful case study analyses, Saint-Onge and Wallace compellingly demonstrate how communities of practice foster learning and facilitate knowledge sharing to add value to an organization and enhance its competitive advantage."

> —**Lynne C. Howarth, Ph.D.**, Associate Professor & Dean, Faculty of Information Studies, University of Toronto

"Hubert Saint-Onge and Deb Wallace point us to the undeniable core foundation of knowledge management—that it is, first and foremost, a collaborative and uniquely human activity. Their book goes beyond a simple focus on technology to provide a wealth of strategies and tools for the more challenging, and ultimately more valuable, work of engaging people directly in the creation and use of knowledge."

> —**Marc J. Rosenberg, Ph.D.,** Senior Director, Diamond Cluster International; author, *E-Learning: Strategies for Delivering Knowledge in the Digital Age*

"Many people talk about communities of practice, but few actually know how to make them thrive and grow! In this book, Hubert Saint-Onge and Deb Wallace generously share their years of experience, from the strategic conceptual plane to the tactical implementation process. It is an essential companion to anyone seriously considering communities in an organizational setting."

> —**Eric E. Vogt**, Founder and Director, Communispace Corporation; CEO, the Interclass Network

"In spite of the billions of dollars we spend on training every year, we now know that most adult learning happens person-to-person and by actively applying new ideas. Communities of practice stimulate and support the type of learning that leads to innovation and better results. This book is a gold mine for understanding how to stimulate and support communities of practice."

> —**Joyce Wycoff**, Co-Founder, InnovationNetwork

LEVERAGING COMMUNITIES OF PRACTICE FOR STRATEGIC ADVANTAGE

LEVERAGING COMMUNITIES OF PRACTICE FOR STRATEGIC ADVANTAGE

HUBERT SAINT-ONGE
DEBRA WALLACE

An Imprint of Elsevier
Amsterdam • Boston • London • New York • Oxford • Paris • San Diego
San Francisco • Singapore • Sydney • Tokyo

Recognizing the importance of preserving what has been written, Elsevier prints its books on acid-free paper whenever possible.

Library of Congress Cataloging-in-Publication Data

A catalog record for this book is available from the Library of Congress.

ISBN-13: 978-0-7506-7458-4

ISBN-10: 0-7506-7458-X

British Library Cataloguing-in-Publication Data

A catalogue record for this book is available from the British Library.

The publisher offers special discounts on bulk orders of this book.

For information, please contact:

Manager of Special Sales
Elsevier
200 Wheeler Road
Burlington, MA 01803
Tel: 781-313-4700
Fax: 781-313-4880

For information on all Butterworth-Heinemann publications available, contact our World Wide Web home page at: http://www.bh.com

10 9 8 7 6 5 4

Printed in the United States of America

To Norma and our kids,
Danielle, Jacqueline, David, and Alain

—HSO

To Ian

—DW

TABLE OF CONTENTS

ACKNOWLEDGMENTS, XV

INTRODUCTION, XIX

Part I: Setting the Context for Communities of Practice   1

CHAPTER 1–INCREASING CAPABILITIES IN THE KNOWLEDGE-DRIVEN ORGANIZATION   3

Creating Value: Assets in the Knowledge Era, 3

Managing Intangible Assets—The Knowledge Capital Model, 9

New Strategies: Communities of Practice, 12

The Knowledge Capital Initiative: Clarica's Knowledge
  Management Strategy, 13

Clarica's Knowledge Strategy, 14

Goals of The Knowledge Capital Initiative, 19

The Strategic Capabilities Unit: Clarica's Organizational Structure in
  Support of Knowledge Strategies, 21

Conclusion, 24

Knowledge Capital in Your Organization—Will It Play in Peoria?, 24

References, 26

CHAPTER 2–COMMUNITIES OF PRACTICE: HIGH-TRUST VESSELS FOR INCREASING CAPABILITIES   27

Knowledge Management Overview, 27

Defining Communities of Practice, 32

Characteristics of Communities of Practice, 34

Communities of Practice Situated in a Strategic Context, 40

Community Life Cycles, 47

Benefits of Communities of Practice, 49

Conclusion, 50

Communities at Work in Your Organization—Will It Play in Peoria?, 51

References, 52

CHAPTER 3–SITUATING COMMUNITIES OF PRACTICE IN A STRATEGIC CONTEXT   55

The New Strategic Context, 55

The Relationship of Communities of Practice to Strategy, 59

Communities of Practice as a Vehicle for Creating
    Competitive Advantage, 61

Communities of Practice in the Context of an Enterprise-Wide
    Knowledge and Learning Strategy, 63

The Business Case for Communities of Practice, 68

The Strategic Nature of Communities at Clarica, 70

Conclusion, 74

Communities as a Strategic Lever—Will It Play in Peoria?, 74

References, 75

Further Reading, 75

CHAPTER 4—A BLUEPRINT FOR BUILDING COMMUNITIES OF PRACTICE 77

Creating the Community Environment, 77

The Architecture of a Community of Practice, 78

Components of Communities in a Strategic Context, 91

Precursors for Building Effective Communities of Practice, 105

Community Success Criteria, 111

Community Evolution, 114

Conclusion, 114

Creating the Foundation—Will It Play in Peoria?, 116

References, 117

Part II: Building Communities of Practice in a Strategic Context 119

CHAPTER 5—COMMUNITY DEVELOPMENT PROCESS MODEL OVERVIEW 121

A Bit about Clarica, 121

Characteristics of a Knowledge-Sharing Organization, 123

The Agent Network—Developing a Community with a Strategic Purpose, 128

Three Strikes and You're Out: Learning and Knowing, 130

A Process Model for Developing Communities within a Strategic Context, 136

The Five C's, 140

Conclusion, 141

Strategy and Process—Will It Play in Peoria?, 141

References, 142

CHAPTER 6–PHASE I: COMMUNITY DESIGN AND LAUNCH   143

Overview, 143

Step 1—Define the Community Project, 145

Step 2—Establish Community Components, 153

Step 3—Launch the Community, 165

Conclusion, 170

Design and Launch—Will It Play in Peoria?, 171

References, 172

CHAPTER 7–PHASE II: COMMUNITY IMPLEMENTATION AND GROWTH   173

Overview, 173

The Community Members, 174

Community Implementation and Growth, 175

Step 4—Establish the Community, 176

Step 5—Checkpoint: Assess Community Progress and Value, 183

Step 6—Grow the Community, 188

Step 7—Evaluate Purpose and Direction, 196

Step 8—Expand the Community, 199

Conclusion, 204

Community Building—Will It Play in Peoria?, 207

CHAPTER 8–ESTABLISHING COMMUNITY VALUE: MEASUREMENT AND REFLECTION   209

Assessing Value, 209

Communities of Practice: Measuring the Value Proposition, 210

Clarica's Measurement Approach, 213

Recommendations—Next-Step Suggestions, 224

Conclusion, 225

Measuring Value—Will It Play in Peoria?, 226

References, 226

Part III: Creating Communities: A Course of Action 229

CHAPTER 9—COMMUNITY DESIGN AND LAUNCH: ILLUSTRATION OF ACTIVITIES 231

Process Model to Practice, 231
Step 1—Define Community Project, 232
Step 2—Develop Community Components, 249
Step 3—Launch Community, 267
References, 271

CHAPTER 10—COMMUNITY IMPLEMENTATION AND GROWTH: ILLUSTRATION OF ACTIVITIES 273

Process Model to Practice, 273
Step 4—Establish the Community, 274
Step 5—Checkpoint: Progress and Value, 280
Step 6—Grow the Community Value, 282
Step 7—Evaluate Purpose and Direction, 293
Step 8—Expand the Community, 300
References, 311

CHAPTER 11—COMMUNITIES AS CATALYSTS FOR CHANGE 313

Communities at Work, 313
Communities of Practice Intertwine with the Organization's Accountability Spine, 317
Communities of Practice as Catalysts for Change, 319
Community Maturity Model, 323
Challenges to Communities as Change Agents, 326
Communities—The New Frontier?, 328
Conclusion, 330
Communities as Agents of Change—Will It Play in Peoria?, 331

APPENDIX—COMMUNITY DEVELOPMENT:
QUICK-START TOOLKIT, 333

INDEX, 355

ABOUT THE AUTHORS, 371

ACKNOWLEDGMENTS

A case study and practitioner's guide of this type reflects the work of many people involved in the original project as well as in the creation of the book. We would especially like to thank members of the Strategic Capabilities Unit at Clarica who were instrumental in shaping this project and providing input for the book:

Mary Lynn Benninger, Knowledge Architect

Bob Forrester, Knowledge Exchange Architect

Jacqueline J. Smits, Community Consultant and Facilitator

Marianna Martisek, Research Analyst

Lee-Ann Simpson, Research Analyst

Susan Milne, Plain Language Consultant

The founding members of the Agent Network Steering Group at Clarica deserve special recognition as the people who provided the leadership that was key to forming our approach to community building. Our thanks for all the efforts from:

Paul Doesburg, representative of the experienced agent community

Norm Steele, representative of the developing agent community

Frank Brisbin, Sales Force Development

John Lanni, Vice President, Sales Force Development

We'd also like to thank our colleagues at Communispace Corporation who understood our need to represent their software product and consulting services in a nonpartisan manner in this book. Their experience on how communities function and contribute to an organization's success provided us with invaluable insights. We worked with a whole team of excellent people, but particularly, we'd like to thank:

Maria Rapp, Director, Strategic Accounts

Diane Hessan, President and CEO

We belong to a vibrant community of knowledge management practitioners and thought leaders—people who have provided us with the ability to shape and revise our approaches to community development through a dynamic exchange of productive inquiry. In particular, we owe a great deal to Etienne Wenger for his thought leadership. Etienne has always been very generous with his knowledge and his support of our work. In fact, it was Etienne's online learning program on communities of practice that provided the spark of energy and enthusiasm we needed to launch the Agent Network. We also would like to recognize the mentorship of Eric Vogt, Chairman, Communispace Corporation, one of the leading thinkers on how to learn through communities. Eric's vision, courage, and entrepreneurial spirit have been a constant inspiration to us.

A pioneer in knowledge management research, Chun Wei Choo, of the Faculty of Information Studies at the University of Toronto, provided us with a valuable framework to help organize and present our thinking about communities of practice. And Brian Hall should also be recognized as a beacon of wisdom in the area of values—work that has influenced our directions in many ways.

Without the support of Bob Astley, Clarica's CEO, our ideas may not have had the concrete manifestation in the organization. He provided the leadership context, and encouraged us to share our experiences.

In addition, we were supported by an incredible group of people while writing this book:

Jaylyn Olivo, Content Editor

Denyse Rodrigues, Graphic Designer

Karen Maloney, Senior Acquistions Editor (Butterworth-Heinemann)

Not only did we learn that it takes a community to build a community, we now know first hand that it takes a community to write a book!

However, our largest debt of gratitude goes to the 150 founding members of the Agent Network. Without their enthusiasm and commitment to developing their community of practice, this story would never have been told. They are the true stars who brought the community to life and continue to grow its potential beyond our wildest expectations.

Hubert Saint-Onge
Debra Wallace
Waterloo and Toronto, Ontario
April 2002

Introduction

Communities at Work

Communities of practice have existed at Clarica for as long as the company has been around. Informal groups getting together to figure out how to do their jobs better—talking in the cafeteria, around the water cooler, or after department meetings. Face-to-face, on the phone, or via e-mail, the need to collectively solve problems drew them together to bounce ideas off one another, get feedback on an idea proposed the week before, or roll up their sleeves to conquer a new beast.

Some of these communities of practice have been supported by senior management in a variety of ways through forms of encouragement, recognition, and the provision of resources. In mid-2000, Hubert Saint-Onge, Senior Vice President, Strategic Capabilities, encouraged Clarica management to take a further step in formally supporting the development of a specialized community. With John Riley, Vice President, Sales Force Support and Jack Garramone, Vice President, Career Sales Force, Saint-Onge and Knowledge Architect Mary Lynn Benninger began planting the seeds for a new form of community, an online community of practice for Clarica's 3,000 independent agents spread across Canada.

Realizing that there was a predisposition to knowledge sharing throughout the agent group, the first hurdle was already passed. To provide a foundation (i.e., a common vocabulary, list of characteristics, range of approaches, and benefits), a small group of agents participated in an online course about communities of practice. The nucleus of a Steering Group resulted—agents from the course who said, "Why can't we put one of these in place for us?"

A project manager was hired, a project plan was developed, and the community was launched. The lapsed time to accomplish? It depends on where you start the clock—six years from when Saint-Onge was hired to implement a vision of Clarica as a knowledge-enabled organization? Six months from the start of the online course led by community of practice guru Etienne Wenger? Three months from hiring Wallace as the project manager? Or 130 years from the inception of the company?

The development of the Agent Network took the concerted effort of a nucleus of committed Clarica independent agents, a Steering Group, a full-time project manager, members of the Knowledge Team from the Strategic Capabilities Unit, a network of Clarica employees from across the company—including Corporate Communications, Market Research, Graphic Services, Information Technology, Sales Force Development, Brand, Membership Services, Plain Language, senior management project sponsors, and staff from Communispace Corporation, the vendor of the community software application.

The time spent preparing for the "launch," when the virtual community was made available to the members? Once again, depending on when the stopwatch started, at least nine months.

As part of the Agent Network project, Clarica management suggested that the process be analyzed with the objective of creating a process model—a best practice guide for developing communities. Applying knowledge management principles to practice, management wanted to ensure that the lessons learned from the initial project could be transferred to other projects to take advantage of previous experience and reduce the time, and therefore the resources, that would be required to put a community infrastructure in place.

Following the success of the Agent Network, Clarica launched a second community for agency management personnel within eight weeks; a third community of innovation stewards was launched within five weeks; and a fourth community for Group Insurance account executives was launched in just over three weeks. Each of these communities has a distinct membership, purpose, and personality. The common thread is the approach used to develop the community infrastructure, a process that we've improved upon with each implementation. Herein lies the reason for writing this practitioner's guide to organizationally supported, strategically situated communities of practice.

Just as the transfer of knowledge benefited subsequent internal communities, we believe that our experience at Clarica can be used by other organizations to support the development of communities of practice in an efficient and cost-effective manner.

ABOUT THIS BOOK

Borrowing from O'Dell and Grayson's (1998) book title, *If Only We Knew What We Know*, this practitioner's guide presents one organization's experience for the benefit of others who are embarking on the development of communities of practice or want to learn about how to leverage existing communities in a strategic context. Here's the opportunity for you to know what we know, to learn from our mistakes, and to adopt an approach for your own organization.

In this book, we've made a concerted effort to link theory and practice—to talk about *why* we did something in conjunction with *how* we did it. It's a reflection of the way we work at Clarica:

- Innovation is encouraged and supported with resources.
- Analysis and reflection are key parts of any initiative.
- Productive conversations drive our development of capabilities.
- Learning and knowledge exchange are natural extensions of our work.
- Partnerships strengthen our approaches.
- Technology fuels our agility.

With one case study, we in fact present two perspectives on creating communities. First, there's an internal focus; we show how to create a community for an internal group of people working within the same practice across an organization. Second, there's an external focus; we realized that the Agent Network could also be described as an external community. Clarica's agents are not salaried employees. They are independent business people who have come together to learn and collaborate in order to better perform their practice. The Agent Network could be described as an external community that interacts with an organization, joined in a purpose of making the organization stronger.

The possibilities for creating communities that contribute to individual and organizational capabilities are endless, especially when you consider internal and external possibilities. This book provides you with a platform for community building that can lead you in many different directions—directions that, in the end, could establish a whole network of internal and external communities that are joined in a common purpose.

At the heart of Clarica's brand promise is *clarity through dialogue*. Conversations and productive inquiries are the keys to our competitive advantage—listening to our customers and building on one another's expertise improve our performance. By telling our story, we hope to provide you with enough information to start the conversations in your organization—to begin the productive inquiry process by asking, "How can we use communities of practice to increase our strategic capabilities?"

HOW TO USE THIS BOOK

As practitioners, our purpose is to provide a context for our work and illustrate a course of action from a variety of perspectives that are grounded in our experience. Our challenge has been to provide a strong conceptual framework and outline a concrete application, while highlighting the contribution of knowledge-focused work to improving the performance of an individual, a practice, and ultimately, an organization.

This book should be of interest to senior managers who would like to understand how they can leverage communities in their own organizations and to practitioners who support the development and growth of communities.

Although this book is created as a practitioner's reference manual, it has been designed as a series of building blocks that create an image based on an iterative process. The three main parts of the book not only form the framework for analyzing communities of practice from various perspectives, but also act as a guide that develops your thinking from the conceptual to the tactical to the operational (see Figure I.1).

Part I: Setting the Context for Communities of Practice

We begin our story of building communities of practice by setting the stage, identifying the context for communities with a discussion of the vital need to increase capabilities, in both individuals and organizations. We provide a brief overview of the field of knowledge management to situate our community work in the bigger picture of developing a knowl-

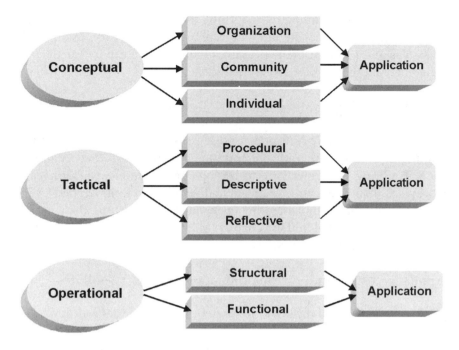

Figure I.1.
A Practitioner's Guide to Process

edge-driven organization. We introduce the concept of *strategic capabilities* in terms of the demands of the knowledge-based economy and show how Clarica has aligned a knowledge strategy with business imperatives, brand development, and our culture.

Part II: Building Communities of Practice in a Strategic Context

The second part discusses the process model that we identified for establishing structured communities of practice. If you're looking for guidance on process, here's the place to spend most of your time. It outlines our tactical approach for establishing structured communities.

We begin this part by telling the story of how we developed a successful strategically situated community of practice—the Agent Network. We set the context for the community development and provide a narrative perspective on how the community was put in place. We outline the process from two additional perspectives: procedural—a graphical representation of the process steps followed; and reflective—an analysis that identifies lessons learned. In addition, we continue the narrative description of the resources (human and material) that were required to accomplish the process steps and produce the deliverables (such as, the explicit or tangible outcomes and the documents) at each step.

Part III: Creating Communities: A Course of Action

In the third part, we continue our discussion of how we implemented a community of practice, with illustrations of actual work that we undertook. We bring our experience to the operational level with samples of workplans, communications, and guidelines that were developed in the course of designing, implementing, growing, and evaluating the community. The level of detail in these chapters is intended to provide practitioners with working references.

Appendix: Community Development: Quick-Start Toolkit

In the final part of the book, we present the toolkit that was developed by Clarica's Knowledge Exchange Architect and our Community Facilitator and Consultant. We use these materials in conjunction with a community consultant to help new communities get up and running within a short timeframe. The exercises move community developers through a series of questions that help put the major building blocks in place—to create the platform from which to launch the community.

In all parts of the book, our goal has been to model *productive inquiry*—the dynamic process that is used within communities to learn. By posing the simple question "How do you build a community of practice?" we start the process of answering that question. Information is accessed from all available sources. Advice, opinions, and insights are offered by practitioners, who validate the information and offer an approach that is situated in their experience. An idea is refined and crystallized to address the question, then codified as new knowledge and stored in a repository for access at a later date, possibly to answer another query in the same vein.

As project managers, we would have welcomed a guide to help us systematically build a community of practice. As knowledge management practitioners, we are pleased to share our knowledge with other practitioners in hopes that you will take our experience and improve on our practice.

What this Book Isn't . . .

This book is not intended as a primer on knowledge management or even communities of practice for that matter. It is intended as a contextual framework and a process guide for practitioners who are planning to implement a community of practice or want to understand the bigger picture of where communities of practice are evolving—how they can be used to create a strategic advantage.

We assume that the reader has some understanding of knowledge management concepts and has developed or is developing a knowledge strategy in his/her organization. We also assume that you as a practitioner or a senior manager are interested in developing a community or are responsible for providing knowledge access and exchange in your organization, so that you are somewhat familiar with the basic concepts of communities of practice. However, to help set the stage for the work we've done, we offer an overview of knowledge management to refresh your memory and to build a common frame of reference for where communities of practice fit into an enterprise-wide knowledge strategy.

A Word about Terminology

In any emerging field of study, one of the biggest challenges is establishing a vocabulary with a concise set of terms to describe the principles and concepts, tools and approaches, and the value proposition.

We have tried to minimize the jargon, buzz words, and acronyms that are prevalent in the literature on knowledge management. A list of standardized terms helped keep our word use consistent. One exception is shortening the term *communities of practice* to *communities*. This practice may cause some confusion because there are other kinds of communities at work in an organization.

To help remind you of the central focus of the book, we use the full term every so often just to jog your memory that *communities of practice* are indeed what we are talking about. But we have chosen to shorten the phrase to *communities* rather than to use the sometimes popular "CoP." Somehow, even with the use of upper and lower case letters, the resulting acronym directly conflicts with the whole philosophy of communities—especially communities that function as a strategic resource in the organization.

ABOUT THE QUESTIONS AND SUGGESTED REFLECTIONS

One of our goals was to write a book that would help readers think about what they wanted to do or could do with the ideas we presented. At the end of most chapters, we include a series of questions to help you place the concepts and approaches outlined in the text in your own situation. The application of new knowledge to an organization is the most challenging aspect of learning. "That's all well and good, but it won't fly at my company" is a very common response to new ideas.

We didn't want to just provide you with information that might follow the proverbial "in one eye and out the other" route. We wanted to help you take information, reframe it for your own situation, and not only ask the question "Will It play in Peoria?" but find a way that it can!

We hope that this book will stimulate your thinking about developing communities of practice and the strategic role that communities can play in the transformative process that is underway in organizations today—a process that is necessary to create innovative structures that will support organizations in the knowledge era. To add to the growing knowledge about communities of practice, we encourage you to join a discussion on leveraging communities of practice as a strategic resource on our Website, hosted by Know Inc. (www.knowinc.com).

We look forward to learning about your experiences with communities of practice!

Part I

SETTING THE CONTEXT FOR COMMUNITIES OF PRACTICE

The emerging knowledge era presents challenges to every aspect of how our society and the economy functions. With advancements in technology fuelling rapid change, customers are demanding products that few organizations can deliver on their own. Value creation networks, based on individual strengths, are formed to offer integrated solutions. New organizational values, capabilities, and structures are needed to support this new business model.

In Part I, we begin the discussion of communities of practice as a strategic resource with an overview of a conceptual framework—what is driving the need for reframing our thinking about value in an organization, increasing strategic capabilities, and learning to leverage our knowledge assets? What strategies do we need to develop to secure our organization's viability, and

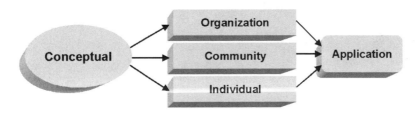

Figure PI.1.
Conceptual Framework

leverage technology so that we keep ahead of change instead of lagging behind?

Communities of practice in a strategic context are a new expression of an age-old structure that fosters collaboration and learning. The concepts are fairly straightforward—give people with a like-interest some time, attention, and resources so that they can collectively solve problems encountered in the workplace. But to meet the accelerated pace of change in the knowledge era, organizations will need to leverage communities to increase capabilities with greater speed and use them with greater agility. Our key thesis is that organizations will need to provide more than casual support in order to maximize the value produced in communities.

We set the context for building communities by looking at the principles of knowledge creation and exchange from the perspectives of the individual, the community, and the organization and explore the foundation needed to encourage the development and growth of communities of practice as a key component of a knowledge strategy.

Chapter 1

INCREASING CAPABILITIES IN THE KNOWLEDGE-DRIVEN ORGANIZATION

The emerging knowledge era is providing opportunities to reframe our thinking about how organizations work—what they value, what their assets look like, and how they create the capabilities needed for effective performance to stay ahead as opposed to lagging behind the curve of rapidly changing market demands. Chapter 1 sets the stage for the development of communities of practice within organizations by discussing the fundamental changes in business concepts and the need for new mindsets and approaches illustrated with Clarica's development of an enterprise-wide knowledge strategy.

CREATING VALUE: ASSETS IN THE KNOWLEDGE ERA

With the dawn of the knowledge era, an organization's intangible assets are widely recognized as key to its ability to create and sustain a competitive advantage and to grow at an accelerated pace. As a result, organizations are beginning to pay attention to leveraging knowledge as a way to create value.

Tangible assets are required for business operations. They are the "bricks and mortar" of an organization—things that are readily visible, can easily be duplicated and quantified, and tend to depreciate with use: buildings, equipment, supplies, and other elements of an organization's physical infrastructure.

3

In contrast, *intangible assets* encompass an organization's intellectual or knowledge capital. They are for the most part invisible and difficult to quantify and track, can't be easily duplicated, and appreciate with purposeful use: business processes, customer loyalty, and areas of employee expertise.

An organization's intangible assets, its *knowledge capital*, are what give it a competitive edge in the knowledge era. Yet, most organizations focus on managing their tangible assets and systematically neglect their intangible assets. To fully leverage intangible assets, organizations require a different leadership and strategic approach to creating and sharing knowledge—an approach that makes the most of their knowledge capital.

The key strategic issues that face organizations today include:

- Escaping the limits of performance to keep growing at an accelerated pace.
- Applying knowledge in different ways, in multiple places across the organization to constantly innovate.
- Building an environment where learning is the norm to acquire capabilities at a faster rate.

In this context, knowledge is a critical commodity, and the organization's knowledge strategy is central to the organization's competitive advantage in the marketplace.

Rationale for Increasing Capabilities

The knowledge era is transforming the rules of business. Many strategies used in organizations today come from the industrial era, a time when financial capital was scarce. In the industrial era, the key to an organization's strategic development was the allocation of limited financial capital to the business activities with the highest yield. In the business context of the knowledge era, the globalization of capital and its greater availability means that a lack of funds is no longer a bottleneck to growth. There is now, in most businesses, a surfeit of financial capital. The new bottleneck is providing the *capabilities* required to create opportunities where financial capital can be applied with an appropriate yield.

By capabilities, we mean a collection of cross-functional elements—attributes, skills, and knowledge—that come together to create the potential for taking effective action. Capabilities are the link between strategy and performance. Stalk, Evans, and Shulman (1993) define capabilities as:

". . . a set of business processes strategically understood" (p. 26). We prefer to discuss capabilities in broader terms that encompass the full range of assets available within an organization—intangible assets that are held individually by the employees and collectively by the organization. We define these two groups of capabilities as:

> *Individual capabilities*: the attributes, competencies, mindsets, and values of an individual within an organization.
>
> *Organizational capabilities*: the strategies, systems, structures, leadership, and culture that make up an organization.

Mindsets are part of a person's ability to take effective action. They reflect a unique set of beliefs and assumptions that are formed through experience. Mindsets are used to filter and interpret what we see and do. They influence our decision-making processes and patterns of behavior.

The equivalent of mindsets at the organizational level is culture—culture reflects collective mindsets. In fact, we define culture as the aggregate of collectively held assumptions and beliefs of individuals in an organization. This definition explains the link between mindsets at the individual level and culture at the organizational level.

To be a successful organization, it's important to have a strong link between individual and organizational capabilities. This link occurs between the individual's mindsets and values and the organization's culture in a number of ways, but the most effective link for transformation is between the mindsets of the individual and the culture of the organization (see Figure 1.1). People may have the necessary attributes and the right competencies to do the job, but their mindsets about how the business works could lead them to apply what they know in counterproductive ways.

Culture is the most difficult element of organizational capability to enhance and move dynamically. Structures, like communities of practice, play an important role in shaping an organization's capabilities because they provide a context where people can apply their capabilities to better perform their role.

The structure of an organization can have a key role to play in either restricting or fostering the collaboration and learning that flow from exchanging knowledge.

While it is useful to think of capabilities on two levels (individual and organizational), the full effect of competing on strategic capabilities comes from the combination of the two. The most effective way of breaking the

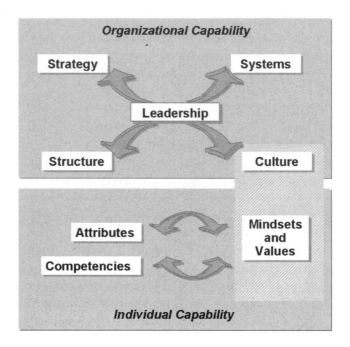

Figure 1.1.
Linking Individual and Organizational Capability

retaining walls of organizational culture is to help individuals question the mindsets that they may have about the business. As we move more squarely into the knowledge era, a disconnect between individual mindsets and organizational culture will hamper the ability to increase the capabilities required to achieve the organization's strategic goals.

Increasing and leveraging capabilities must become the focus of the organization's strategic planning framework. The organization's objectives, responses, and business models should be calibrated on the basis of its capabilities. Market demands and expectations continue to increase relentlessly. The pace at which an organization can grow is determined by the speed at which it can generate and reconfigure its capabilities in response to the challenges of its changing marketplace. Figure 1.2 illustrates the relationship between market expectations and the planning framework needed to create business strategies that are driven with customer needs.

The organization that fails to put sufficient capabilities in place in response to marketplace changes stands to lose ground, probably at an alarming rate. This inability to identify and generate the required capabil-

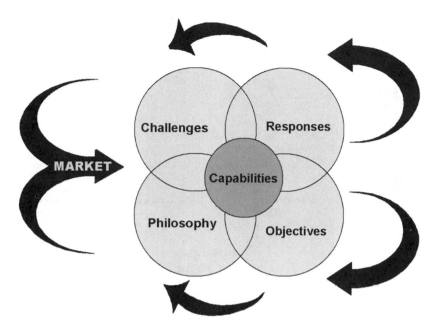

Figure 1.2.
Market Influences on Capabilities

ities will cause a competitive advantage deficit as opposed to creating a sustainable competitive advantage. Ultimately an organization's very existence can be in jeopardy.

The rapid shift of customer preferences and market trends imposes a need for organizations to rapidly acquire and use capabilities. Each competitor aims to shape the market to its strengths in order to achieve a preeminent position—to be the market leader. With increasingly intense competition, these rapid marketplace changes are now a major factor in an organization's continued success. For example, introducing a new product or service that lags behind the competition may mean the offering enters the marketplace when much of the profitability margin has already been lost. Therefore, the accelerated development of capability is a precondition for leading and shaping the marketplace in line with organizational strengths. This is at the heart of creating a competitive advantage.

In all markets, customers are more demanding of how they want their needs and expectations met. In response, organizations are developing solutions and services that are increasingly customized, integrated, and complex. One of the key limitations that organizations encounter in this change process is the ability to generate and introduce new solutions at a

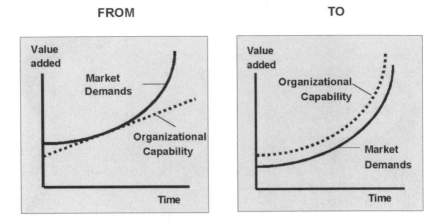

Figure 1.3.
Market Demand

pace that meets the rapidly evolving needs of customers and outdistances competitors' offerings. To fuel this innovation, unprecedented demands are placed on the creation and exchange of knowledge at all levels: inside the organization, outside with partners involved in creating an integrated solution, and with customers.

An organization's ability to acquire and apply new knowledge becomes the determining factor in introducing new solutions to customers. Accelerating the pace of learning, of generating new capabilities, which results in the creation of knowledge capital, is key.

Customer Demands for a Knowledgeable Workforce

With the increasing complexity of marketplace solutions, it is not surprising that customers express a high level of frustration in understanding exactly what products and services are available from an organization. Evidence shows that customers are demanding clearer information from their solution providers—information that enables the customer to be more self-reliant. Therefore, to deal successfully with customers, organizations must, more than ever before, have the necessary knowledge at employees' fingertips. The capabilities of employees interacting with customers must constantly be renewed and enhanced to meet ever-increasing customer requirements.

The performance and growth of today's organizations rely on the capabilities of the organization, which in turn depend on the capabilities of its people. In the industrial era, people were easily recruited and retained to fill an established, unvarying set of roles and standardized tasks. The knowledge era brings with it a much more competitive marketplace for talent. As people experience unprecedented employment volatility, they place a greater value on working in an environment that affords opportunities to actively develop their own capabilities.

At the same time, customers are putting a high value on learning. They want the opportunity to increase their own knowledge. As a result, customers highly value an organization that enables them to enhance their own capabilities—an approach that also strengthens the relationship between the customer and the organization.

To succeed, the organization must implement a multilevel strategy in which:

- Employees are encouraged to learn and increase individual capabilities.

- Increased capabilities are used to bring new solutions to the marketplace.

- The organization assists customers in increasing their own capabilities to effectively utilize the organization's solutions.

- Customers become more knowledgeable and self-sufficient with every interaction with the organization.

The knowledge capital built through increasing individual and organizational capabilities provides the organization with stronger customer relationships and a sustainable competitive advantage.

Managing Intangible Assets— The Knowledge Capital Model

In today's business context, an organization's value proposition (i.e., what creates value) has radically changed. Intangible assets now represent the most important source of value creation—a substantial change from the industrial era when tangible assets played a more prominent role. However, the overall blueprint of today's organization has, for the most part, been inherited from the industrial era, leaving organizations ill equipped to manage their intangible assets.

At Clarica, we developed The Knowledge Capital Initiative to provide a new perspective for creating a *knowledge-intensive* organization where intangible assets are leveraged. Managing the knowledge capital of an organization consists of systematically developing, maintaining, leveraging, and renewing intangible assets. Intangible assets are described in terms of:

- *Human capital:* the attributes, competencies, and mindsets of the individuals who make up an organization. The individual capabilities that are required to provide customer solutions.

- *Structural capital:* the strategies, structures, processes, and culture that translate into the specific core competencies of the organization (e.g., the ability to develop solutions, manage risk, engineer processes). The organizational capabilities that are necessary to meet market requirements.

- *Customer capital:* the sum of all customer relationships, defined as the depth (penetration), breadth (coverage), sustainability (durability), and profitability of the organization's relationships with all its customers.

Figure 1.4 illustrates the relationships among these three types of capital that comprise the intangible assets of an organization. The often unrecognized component of an organization's collective assets, knowledge capital plays a key role in capability generation because it is the knowledge assets that feed the productive inquiry cycle that is central to learning and collaboration.

The organization creates value when individual employees interact with customers. The quality of these relationships will determine the effect on the organization's customer capital. The structural capital interacts directly with customer capital but also serves mainly as the platform from which the human capital can multiply the value created for customers. In other words, structural capital provides employees with the organizational support they need to offer added value to customers.

Two key assumptions can be derived from The Knowledge Capital Model (Figure 1.5):

1. *The intangible assets of an organization are made of capabilities and relationships that are built through the exchange of knowledge.*

    Value creation occurs as knowledge is exchanged among the three types of knowledge capital. Knowledge exchange serves as the basis for accelerating learning and systematically developing

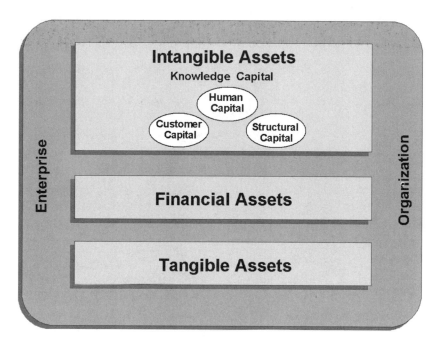

Figure 1.4.
Knowledge Capital

individual and organizational capabilities. It's essential that we promote and facilitate the free flow of knowledge across the organization. The overall level of trust in relationships determines the bandwidth of this exchange and the extent of the value creation potential.

2. *The intangible assets of an organization form a system that must be managed through an integrated approach.*

It's pointless to try to manage customer relationships in isolation from the development of individual and organization capabilities. All three forms of capital (human, structural, and customer) should be developed in an integrated approach, not in isolation.

Applying these two assumptions to strategies for increasing capabilities leads to significantly different approaches from those generally in place today as remnants of the industrial era. New strategies for the knowledge era focus on ways to increase an organization's knowledge capital.

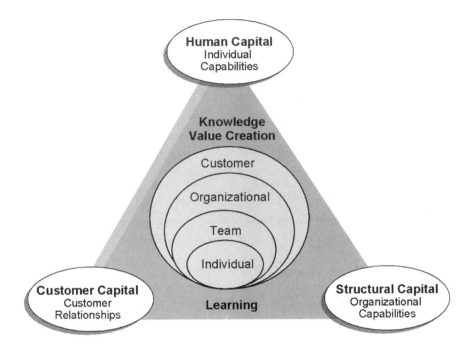

Figure 1.5.
The Knowledge Capital Model

New Strategies: Communities of Practice

With new business rules emerging, strategies are being developed to leverage knowledge capital to create a sustainable competitive advantage. One of the most prominent strategies is developing and supporting *communities of practice* as a vehicle for increasing knowledge creation as well as expanding the extent and accelerating the speed at which knowledge is exchanged across the organization—in other words, for increasing individual and organizational capabilities.

While the idea of communities of practice is not a new phenomenon (people have formed groups to address work-related issues for centuries), the term was first coined in 1991 by Jean Lave and Etienne Wenger in their book, *Situated Learning*. Wenger and a number of other researchers have continued to develop the concept of communities of practice as informal networks of people with a shared interest who come together for problem-solving, innovation, and learning—a means of facilitating knowledge creation, access, and exchange as a basis for generating capabilities.

From our work at Clarica, we've seen that capabilities are most effectively developed through the creation and exchange of knowledge and have come to realize that communities of practice should form a key element of any organization's knowledge strategy. We'll look at the characteristics of communities of practice in more detail in Chapter 2 and then build the case for an organization's involvement in developing and sustaining communities in Chapters 3 and 4. But let's start with an overview of a knowledge management strategy.

THE KNOWLEDGE CAPITAL INITIATIVE: CLARICA'S KNOWLEDGE MANAGEMENT STRATEGY

Clarica's business imperatives are not unlike those of other organizations. Clarica aims to increase earnings and accelerate growth to meet the expectations of its shareholders and provide value to its customers. While Clarica continues to reduce unit costs, it strives to create new business opportunities for growth by providing superior value to customers through integrated solutions that respond to their rapidly changing needs.

With these goals in mind, Clarica launched The Knowledge Capital Initiative. Its purpose is to generate the individual and organizational capabilities that allow the organization to meet current and evolving market challenges. The initiative has five core components:

- Accelerate the generation of individual and organizational capabilities.
- Develop a culture of self-initiative, shared ownership, and collaboration.
- Harness the power of the technology infrastructure.
- Renew people management processes in support of building capability and a culture based on self-initiative.
- Build a systematic and readily accessible knowledge architecture.

The initiative was designed to accelerate the acquisition of new capabilities that are required to serve changing market needs and to launch new income streams in support of business growth. From the perspective of enhancing individual capability, the initiative aims to strengthen the acquisition and retention of critical talent in a highly competitive marketplace.

The initiative also supports faster access to information to:

- Reduce the time required to achieve objectives.
- Eliminate duplication of effort.
- Enhance the ability to sense and respond to changing markets or service issues.

This last objective is, in large part, related to the knowledge strategy that is at the heart of The Knowledge Capital Initiative. In fact, this strategic component provides the fuel for enhanced value creation.

CLARICA'S KNOWLEDGE STRATEGY

Clarica's knowledge strategy outlines a systematic approach to creating and harvesting the knowledge of the organization. The intent is to place our best collective knowledge at the fingertips of everyone in the organization. This allows everyone across all facets of the organization to work in concert to realize business goals.

Some knowledge management approaches begin with narrow, project-specific efforts that may initially appear to be easier, have a greater likeli-

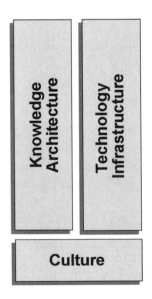

Figure 1.6.
The Knowledge Strategy Pillars

hood of success, and produce a greater impact. However, in the end, they fail to bring sustainable progress at the broader level or across the organization. A knowledge initiative that's narrow in focus without enterprise-wide sponsorship and broad involvement of employees from across the organization, starts as a peripheral effort and will most likely end as a peripheral effort.

The purpose of the knowledge strategy is to leverage the knowledge held by people throughout the organization and utilize the organization's substantial investment in technology. Clarica, like many other organizations, has invested substantially in the creation of a technology infrastructure that isn't utilized to its fullest potential. The creation of a knowledge and learning platform allows us to leverage this technology to a much greater extent. In what is essentially a socio-technical approach that integrates technology and culture, the knowledge strategy provides the context for the development of practices and processes.

A knowledge strategy needs to have a broad base. It must be embedded in how the organization works and creates value. Accordingly, Clarica's knowledge strategy is based on three pillars that support an enterprise-wide approach (see Figure 1.6):

- Knowledge architecture
- Leadership culture
- Technology infrastructure

It's interesting to note that some organizations have chosen not to address knowledge as an explicit strategy, perhaps fearing that their management won't have the patience to understand the underlying concepts or won't see the initiative as relevant to the performance of their business. However, management support is imperative. Without it, very little can be done about knowledge creation and use in a purposeful, sustained manner. The leadership culture must embrace the value of such a strategy and include capabilities and knowledge as part of the organization's vocabulary.

Knowledge Architecture

The knowledge strategy defines how Clarica encourages knowledge creation and exchange. It guides how new and existing knowledge is used to enhance capabilities. It also provides the vision and direction for this investment in building the strength of the organization. The knowledge

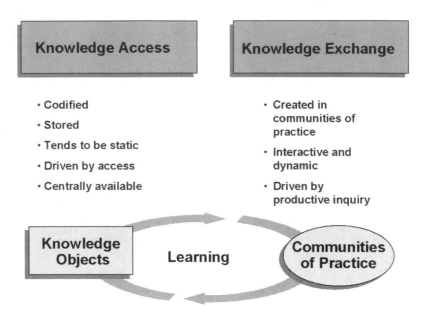

Figure 1.7.
Knowledge Architecture

architecture provides the blueprint for achieving the goals of this strategy—it outlines the approach for placing the collective knowledge of the organization at the disposal of every individual in real time as an integral part of everyone's work. Figure 1.7 shows two key approaches that individuals can apply to utilize the entire knowledge base of the organization through *knowledge access* and *knowledge exchange*.

The *knowledge access* approach provides a platform for storing explicit information. Over 30 knowledge managers at Clarica ensure that knowledge databases directly support information needs of all employees. In addition, considerable attention is given to how the different knowledge databases are linked into a navigable network, making sure that explicit knowledge is easily transferred from one situation to another. On our corporate intranet, The Knowledge Depot provides one stop access to our library of reference documents, best practices, and directories for learning and mentoring.

The *knowledge exchange* approach utilizes the tacit knowledge of colleagues and lessons learned from their experience. Frequently, people on specific projects encounter an issue that they have not seen in the past. They need someone to advise them on how to resolve it. At this point, they need more than stored, explicit knowledge. They need advice on how to assess the situation and proceed from someone who has had a similar experience. In other words, they need the combined strength of explicit and tacit knowledge to attain the level of understanding required to have the confidence to take effective action.

This process is driven by *productive inquiry*—a dynamic questioning and validation process that draws out tacit knowledge to give meaning to explicit knowledge. The answer to a productive inquiry places the knowledge provided in context for formulating a solution. Anyone who encounters an unfamiliar issue, problem, or situation can ask for help or advice within a community of practice where the real expertise lies. Members of the community respond by calling upon the knowledge at their disposal and the experience they have from similar situations. To give advice and interpret information, people need to understand the context in which the information will be used. The community of practice, linking individuals who have a shared purpose, by definition provides that context and effectively enables them to think through the situation and draw on their own tacit know-how. The process requires person-to-person contact, whether face-to-face, by telephone, virtually via electronic media, or through written communication.

Communities of practice are an integral element of the knowledge strategy at Clarica. In an open, collaborative culture, these communities take advantage of a combination of the explicit and tacit knowledge required to answer productive inquiries in a manner that renews the central knowledge repository and generates individual and organizational capability. As new knowledge is created within the community, these knowledge objects are stored in a central location for access at a later time. The community's knowledge is made persistent, collected as the result of a member's need, making it more relevant to supporting the practice and assisting members to take effective action.

The knowledge architecture outlines the plan for the network of tools and resources that provides support to learning—the process of turning information into knowledge, leading to effective action. A combination of art and science, the architecture is the bridge between the strategy and the organization's ability to perform.

Culture

The definition and deployment of values is the foundation on which our knowledge strategy is built. The success of Clarica's knowledge strategy depends on the development of culture and leadership principles based on self-initiation. An entitlement and dependency mentality represents a serious barrier to the creation of an open, collaborative environment. A knowledge strategy can only work when individuals function on the basis of partnership and interdependence and are convinced that their own success is tied to the success of the organization as a whole. The alignment of individual and organizational values is essential to ensure that individual learning contributes to building organizational capability.

Clarica undertook an extensive analysis of the values held by individual employees across the organization—an invaluable early step in our journey to create a knowledge-driven organization. The approach that we used to articulate organizational values was specifically designed to align these values with individual and organizational aspirations. The work we continue to do on values also provides a framework for developing a leadership and organizational culture conducive to nurturing the level of trust and establishing the quality of relationships necessary to create and exchange knowledge across boundaries—key requirements of effective communities of practice.

Technology Infrastructure

Like many other organization, Clarica has made a significant investment in technology over the last decade. As we strive to tap the full potential of this technology platform, the knowledge strategy offers the next level of leverage for enhancing the effect of technology on business performance.

The successful implementation of the knowledge strategy depends in large part on the organization's technology infrastructure. Technology is the conduit for the knowledge network—the pipeline through which knowledge flows throughout the organization. Technology's key role is to convey information in a manner that allows individuals and teams to translate it into knowledge. They do this by interacting with one another, internalizing the meaning, and gearing their actions accordingly. Knowledge strategy requirements must be coordinated with the design of the technology infrastructure and the acquisition or development of new applications.

New applications, including the Internet as well as group-ware tools and templates, help to shape the technology infrastructure. Work to date at Clarica includes:

- A knowledge-based corporate intranet called "Clarica Connects."
- Templates for the effective exchange of knowledge in communities of practice, supporting productive inquiries and knowledge sharing.
- Collaboration tools that allow for synchronous (same time) and asynchronous (different time) interactions.

Our integrated technology platform harvests and stores knowledge. It provides access to knowledge at the lowest possible transaction costs in terms of user time and effort. And, finally, it enhances efficiencies by allowing for the reuse of knowledge objects.

To summarize Clarica's knowledge strategy structure: the knowledge architecture outlines a blueprint of tools and approaches for creating, storing, and exchanging knowledge that is valued by the organization, utilized by a self-initiated culture, and enabled by an integrated technology platform.

Goals of The Knowledge Capital Initiative

The organization's goals and the knowledge strategy's approaches used to attain these goals contribute to many aspects of Clarica's transformation. As an illustration of the knowledge strategy's integral role, we've taken the organization's strategic imperatives and described how the knowledge strategy contributes to achieving each one.

- **Agility**—*Every employee is able to readily contribute to the early detection of internal and external trends and respond with speed.*

  With a comprehensive knowledge architecture, individuals can collaborate to find immediate solutions to problems as issues emerge. This collective awareness of what is happening allows the organization to detect new trends early and respond to them with unparalleled speed.

- **Collaboration**—*Results are achieved just as effectively across organizational boundaries as they are within teams.*

  Knowledge tools reduce the costs related to collaboration and optimize the collective expertise of any given group. Knowledge sharing and exchange allows groups to work at a higher level of collaboration and to maximize the productivity of meetings and other collaborative work. Meetings are more purposefully used to accomplish tasks ineffectively addressed through electronic exchange.

- **Quality and Speed of Decision Making**—*Employees make better and faster decisions through knowledge access and knowledge exchange facilitated by technology.*

  The complexity of the business environment creates decision-making bottlenecks at various levels that paralyze the organization. With an up-to-date view of relevant issues, the information brought in real-time from many perspectives leads to decisions that are timely, of high quality, and widely owned and therefore more likely to be implemented.

- **Accelerated Learning and Capability Building**—*Employees' access to learning opportunities increases capabilities to meet emerging market and business needs.*

  Every employee has ready access to the organization's knowledge and interactive learning modules. Individuals and learning groups can put forward productive inquiries to learn about specific issues they encounter in the course of their work. Together, these elements create a highly effective learning environment in which learning that is integrated with work is always relevant and purposeful.

- **Coherence**—*Employees collectively make sense of what is happening.*

  This rich, knowledge-based context allows employees to understand and interpret the principles that guide them through the choices they have to make. As they work to resolve a situation, the communities of practice give employees a forum to test different approaches with their colleagues. The exchange that takes place in communities engenders continuous and dynamic alignment of the organization.

- **Innovation**—*Employees create value for the customer by building on one another's ideas and capabilities to offer better solutions.*

  People are provided with tools, processes, and communities to help them find new ways of doing things. The forums created through the knowledge architecture engender a high level of collaboration, bringing different perspectives to bear on issues and providing an ideal environment for innovation.

In summary, The Knowledge Capital Initiative brings people, values, knowledge, processes, tools, and technology together, enabling systematic individual learning and the generation of organizational capability.

THE STRATEGIC CAPABILITIES UNIT: CLARICA'S ORGANIZATIONAL STRUCTURE IN SUPPORT OF KNOWLEDGE STRATEGIES

A knowledge strategy can't be realized without the resources to implement and support it. To ensure that we had the right resource structures, Clarica's human resources department was reorganized with a focus on developing individual and organizational capabilities. Renamed the Strategic Capabilities Unit, this group is organized to guide enterprise-wide and individual business unit initiatives within a partnership model (see Figure 1.8).

The Strategic Capabilities Unit provides a focus on capability generation and integrates individual, team, and organizational learning in the service of the customer and shareholder. Knowledge creation and

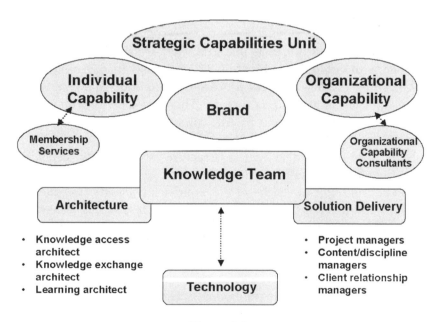

Figure 1.8.
Strategic Capabilities Unit

exchange accelerate learning. To support this belief, we organized our staff resources into four teams, each guided by a practice leader.

- **Individual Capability Team**—to shape and support the people management processes, practices, and tools required to meet the business needs of the organization. Its purpose is to ensure that people management practices are conducive to high levels of performance for individuals and the organization as a whole.

- **Organizational Capability Team**—to align leadership, culture, processes, and structure to ensure that the organization and its business teams can develop and implement superior strategies.

- **Knowledge Architecture Team**—to provide the processes, tools, and technology infrastructure required to provide all employees with access to the knowledge they need to know or learn in real-time in order to best support colleagues and effectively serve customers.

- **Branding Team**—to define and realize the customer brand strategies and the brand experience with an external and internal view where employees live the brand promise reflected to our customers.

The value proposition that underlies the Strategic Capabilities Unit mandate is the unique combination of knowledge management principles, learning and development processes, team, leadership, and cultural norms, and technology infrastructure. This new mandate integrates all human resource management policies, processes, and practices, focusing them on one element—*the generation of capabilities.*

More than a mandate and a structure, the strategic capabilities approach is at the center of Clarica's efforts to transform the organization. The successful implementation of this approach enhances customer relationships, improves our agility and coherence in responding to new market trends, accelerates learning, and increases the acquisition of capabilities. It also reinforces the development of our culture in line with our values. These outcomes help create a customer-centered, high-performing organization that brings superior value to its shareholders. In the end, the strategic capabilities approach is geared to help us shift from a make-and-sell to a sense-and-respond organization with the ability to react more quickly to changes in market trends and customer preferences than any competitor.

	INDIVIDUAL CAPABILITY	ORGANIZATIONAL CAPABILITY	KNOWLEDGE ARCHITECTURE	BRAND	STRATEGIC CAPABILITIES UNIT
DOMAIN	Shape and support people management processes	Ensure that the organization as a whole and its business teams have the capability to realize winning strategies	Build processes and tools for the creation and sharing of knowledge across the organization	Define and implement the focused execution of brand strategies	Link individual and organizational capabilities to the customer and overall strategies of the organization
PURPOSE	Ensure that people management practices are aligned to the core values and are conducive to high levels of performance	Accelerate learning and change to optimize performance	Ensure that the knowledge of the entire organization is readily accessible to support real-time learning	Express a distinctive brand that enhances customer relationships and accelerates growth. Build internal commitment to creating the targeted customer experience	Put in place strategies that will optimize the impact of organization's capabilities on performance
ROLES	Individual Capability Architects; Membership Services Representatives (Tier 1) and Consultants (Tier 2); Individual Capability Consultants (Tier 3)	Organizational Capability Architect; Organizational Capability Consultants	Knowledge Architects; Intranet Gatekeeper; Programmers	Brand Expression Consultants; Brand Experience Consultants	Head of Strategic Capabilities Unit; Practice Leaders; Membership Services Manager; Technology and Business Manager

Table 1.1.
The Strategic Capabilities Community

CONCLUSION

Shaping a new mandate for increasing individual and organizational capabilities isn't without its challenges. It definitely represents a radical departure from more traditional management approaches and interpretations of assets.

This knowledge-intensive context forces us to adopt new ways to accelerate learning and systematically generate capabilities. Understanding and courage are essential to the implementation of this approach. Without courage, it isn't possible to advance ideas that don't correspond to prevailing organizational assumptions. Without the insight and resolve to clearly articulate a new vision, people may be dissatisfied with the current state of affairs, but do not see the choices available to them. Without empathy for the sense of betrayal we all experience when new assumptions displace the ones that have guided us, it isn't possible for people to commit to a new mandate.

Throughout this change in focus, we must remember that people, with their varied experiences, assumptions, feelings, and beliefs are at the center of the organization in the knowledge era. In the end, the success of expanding an organization's knowledge capital through increasing individual and organizational capabilities and of creating and exchanging knowledge across the organization depends on our ability to enlist the commitment of individual employees.

Communities of practice provide one of the most effective ways of increasing capabilities in an organization. Communities based on a high-level of trust, situated in the problems of practice, where knowledge is readily accessed, exchanged, and created can provide organizations with a strategic resource that is unparalleled in traditional organizational structures.

KNOWLEDGE CAPITAL IN YOUR ORGANIZATION— WILL IT PLAY IN PEORIA?

1. Taking Stock—Human capital in your organization; Your individual capabilities.

   - Among the many competencies (knowledge, skills, and attitudes) possessed by your colleagues, which ones do your users or customers value the most? Do these competencies vary by customer type?

- Which competencies are most admired by other employees in your organization?

- What individual capabilities do you require—that are missing in order to meet your customer's needs? What human capital needs to be developed?

2. Taking Stock—Structural capital in your organization; Your organizational capabilities.

    - What processes do you have in place for making decisions, managing information, and communicating with your employees? What do these systems look like?

    - How is your organization structured? How are your accountabilities grouped? What structures define the position and relationships between employees?

    - How would you characterize your organizational culture? What are key characteristics or attributes? What values does the organization jointly hold? How do you know—what process did you follow to identify them?

3. Taking Stock—Customer capital in your organization.

    - How do you attract customers to your organization? How do you build a relationship with your current customers? What are the obstacles to building a stronger relationship?

    - What is your core value proposition to the customer? How does it correspond to your customers' aspirations?

    - How do you evaluate or rate customer satisfaction? What do you do to measure it? What do you do with the results?

    - What individual and organizational capabilities do your customers value most? Why? What do you do to continually improve on these capabilities?

4. Taking Stock—Knowledge Strategies in your organization.

    What strategies and approaches for managing knowledge exist in your organization? By identifying the practice in individual departments as well as across the organization, you can see the foundation of your knowledge strategy. Connect the dots after identifying:

    - Who are your experts on various topics? How do you identify them? How do you get in touch with them if you need their help?

- How do you share knowledge throughout the organization? How do you highlight best practice?

- What opportunities are there for increasing your knowledge? What is the organization's commitment to learning, training, and personal development? How do you share new knowledge?

- What tools exist that help you work collaboratively and share knowledge (could be technology based or other form)? What helps you interact or "connect" with your colleagues?

- How would a knowledge strategy support your mission? What strategies exist that reflect a knowledge sharing vision? How are these strategies aligned with business strategies?

References

Stalk, G., P. Evans, and L.E. Shulman. (1993). "Competing on Capabilities: The New Rules of Corporate Strategy." In R. Howard. (Ed.) *The Learning Imperative: Managing People for Continuous Innovation*. Cambridge: Harvard Business Review, pp.19–40.

Chapter 2

COMMUNITIES OF PRACTICE: HIGH-TRUST VESSELS FOR INCREASING CAPABILITIES

Further to the need of building knowledge assets as outlined in Chapter 1, we provide an overview of the concept of communities of practice. A search of the Web, library catalogues, and online bookstores identified a number of titles discussing the topic, with a corresponding number of definitions, outlines of characteristics, and examples of best practice. However, Wenger's work (with more recent colleagues McDermott and Snyder) dominates. This chapter begins by situating communities of practice within the field of knowledge management and then synthesizes ideas about what communities of practice are and how they benefit organizations. It provides the context for Clarica's initiative to support the development of communities of practice within the organization as a strategic resource for generating capabilities.

KNOWLEDGE MANAGEMENT OVERVIEW

Knowledge management is the field of study that a *community of practice* usually calls home. But the concept of communities is a complex one in which many fields have a stake—organizational learning, business management, and sociology, to name a few. In this chapter, the concept of communities of practice is discussed in order to help practitioners understand this unique structure found in most private-sector and public-sector organizations. A vehicle for learning, a community of practice is a place where people generate new knowledge that increases the stocks and facilitates the flow of knowledge capital in an organization. Let's start by looking at the broader field of knowledge management.

Often labeled the latest management fad, a repackaging of consulting opportunities, or at best an oxymoron (What? Knowledge can't be managed . . .), knowledge management burst into the business literature at the same time that the knowledge era and the knowledge-based economy were being heralded globally by industry analysts and governments. Knowledge management as fact or fiction, fad or foundation, or old wine in a new bottle—its popularity on conference programs and in the press continues to fuel the debate about the role knowledge management plays in creating an organization's competitive advantage or improving the quality of its service.

As with any new field of study, early efforts are focused on establishing concepts and principles, identifying characteristics and elements, building a vocabulary with standardized definitions, and outlining successful applications of the underlying theory. The field of knowledge management has been developed over the last decade by academics, consultants, and a myriad of leading practitioners who were probably "doing" knowledge management well before the term was coined!

Knowledge management pioneers Tom Davenport from the University of Texas and Larry Prusak of IBM's Knowledge Management Institute suggest that ". . . the only sustainable advantage a firm has comes from what it collectively knows, how efficiently it uses what it knows, and how readily it acquires and uses new knowledge" (Davenport and Prusak, 1998, p. xv).

In a nutshell, this statement summarizes knowledge management—a successful organization's value (its competitive advantage based on its knowledge capital) is derived from its ability to learn (increase capabilities and create new knowledge) and apply what it knows (take effective action based on existing and new knowledge). Knowledge management, then, promotes a collaborative environment for identifying existing knowledge, creates the opportunities to generate new knowledge, and provides the tools and approaches needed to apply what the organization knows in its efforts to meet its strategic goals.

The term *knowledge management* has been defined in many ways, from a simple phrase to a complex illustration. The varying definitions reflect the wide range of elements covered in the field coupled with the vagaries of describing an intangible object. A useful way to explain what knowledge management means is to look at it not as a single thing or a neat and tidy management slogan, but as a framework—a collection of elements that work together in varying combinations to accomplish the goal of leveraging an organization's knowledge capital.

Chun Wei Choo, a professor in the Faculty of Information Studies at the University of Toronto, bases his definition of knowledge management on this framework approach:

> *Knowledge management is a framework for designing an organization's goals, structures, and processes so that the organization can use what it knows to learn and to create value for its customers and community. (Choo, 1999)*

Worth a book on its own, but briefly described here, Choo's framework illustrates the wide range of possible components of a knowledge management strategy (see Table 2.1). He organizes these components in a matrix where the horizontal axis is divided into three types of knowledge with

	TACIT KNOWLEDGE KNOWLEDGE CREATION	EXPLICIT KNOWLEDGE KNOWLEDGE SHARING	CULTURAL KNOWLEDGE KNOWLEDGE USE
VISION STRATEGY	Scenario planning Future search	Knowledge audit Action agenda	Leadership Commitment Communication
ROLES STRUCTURES	Subject experts Mentors X-Functional teams	Knowledge editors Knowledge analysts Knowledge architects	CKO Champions Evangelists
PROCESS PRACTICE	Communities of practice Lessons learned Improvisation	Knowledge organization Intellectual asset management Workflow	Motivation Training & development Knowledge valuation
TOOLS PLATFORMS	Expertise access management Collaborative work tools & systems	Data mining Information architecture Knowledge repositories	Enterprise information portals Community building

Table 2.1.
Managing Knowledge: A Planning Framework

related processes: tacit knowledge and knowledge creation; explicit knowledge and knowledge sharing; and cultural knowledge and knowledge use. The vertical axis identifies four layers of organizational enablers: vision and strategy; roles and structures; process and practice; and tools and platforms. The windows of the framework are populated with examples of activities and resources that reflect the intersection of one of the three types of knowledge and one of the four components of an organization (Choo, 1999).

This framework approach can guide an organization's design of a knowledge management strategy based on its strengths and targeted at its weaknesses. Rather than identifying one standard approach to designing a knowledge management strategy, it facilitates the creation of a unique strategy that meets the needs of any given organization.

Knowledge management handbooks or manuals shouldn't be seen as a cookie-cutter approach to success, complete with a list of ingredients and a step-by-step guide to designing, implementing, and evaluating a prescribed process. Instead, a knowledge management approach needs to be based on a unique combination of strategies, roles, processes, and tools working in concert to take advantage of an organization's knowledge capital in order to successfully meet and, with luck, exceed its goals.

Debating the Value of Knowledge Management

After a decade, the debate over knowledge management's value continues, pitting knowledge management practitioner against critic. The victor? The jury for some may still be out, but time will tell as more organizations attribute their successes to an effective knowledge management strategy.

IDC Corporation of Framingham, Massachusetts suggests that the global market for knowledge management software and services will increase from $1.4 billion in 1999 to $5.4 billion in 2004 (Wintrob, 2001). This level of investment shows that many organizations are already paying attention to identifying, increasing, and utilizing their knowledge capital and that many more will investigate and implement knowledge management strategies and approaches over the next several years.

Organizations such as Hewlett-Packard, General Motors, The United States Army, and Dow Chemical lead a long list of knowledge management success stories—instances where concerted efforts to manage knowledge assets have resulted in a significant competitive advantage and/or increased service efficiency.

Professional service organizations (e.g., McKinsey & Company, Ernst & Young, PriceWaterhouseCoopers), whose core business relies on the expertise of its employees, were in the forefront of capturing, storing, and accessing their knowledge capital. Companies with distributed personnel working on similar problems, such as Xerox's service technicians, implemented systems to share "tricks of the trade" that practitioners had developed over time, thus reducing costs and increasing customer satisfaction. Global relief organizations, such as the World Bank, gathered examples of best practice in order to more rapidly deploy relief resources in disaster situations on the basis of past experience.

Central to all of the recognized success stories of knowledge management initiatives is an ability to innovate, to collaborate in situations where existing knowledge is applied or new knowledge is created to solve a problem or identify a new way of doing business.

One of the first tangible illustrations of knowledge management in action, communities of practice have emerged as an example of what an organization actually does in a knowledge strategy. As noted earlier, many discussions of knowledge management are at a conceptual level—abstract terms used to talk about intangible things that may be somewhat outside the realm of recognized business language. Many of these abstract discussions lead to a misunderstanding about the real value of "knowing what you know." They continue to fuel the debate about whether or not knowledge management makes a significant contribution to creating a competitive advantage or an increase in service quality. But debate is healthy! It forces practitioners and theorists alike to support their positions with comprehensive evidence.

Knowledge Management and Communities—Where's the Fit?

Early analysis of knowledge-based organizations identified groups of employees getting together to solve work-related problems without management directive or involvement. Recognizing the level of learning that took place within the group and the ability to innovate and problem solve, management began to pay attention to these loosely formed, often organic structures that are now called *communities of practice*. Through a meeting of the minds, community members are able to pool their expertise, share their experience, test new ideas, improve on past processes and procedures, and find solutions that result in increased capability and improved performance.

The Xerox service technicians' story is perhaps the most often cited early example of a community of practice, a concrete illustration of managing knowledge, which until the mid-1990s was considered a somewhat "soft" management approach. Using a blend of expertise and technology, the technicians were able to build a database of tips about service calls—things that weren't found in the manual or taught in a course, but were learned from trial and error over repeated repair situations. With the help of an information technology infrastructure, these tips were organized and stored for online access by technicians in the field. The length of service calls was shortened and customer satisfaction was significantly improved. The perfect combination of reducing costs while strengthening customer relationships was achieved by applying knowledge to a problem of practice. Xerox's investment was relatively small—an existing technology platform with some added database structure and access. But the return on leveraging the service technician's knowledge was, as the credit card motto says, PRICELESS!

Communities of practice have been recognized in some organizations as an integral structure in which employees (and sometimes colleagues from other organizations) join together in informal groups to talk about common issues, concerns, and challenges. The community's activities are focused on learning: finding solutions to existing problems, creating understanding about business-related issues, improving current practice, and ultimately increasing the community members' individual capabilities and contributing to organizational capabilities as a whole.

Defining Communities of Practice

As with many new terms, it takes a bit of time for a consensus on a definition to emerge, and early attempts to define the term often result in the creation of some pretty distinct boundaries—a black and white interpretation of the new term. *Communities of practice* is no exception. If we think of an organization, a multitude of structures comes to mind—business units, departments, functional areas, project teams, cross-functional teams, working groups, project clusters, sections, centers, networks. At the same time, if we look at communities in an organization, chances are we'll see a wide range of types: communities of interest, communities of purpose, knowledge networks, communities of commitment, communities of expertise, professional communities, learning communities, and so forth.

While many different types of communities exist within an organization, our focus for this book is on *communities of practice* in which a group of individuals make a collaborative effort to improve their practice.

Combining two words to describe another entity seems a good way to provide a rich definition—the sum of two meanings to more thoroughly illustrate a third concept. However, when the two words are in and of themselves complex terms, the resulting definition may be mired in confusion rather than made clear.

Community has been labeled one of the most difficult and controversial concepts in modern society. With numerous meanings and interpretations, it stands as an elusive and vague concept and is thought to be the most widely used and abused term in sociology.

Practice is another complex term that conjures up a range of images—painful hours of endless scales on an ill-tuned piano, a collection of clients who obtain services from a professional such as a dentist or lawyer, or an unacceptable behavior as echoed in "oh what a tangled web we weave when first we practice to deceive!"

The term *community of practice* is attributed to then Institute for Research on Learning researchers Jean Lave and Etienne Wenger, who first used the phrase in their book, *Situated Learning* (1991). Wenger has since become an internationally recognized expert in the study of how organizations collectively create and share knowledge. Dubbed "Mr. Communities of Practice" (Stamp, 2000), Wenger has extensively researched, written, consulted, and taught about the subject. With colleagues McDermott and Snyder, he defines *communities of practice* as:

> *Groups of people who share a concern, a set of problems, or a passion about a topic, and who deepen their understanding and knowledge of this area by interacting on an ongoing basis. (Wenger et al., 2002, p.4)*

This general definition provides a springboard from which other definitions are developed—variations on a theme or refinements to meet the needs of unique situations in other organizations. In Chapter 9, we'll look more closely at creating a definition that is meaningful to your organization.

We can also look at communities of practice from two perspectives. First, we can talk about communities of practice in general terms as an approach or methodology for creating and sharing knowledge. In the generic sense, communities are a representation of a phenomenon that has been identified in the study of organizations that embrace the principles of knowledge management, a way for people to connect, to collectively learn from each other. Second, we can look specifically at a community itself—not as a tool or approach, but as a result or outcome. From this perspective, the purpose and activities of an individual community are the focus—what the community accomplishes, what new knowledge it creates and stores, what successes it represents in building its members' capabilities, or how the community collectively improves the performance of its practice.

Characteristics of Communities of Practice

Wenger (1998) provides a thorough discussion of the underlying theory plus a description of a community of practice in his book, *Communities of Practice: Learning, Meaning and Identity.* This seminal work may be somewhat difficult to digest in one reading, but Wegner provides a comprehensive look at communities from educational, organizational, and social perspectives. It serves as a reference for most writing on communities of practice.

Various key components of a community of practice have been described in the literature. We offer you an overview of three perspectives from researchers, consultants, and practitioners on the main elements of communities (see Table 2.2).

Many people working in the field of knowledge management and with communities of practice in particular have outlined a variety of characteristics. We'd like to add to this discussion of community characteristics by first outlining a range of types of communities of practice that we've observed.

A Range of Community of Practice Types

Many discussions of communities of practice situate them in a range of different community types—communities of interest, communities of learning, communities of commitment, and so on. Communities of practice are discussed as a certain "type" of community that exists within an organization. They form a range from organic communities that may meet just to exchange ideas, but have no plans to commit to further development, to highly structured communities of practice that are situated in a strategic context and are funded by the organization. Many labels have

AUTHOR & PERSPECTIVE	ELEMENTS		
Wenger, McDermott, Snyder (consultants and researchers)	Domain: the community's knowledge base and understanding of the field in which it resides	Community: the collection of people and their corresponding roles that form the community	Practice: the "work" of the community: its actions, learning activities, knowledge repositories, etc.
Lesser, Fontaine, and Slusher (consultants, IBM Institute for Knowledge Management)	People: those who interact on a regular basis around a common set of issues, interests, or needs	Places: gathering points, face-to-face or virtual, that provide a meeting ground for the community members	Things: the knowledge objects generated by individuals or collectively by the community
Saint-Onge & Wallace (KM Practitioners)	Practice: the knowledge base, processes, and procedures that inform a collection of actions in the delivery of a product or service	People: the community of practitioners who join together to find ways to rebuild capability required to realize business strategies	Capabilities: the knowledge base, skills, abilities, attitudes, brands, processes, and relationships that result in the ability to undertake actions within the practice. The "link" between strategy and performance

Table 2.2.
Elements of Communities of Practice

been assigned to these various types of communities of practice—informal/formal; organic/structured; or natural/engineered.

As we've worked with communities, we've seen a broad range of types of communities of practice. At one end of the range are informal communities that are grass-roots structures, loosely organized, and formed by people who have a common need to discuss topics related to their work. We call this type an *informal community of practice.*

CHARACTERISTIC	INFORMAL	SUPPORTED	STRUCTURED
Purpose	Provide a discussion forum for people with affinity of interest or needs within their practice	Build knowledge and capability for a given business or competency area	Provide a cross-functional platform for members who have common objectives and goals
Membership	Self-joining or peer invited	Self-joining, member invited, or manager suggestion	Selection criteria outlined Invited by sponsors or members
Sponsorship	No organizational sponsor	One or more managers as sponsors	Business unit or senior management sponsorship
Mandate	Jointly defined by members	Jointly defined by members and sponsor(s)	Defined by sponsor(s) with endorsement of members
Evolution	Organic development	Purposeful development, co-determined by sponsor(s) and members	Organizationally determined development based on business objectives and alignment of purpose
Main Outcomes	Individual capability development Codification of knowledge useful to members Increased levels of trust and collaboration in the organization Greater retention of talent	Sharing and building of organizational knowledge Focused development of capability relevant to achieving organizational goals Greater collaboration across organizational segments	Systematic orchestration of communities of practice across the organization Speed of execution Enterprise-wide alignment Creative, integrated solutions Enhanced effectiveness of organizational structure Ability to respond to market needs

Accountability	Not attached to formal accountability structure	Contributes to the realization of business objectives	Forms an inherent part of the accountability structure with specific objectives to achieve as outlined by the purpose
Organizational Support	General endorsement of communities of practice Provision of standard collaborative tools	Discretionary managerial support in terms of resources and participation Supplemented array of tools and facilitation support	Full-fledged organizational support on the same basis as organizational segments Budget allocation as part of business plans
Infrastructure	Most likely meets face-to-face for primary contact Has a means of communication for secondary contact	Uses collaborative tools Meets face-to-face on a regular basis	Uses sophisticated technology infrastructure to support collaboration and store knowledge objects generated in the community Highly enabled by technology
Visibility	So natural, may not even be noticed	Visible to colleagues affected by the community's contribution to practice	Highly visible to the organization through targeted communication efforts that are stewarded by sponsors

Table 2.3.
Community of Practice Characteristics

In the middle of the range, we've identified communities of practice that are more fully developed. They have sponsorship at some level within the organization and a more purposeful focus on developing new knowledge that furthers their capabilities within their practice. We call this type a *supported community of practice.*

And at the far end of the range, we've seen communities of practice that are highly motivated, aligned with strategic imperatives that significantly contribute to an organization's performance. They utilize new capabilities that have been purposefully generated within the community through collaboration and learning that is focused on needs in their practice. We call this type a *structured community of practice.*

In a sense, these three types of communities form a continuum—they range from informal to semi-informal or semi-formal to formal. But a continuum may suggest that there is a developmental cycle expected—that a community would naturally "grow" from informal to formal. We don't believe that's the case. While communities of practice might evolve to a different type over time, they don't inherently do so. Many will stay as either informal or supported simply because that's where the community wants and needs to be. Other communities may start as a grass roots effort, find support for their collaboration, and eventually become a strategic resource to the organization due to increased capabilities and possible alignment with the organization's strategic imperatives.

To continue our discussion of communities of practice characteristics, Table 2.3 outlines the characteristics we've observed according to three points in a range of possible types of communities of practice. We'd also like to note that, while the demarcations are useful for neatly organizing categories, there are ranges within each category—shades of gray that we've tried to illustrate at a median point.

Common Characteristics of Communities of Practice

We started our discussion of community of practice characteristics by organizing them in three types of communities within a range. We'll expand that view and suggest that there are a number of characteristics that can be seen across all of the communities of practice that we've observed. Generally speaking, communities:

- **Utilize productive inquiry**—communities of practice exist to find answers to questions that are situated in practice. Members have a high degree of "need to know" and have found that by asking questions within the community, the responses are situated in experience and directly related to the realities of work.

- **Self-manage through a governance structure, principles and conventions, the shared leadership of members, and some form of facilitation**—communities are not just amorphous shapes that lumber along. They have purpose and direction and a way to self-organize to meet their goals.

- **Generate knowledge that supports the practice**—through productive inquiry, access to internal and external information, and contributions of members, new knowledge objects are created by the community that forms the content or domain of their practice.

- **Self-govern on the basis of agreed-upon conventions**—the members govern the community through norms and guidelines that have been developed through consensus within the community, not imposed by the organization.

- **Assume accountability for supporting one another**—the community exists as a resource for its members. It takes full responsibility for providing an effective and productive forum. Within this context, each member assumes the responsibility to support fellow members as required.

- **Collaborate via multiple channels**—communities utilize a variety of synchronous and asynchronous forms of collaborative tools, including face-to-face meetings, to enable their discussions.

- **Receive support from the organization**—while the organizational support may not be directly given or accepted by any given community, there exists within the organization an acknowledgement of the social nature of learning and the benefits of providing opportunities for employees to collaborate and learn.

Communities of Practice Share a Common Purpose

At Clarica, we have identified over 30 communities of practice, most with unique characteristics. Some meet regularly, others are loosely knit groups that come together as needed. Some have a fairly static membership; others fluctuate in membership depending on the current focus and interest of the members. Some are highly motivated to find a solution to a specific problem that is hampering the members' ability to do their work. Others are intensely curious about a wide variety of topics—some applicable today, some looking toward the future. Some communities meet casu-ally over coffee, while others have planned agendas with guest speakers. Some have sophisticated technology tools to support collaboration and conversations, others work through e-mail or the telephone. The commu-nities of practice at work at Clarica are extremely varied, but they share a common purpose:

- A desire to collaborate with colleagues
- A commitment to learning and generating new capabilities
- A need to find a solution to issues or problems related to their area of practice.

In his description of creating knowledge assets, Stewart (2002) identi-fies a principle that relates beautifully to communities of practice: "Like pearls, knowledge assets form around irritants, such as real business needs" (p. 85). Communities of practice could be compared to these knowledge assets—they form around a particular need related to the members' practice.

Communities of Practice Situated in a Strategic Context

To the range of communities we discussed earlier, we add another dimension. One might argue that communities of practice that are aligned with a strategic purpose are still "structured" communities—and we'd have to agree. But we think they are different in a number of ways and merit their own category.

At Clarica, we've identified communities along the entire length of this continuum. But for the purpose of this book, we'll be focusing on com-munities of practice that have been purposefully built to meet a strategic objective. We see these communities as the most highly structured type of community of practice. Leveraging the knowledge capital of this specific type of community has the most significant effect on creating a competi-tive advantage because the community is aligned with an organization's strategic imperatives.

Let's look at communities that function as a strategic resource using, once again, Choo's framework.

Vision and Strategy—Communities with a Strategic Purpose

A community of practice with a strategic purpose exhibits all of the characteristics of the formal, highly structured, or engineered community. That is, the community is:

- Supported by corporate resources (e.g., infrastructure, facilitation, materials).
- Encouraged by the sponsors through recognition of the members' efforts.
- Promoted to the organization and industry as an example of best practice.
- Valued by senior management for its contribution to the organization.

A community situated in a strategic context has a high sense of purpose that is developed from three perspectives. First, the members are highly committed to collaborating on solving the problems of their business practice and increasing the capabilities that will, in turn, make them high performers. Second, while the members are an obvious focus of the capability generation, the community as an entity has a purpose in providing the structure or space to which the members are drawn and creating a repository that facilitates access to the community's explicit knowledge. Third, the organization is interested in supporting focused opportunities for employees to increase capabilities that will increase performance and achieve strategic goals.

These perspectives are not at cross-purposes. In fact, they are closely aligned, if not interwoven. In the end, the individual member, the community, and the organization all want to realize maximum benefit from the excellence in performance that is developed through increased capabilities generated within the community.

Communities that are aligned with a strategic purpose can make a significant contribution to creating an organization's competitive advantage. We'll talk more about the strategic placement of communities in the next chapter as we move our discussion from the general concepts of communities to the creation of a specialized type of community of practice that is a strategic resource in an organization.

Roles and Structures—Who Makes up a Community of Practice?

Who belongs to these communities? What are the roles and responsibilities of the people involved? How do they interact to make the community work?

Think of the community where you live. It's made up of a collection of people who hold different positions with specific responsibilities—for example, residents, politicians, service providers, and business people. A community of practice is similar in that there are distinct roles with corresponding responsibilities necessary to keep the community moving ahead.

Little has been written about the various types of people who make up a community of practice. In one discussion, Nichani (2001) proposes an interesting adaptation of Gladwell's work on what "tips" social change. Nichani argues that, given communities are social structures, Gladwell's identification of three types of people who make a difference in getting things done in a social setting applies to communities of practice as well. These types of people can be grouped by their behavior within the community:

Connectors: The people who know lots of other people. They have the extraordinary knack of making friends and acquaintances. "Their ability to span many different worlds is a function of something intrinsic to their personality, some combination of curiosity, self-confidence, sociability, and energy" (Nichani, 2001, pg. 49).

Mavens: The people who connect other people with information. They are information specialists or "information stewards." They collect information and want to tell other people about it.

Salesmen: The people who are the persuaders. They reach out to the unconvinced and persuade them to accept change or to try something new. They are "very good at expressing emotions and feelings, which means that they are far more emotionally contagious than the rest of us" (Nichani, 2001, pg. 85).

To this list, we add the roles we've observed in the communities of practice at Clarica, starting with members and moving to the people who work either directly or indirectly in support of the community:

Members

The heart and sole of the community. The collective of people who collaborate to further the community's purposes. Their participation varies depending on circumstance or perhaps the topic or focus of community activity. Within the membership, we've observed:

- **Sparkers—the debate triggers.** They identify gaps in the practice or needs for new capabilities or approaches, ask questions, pose problems, and point out shortfalls and discrepancies. They may or may not contribute to the resolution, but they are first to identify an issue that needs to be resolved and are soon on to the next.

- **Synthesizers—the summarians.** They help the community create meaning. They set the context, provide the history and outline the successes or failures that came before the current issue. They summarize how far the community has come, marking the tally of accomplishments.

- **Sole Contributors—the FYI advisors.** They come into the community discussion and contribute from their own vantage points. They provide a rather "take it or leave it" response, contribute a possibility, and do not actively try to persuade anyone to their viewpoint. They state their case and offer their situation as an example, and that typically ends their participation for the time being.

- **Witnesses—the testimonial providers.** They support a position and idea with their "vote of confidence." They provide credibility to an idea, reinforcing a point of view with their own experience.

- **Champions—the cheerleaders.** Probably the most actively involved member(s) of the community. People who have a keen interest in the success of the community and assume a leadership role. They have something to say about everything, out distance the pack in log-ins and contributions. They know the community inside and out and actively promote the community's value to the outside world.

- **Lurkers—seen but not heard.** They visit the community on a regular basis, but their participation is limited to viewing the community contributions. They don't contribute themselves, but find value in seeing what is being said and using the resources that are provided.

Support Roles

- **Steering/Advisory Group Members:** Members of the community and possibly the organization who take a leadership role, drafting policies, identifying procedures, and encouraging the community's development.

- **Facilitator:** The dedicated resource who coordinates community activities and facilitates the community's purpose. Often a liaison to sponsors and other stakeholders.

- **Sponsors:** The managers or executives who provide support and resources, encouragement, and public relations. They recognize the value of the community's commitment and champion its cause.

- **Management Supporters:** While the sponsors may have a lot of influence in the organization, a community needs a wider range of supporters (who may also be stakeholders), especially when the community may have some special form of status (i.e., the Agent Network that has no management involvement).

Process and Practice—What Keeps a Community Humming?

How communities work, or the practice of communities, is based on the knowledge architecture we introduced in Chapter 1—knowledge access and knowledge exchange (see Figure 1.7). Productive inquiry is the catalyst. Knowledge objects (or codified knowledge) form the knowledge base that can be referenced, tacit knowledge is exchanged based on member experience, and new knowledge is created during the act of finding an answer to a question or a productive inquiry.

The community's practice, then, is based on three components:

- **Access to existing knowledge** that is primarily codified or explicit (e.g., knowledge objects stored in a database).

- **Knowledge exchange** gained through sharing experience that is primarily tacit, but may also be explicit; a validation of information (e.g., conversations in the community).

- **Creation of new knowledge**—through collaborating on innovations (e.g., result of a problem-solving exercise based on a productive inquiry).

Access to existing knowledge. The community may have a variety of knowledge bases that it can access within the community's collaborative space or externally through multiple sources (e.g., organization's intranet, affiliated professional organization's Internet site, personal sources). Our experience is that plenty of information exists—the challenge is getting what you really need without experiencing the "drinking from the fire hose" syndrome that is so prevalent with access to the Internet. What is lacking is access to real knowledge—what O'Dell and Grayson (1998) have observed as drowning in information, but starved for knowledge.

Knowledge exchange. The method used to exchange knowledge depends on the nature of the productive inquiry that begins the conversation. Depending on the collaborative tool used to support the community, the conversations that build may be initiated in an asynchronous dialogue or discussion space, a comment made in a synchronous chat or online presentation, a question raised by a summary of a recommended book, or the contribution of material to the reference center or community library. These conversations may flow naturally, posed by a member confronted with a situation about which he or she needs some advice. Or they may be nurtured through facilitation in which key contributors are contacted to contribute or expertise outside the community is consulted. The knowledge that is exchanged has been validated by a member's experience—situated in practice with a view of "what worked" and "what missed the mark."

Creation of new knowledge. A productive inquiry might be satisfied by material in the knowledge repository or by a brief conversation with another member. But the real value of the community is realized through its ability to innovate—to move the practice forward. The creation of new knowledge may be manifested in an incremental improvement of an idea that results from the synthesis of several members' contributions in a brainstorming session. Or new knowledge can be created through significant efforts in collaborative problem-solving facilitated over a period of time, supported by external expertise and access to additional resources.

The process and practice of the community is at the heart of community building, achieving its purpose and creating value. Although shaped by governance structures (guidelines and rules, the norms of the community) and facilitated through technology (the collaborative tool or workspace), the practice of the community isn't dictated by either. Instead, the community members outline practice in their preferred method of satisfying their need to find answers that will further their practice and improve their performance.

Tools and Platforms—What Infrastructure Supports the Community?

Technology plays a key role in the development and support of communities. Although technology comes last in the sequence of key characteristics of communities, "last but not least" certainly applies! Its position late in the discussion is not a deliberate attempt to put technology in its place as an enabler or support tool, but a reflection of our philosophy about technology and communities.

Clarica has an impressive technology infrastructure. In our knowledge strategy, technology is identified as one of the three pillars. A key objective of the knowledge strategy is to leverage the substantial investment that Clarica has made in computers and network communication. Thus, technology plays a significant role in how we approach our business, how we accomplish our work, and how we see ourselves as a company.

In each of our communities with a strategic purpose, technology is a key factor. From simple e-mail to a Webified version of a Lotus Notes Discussion Database to a sophisticated Web-enabled application called Communispace, our communities use technology to communicate with each other, engage in activities, and create, store, and access resources in an exchange of explicit and tacit knowledge.

In 1998, we participated in a collaborative research project with Anheuser-Busch and Shell Oil (NB—Clarica was called The Mutual Group at that time) that was conducted by Arthur Andersen's Next Generation Research Group. The project included:

- A search of the literature
- Conversations with consultants, solution providers, and other people active in the online communities marketplace
- Interviews with people who coordinated or facilitated online communities in 15 organizations.

The report provided a wealth of understanding about how online communities operate, what they contribute, how they are valued, and where they are headed. But the most telling comment about the role of technology is reflected in a discussion of the definition of the term *online community*:

And what about online community? In fact, the respondents reminded us that the central issues of OLCs [online communities] are people issues, not technology issues, and that online is simply a tool for helping people come together (Arthur Anderson, 1998, p. 5).

This comment tells us what communities are all about. Whether they are online or not, communities have people, not technology, at the center of their opportunities and issues. However, our experience with virtual communities suggests that "simply a tool" is somewhat misleading! Even with our extensive use of technology throughout the organization, the technology component of communities is a challenge, and a major focus of continued efforts is to manage technology issues.

As an enabler, technology more than likely plays a significant role in any kind of community, not just a virtual community. Given the realities of a geographically dispersed organization, technology provides the vehicle for creating communities where face-to-face conversations are not possible. In Chapter 4, we take a more comprehensive look at the benefits, approaches, and challenges of technology as one of the critical success factors for communities.

Community Life Cycles

In a book on entrepreneurship, Cammarano (1993) notes that 50% of new companies fail by the end of their first year. By the end of their third year, 80% of the remaining companies have failed. Only one out of every 10 new companies is still in business going into its fourth year. Similarly, most companies that make the Fortune 500 list won't celebrate a golden anniversary on the list. They are the target of either acquisition or merger, no longer meet the selection criteria, or go out of business. It stands to reason that communities, like a product, service, or even a business, follow a cycle of birth, death, and rebirth.

Wenger et al. (2002) have identified this community life cycle in five stages of development (see Figure 2.1). They note that these stages are a collective representation of communities that they've studied. Individual communities may follow a very different sequence, but generally speaking, a cycle can be observed:

- **Potential:** People with similar issues and needs find each other and identify the potential for forming a community.

- **Coalescing:** The community is formed as activities develop to meet the needs of the community members.

- **Maturing:** Community members begin to plan directions, set standards, and engage in joint activities. The value of the community has been established. It begins to clarify its focus, role, and boundaries.

- **Stewardship:** The community begins to plateau. Although energy and activity continue, members who were once enthusiastic may take a sideline position. The main issue for the community is sustaining its momentum, recognizing the natural changes in practice, membership, and relationship to the organization.

- **Transformation:** People leave the community when it's no longer useful or pertinent to them. New people join and the focus changes, returning the community to a new growth stage or moving it toward closure.

These stages aren't linked to a timeline. Each community will develop at a different rate, although the pattern of development can be identified. While time is linked to the horizontal axis, the focus is on the level of energy and visibility, represented by the vertical axis (Wenger et al., 2002, p. 69).

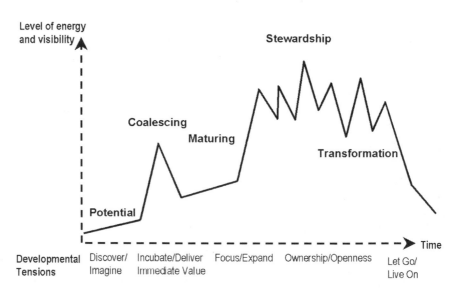

Figure 2.1.
Community Life Cycle

In the process model that we'll discuss in Part II, we focus on the first three stages of this life cycle, with an emphasis on "Maturing" because that's where the greatest value for all parties involved can be leveraged. As communities mature, they get better at being a community, push their capabilities through community building to new heights, and eventually may form the single largest vessel for creating knowledge assets in an organization.

Benefits of Communities of Practice

The value of communities of practice, like the field of knowledge management itself, continues to been debated. Managers who have seen an effective community at work value its contribution to the organization and continue to support the community's development. In other organizations where communities are mired in gripe sessions, creating a forum primarily to air concerns and challenge corporate policy, management is less than enthusiastic about the perceived benefits.

Verna Allee (2000), a prominent consultant in knowledge management and organizational development, has provided a synthesis of benefits from the perspectives of the business, the community, and the individual community member.

For the Business:

- Helps drive strategy.
- Supports faster problem solving both locally and corporately.
- Aids in developing, recruiting, and retaining talent.
- Builds core capabilities and knowledge competencies.
- More rapidly diffuses practices for operational excellence.
- Cross-fertilizes ideas and increases opportunities for innovation.

For the Community:

- Helps build common language, methods, and models around specific competencies.
- Embeds knowledge and expertise in a larger population.
- Aids in the retention of knowledge when employees leave the company.
- Increases access to expertise across the company.

- Provides a means to share power and influence with the formal parts of the organization.

For the Individual:

- Helps people do their jobs.
- Provides a stable sense of community with other internal colleagues and with the company.
- Fosters a learning-focused sense of identity.
- Helps develop individual skills and competencies.
- Helps a knowledge worker stay current.
- Provides challenges and opportunities to contribute.

A method for accurately measuring these benefits is perhaps closer to the center of the debate than the question of whether or not communities are of value to an organization. In Chapter 8, we take a further look at the metrics for assessing the community's contribution to the organization, with a focus on achievement in collaboration and the organization's ability to leverage the community's assets rather than a formulaic calculation of return on investment per se.

CONCLUSION

Communities of practice may be the most significant, tangible example of knowledge management at work in an organization. They are groups of people who are drawn to each other because of a common purpose. They get together to share their existing knowledge, create new knowledge, and apply their collective knowledge to either increase their own capabilities as practitioners or improve their practice—the sometimes technical processes to the extreme art that is required to succeed at their work. These communities come in many shapes and sizes. Their activity levels fluctuate over time as their need to learn new things or solve a particular problem related to their work changes.

In essence, a community of practice is a vessel for conversations to take place, conversations that lead to increasing capabilities. In order for people to commit to these productive conversations, there needs to be a purpose, a sense of achievement that flows out of their collaboration, an ability to measure improved personal performance or identify advances to the practice.

Professionals often learn best from one another. Sharing experience and expertise within a community of practice is very pragmatic, tied to the business, and, for the most part, based on actual situations from the members' environment. More than likely there is little, if any, discussion of theory. The knowledge creation and exchange are focused on a particular dilemma, and the result is improved capabilities directly related to performance.

Whether actively supported or unnoticed by the organization, these communities provide a vessel for learning for their members and innovation for the practice. A knowledge asset that can be leveraged by the organization, communities of practice provide an opportunity for individual or organizational capabilities to be significantly increased. And, if properly leveraged, this knowledge asset, like Stewart's pearl, can be harvested—adding significant value to the organization.

Communities at Work in Your Organization— Will It Play in Peoria?

1. Identify the communities of practice at work in your organization and characterize several according to the following chart. Chances are if you're aware of them, they are successful to some degree. So, what makes them successful? Can you see a trend or pattern for success across the communities?

Name	Interest or Subject Area	Membership	Size/Age	Method of Communicating	Level of Organizational Involvement

2. Have a look at your organization's objectives, strategic imperatives, or business goals—whatever you call them. Can you match existing communities to the goals in your strategic plan? If not, what communities might the organization need to put some

resources towards creating and supporting in order to achieve your goals?

Organization's Goal	Community of Practice	Key Strategic Contribution

3. Among the communities that you are aware of, what benefits have they provided to their membership, their practice, and the organization? How has the community's value been recognized?

References

Allee, V. (2002). "Knowledge Networks and Communities of Practice." *OD Practitioner*, 32 (4). http://www.odnetwork.org/odponline/vol32n4/knowledgenets.html

Arthur Anderson. (1998). *Online Communities Research Study. Phase 2 Report.*

Cammarano, R.F. (1993). *Entrepreneurial Transitions: From Entrepreneur Genius to Visionary Leaders.* Cited in "Entrepreneurial personalities from start-up to Fortune 500" by W. Harrell. http://www.atlanta.bcentral.com/atlanta/stories/1996/12/02/smallb3.html

Choo, C.W. (1999). The FIS Knowledge Management Institute, session presentations. Faculty of Information Studies, University of Toronto. http://www.choo.fis.utoronto.ca

Davenport, T. H. and L. Prusak. (1998). *Working Knowledge: How Organizations Manage What They Know.* Boston: Harvard Business School Press.

Lesser E.L., M.A. Fontaine, and J.A. Slusher. (2000). *Knowledge and Communities.* Boston: Butterworth-Heinemann.

Nichani, M. (2001). "Communities of Practice at the Core." Learningpost. http://www.elearningpost.com/elthemes/kmcore.asp

O'Dell, C. and C.J. Grayson. (1998). *If Only We Knew What We Know: The Transfer of Internal Knowledge and Best Practice.* New York: The Free Press.

Stamp, D. (2000). "Etienne Wenger: Mr. Communities of Practice." *Training,* 37 (11), pp. 78–79.

Stewart, T.A. (2002). *The Wealth of Knowledge: Intellectual Capital and the Twenty-First Century Organization.* New York, Doubleday.

Wenger, E. (1998). *Communities of Practice: Learning, Meaning, and Identify.* Cambridge: Cambridge University Press.

Wenger, E., R. McDermott, and W.M. Snyder. (2002). *Cultivating Communities of Practice: A Guide to Managing Knowledge.* Cambridge, MA: Harvard Business School Press.

Wintrob, S. (2001). "Sharing Knowledge: The Smart Thing to Do." *Information Highways,* 8 (5), pp. 14–16.

Chapter 3

Situating Communities of Practice in a Strategic Context

Communities of practice can play a vital role in an organization, but their greatest value comes when they can be leveraged for the strategic capabilities that they generate. Building on what we know about the changes that a focus on knowledge capital has brought to the economy and the nature of communities of practice, we shift to our main purpose for writing this book—to explore how organizations can leverage communities of practice to create a competitive advantage. In this chapter, we begin the discussion by placing communities of practice in a strategic context. How are they related to strategy? Where are they situated in the "bigger picture?" With the need to build the case for communities, we outline the benefits and suggest how you can position them to gain support for their development.

The New Strategic Context

Is technology really changing anything? The answer is an unqualified and emphatic YES!

As we start this new millennium, computer and telecommunications technology continue to create enormous change in the way the economy works. As technology dramatically reduces the cost of transactions within and between organizations, value networks will be built out of multiple participants in which each organization or component in the value network contributes where they have the most expertise. These value networks are supplanting value creation based on vertical integration within the organization. These emerging value creation networks are made up of external partners who bring together their expertise, creating a network of organizations each with a world-class advantage in a particular area (see Figure 3.1).

For example, a customer who holds policies with Insurance Company A is interested in purchasing a particular form of critical illness insurance. However, Insurance Company B already has a world-class critical illness product. Recognizing the value of partnering instead of trying to compete in an area where they have little expertise, Insurance Company A purchases the critical illness product from Company B. A two-participant network to the customer is formed. Insurance Company A is better at reaching a certain customer base and Insurance Company B has a superior product. There could be a third participant in this network because Insurance Company B gets its underwriting from another company that is the top underwriter in this field. A third organization is brought into the value creation network.

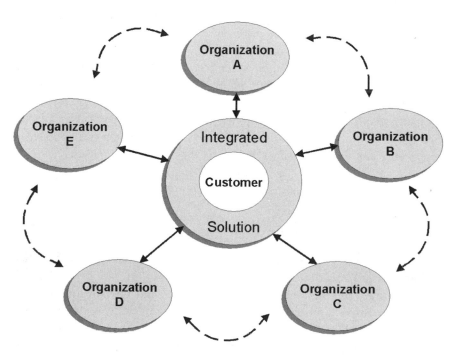

Figure 3.1.
A Value Creation Network

The customer is better served through the network because Insurance Company A, using its ability to attract the customer in their customer file, comes to Insurance Company B because it's the best at administering and issuing the policy, and Insurance Company B in turn uses an underwriter to manage the risk that is inherent in the critical illness product.

As a result, we have a multiple-participant network that creates value for the customer based on each organization's contribution of a specific capability domain in which they have a clear advantage. The reason these networks are successful can be boiled down to several factors. All of the organizations participating in the network:

- Understand the value of the network strategy.
- Know their customer's needs.
- Have the capabilities to partner.
- Leverage technology to realize their strategy.

Facilitated by technology, these multiple-participant networks demand new business strategies that leverage the capabilities of multiple participants in order to deliver a product or service to the customer. As organizations' structures inevitably take on the shape of these networks, they will define themselves as assemblies of capabilities and relationships. This form of collaboration sets the context for communities of practice as the ramp you build to enable an organization to participate in networking. Value creation networks will also redefine the traditional boundaries of organizations to include, in addition to their employees, their customers and suppliers.

Not only are these networks transforming the fundamental rules of business, they also have the potential to help us transform the way we create value within an organization. The network model (organizations partnering to create an integrated solution for a customer) highlights the capabilities that organizations will need internally in order to cope with the new rules of business that are being driven by changes in the market environment. What we need to do is essentially infuse the organization with the same characteristics that are affecting the marketplace. In other words, our organizations must internally reflect the emerging characteristics of the marketplace.

The problem is that, for the most part, we haven't found a way to make this change because organizations are slower to move than their markets. Markets do not have the resistance factors inherent to organizations. Consequently, markets generate change faster than organizations. Organizations have built-in resistance because they can't quickly change their culture or the mindsets of individuals. The need to maintain the status quo is a powerful force that is difficult to overcome.

Beyond its tremendous effect on efficiency and productivity, networking becomes a strategic resource. It helps us change the organization. Networks facilitate the purposeful "connectedness" that enables organizations to develop their collaborative infrastructure. And communities of practice play a significant role in developing this infrastructure by modeling collaboration and showing the benefits of knowledge exchange.

The multiple relationships engendered by these networks bring to organizations the creative tension they need to keep evolving at the pace of their markets. The fast-evolving identity, purpose, and capabilities of these organizations will be reflected in the networks for all to access and fashion dynamically in order to meet emerging market challenges. Communities of practice are fundamentally a change agent for the organization, providing a model for a collaborative infrastructure that readies the organization to participate in these new networks.

While technology makes networks of organizations possible, the quality of the participants' relationships that are formed in the network will determine the network's effectiveness. As we learn to leverage emerging business networks, we will find that knowledge creation is the key contribution of networks. Yet, knowledge creation relies on relationships that are only possible with shared values. Through shared values and mutual accountability, we can form the foundation for the effective creation and exchange of value within business networks. One of the key outcomes of this network configuration will be a new form of collective "knowing"— the result of sharing knowledge across the network. Again, communities of practice model this important capability through the high degree of knowledge sharing and collaboration that exists within the community's self-organized structure.

There are plenty of signs that these external value creation networks and the knowledge that travels through them will have a transformative effect on marketplaces and organizations. Hardly a single aspect of business will be left untouched. Organizations are already assuming a network shape evidenced by the new technology tools (e.g., local area networks) they are adopting. Changing our tools changes how we work and create value. It's ironic that technology may be the most significant force in creating a context that maximizes human potential through relationships.

It's essential to the long-term prosperity of organizations that they develop their readiness for this new strategic context. Working online helps create the readiness for taking an active part in these networks. And this is again where communities of practice can play an important strategic role. As communities of practice are created throughout an organization, the organization conditions itself to gradually enter the larger context of knowledge-driven networks. The organization develops the ability to function in this mode and enhances its readiness to become an integral part of networks when they become strategically relevant to the organization's niche in the market.

Organizations without a level of readiness will not be able to effectively participate and will find themselves at the mercy of those who can proceed with confidence into the new network configuration. With the experience of participating in communities of practice, an organization is well positioned to gain from early adoption of this new configuration for value creation.

The Relationship of Communities of Practice to Strategy

Identifying the path for developing competitive advantage has always been the key purpose of strategy. Strategy sets direction, focuses efforts, and encourages consistency. However, the notion of what constitutes strategy has changed significantly. For many years, competitive advantage has been considered a function of positioning the organization within a market or industry by understanding the organization's strengths, weaknesses, opportunities, and threats.

Recently, a new way of thinking about creating a competitive advantage based on an organization's capabilities has begun to emerge (e.g., Dosi, Teece, and Chytry; Hamel and Prahalad). According to this new view of strategy, capabilities generate the organization's value and produce results in the marketplace (see Figure 1.2 in Chapter 1).

The focus for strategy development is on creating a distinctive set of organizational capabilities that will meet market-driven demands. The value-creation model underlying this thinking is that capabilities represent the focal point from which strategies are built. In turn, the organization's performance depends on the quality and reach of its strategies and its ability to provide the necessary individual and organizational capabilities that enable employees to take effective action (see Figure 3.2).

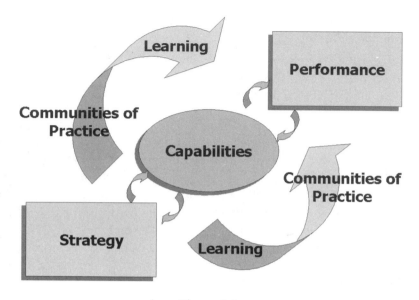

Figure 3.2.
Strategy, Capability, and Performance

Meta-Capabilities: Capabilities that Enable Capability Generation

The ability to continuously build new capabilities is at the heart of competitive advantage in markets characterized by rapid change. Keeping up with the demand for continually increasing capabilities means that we need to systematically build generative capability into the organization. By generative capability, we mean the capability to generate new capabilities, which is also referred to as a *meta-capability*.

Meta-capabilities enable the continuous generation of more specific capabilities over time and at an accelerated pace. In our view, there are two key meta-capabilities: learning and collaborating. Learning is the ability to acquire new sets of capabilities on an ongoing basis. Collaborating is the ability to work and learn across functions and business segments. In a sense, collaboration distributes and generalizes learning throughout the organization—the two are fundamentally linked. These meta-capabilities guide the development of organizational strategies and the building of an infrastructure that is required to generate new capabilities.

The art of building and sustaining collaborative relationships is a fundamental prerequisite for competitive success in the knowledge network era. And at the heart of this dynamic new form of creating a competitive advantage lie learning and collaboration as the key basis for generating the new capabilities an organization will need to succeed.

COMMUNITIES OF PRACTICE AS A VEHICLE FOR CREATING COMPETITIVE ADVANTAGE

Communities of practice embody the ability to learn and collaborate. In other words, communities of practice provide an essential platform that fosters learning and collaborating across the organization. Communities function as tangible vessels that enable organizations to meet important challenges presented by the knowledge era.

In the last several decades, organizations tended to create functional structures under which people were grouped and often siloed by their type of work—groups based on functional area or discipline such as actuaries, accountants, or lawyers within the organization. The problem with this structure was that people became more interested in their functional discipline than the business. To address this problem, organizations implemented new structures around responsibilities for different business segments in order to enhance performance. By creating clear accountability and responsibility for the profit and loss of business segments, managers could be motivated for the profit and loss of business elements that encompassed multiple functional areas.

This shift from the functional organizational structure to a broader business segment accountability structure has significantly enhanced the performance of organizations in the last two decades. But now we're coming to the end of the yield that this restructuring brought. Just going harder at the profit and loss base isn't going to continue to bring value to an organization. The market is driving organizations in a new direction.

More and more, customers are insisting on integrated solutions instead of asking for single products. For example, customers don't want to just buy insurance—they want to meet their total financial planning needs, of which insurance is only a part. One way that organizations have sought to create new organizational structures that go beyond the earlier functional and business segment boundaries is to create client service teams. These teams are placed on top of business segments with a focus on providing integrated solutions to meet the total needs of the customer, not to provide a specific, standard product.

However, it's important to remember that customers don't make a distinction about what they want from an organization based on how the organization wants to structure itself. In fact, customers don't even care how the organization is structured. But their demands do shape how the organization should be structured in order to meet market needs.

This new collaborative, cross-functional structure is wreaking all kinds of havoc in organizations, mainly because they aren't ready to deal with the change. They haven't put an emphasis on cross-functional collaboration, which means that they are not able to pull together a solution based on elements that may be spread out across the organization.

The traditional "boxes and lines" drawing that represents a hierarchy of accountability is more conducive to internal competition than to the level of collaboration required for creating integrated solutions. It's not difficult to see the challenges of fostering greater collaboration. The problems encountered in working across functions or lines of business often seem to outweigh the benefits in organizations where turf protection has been the norm. In this context, effective collaboration is difficult to achieve. The collaborative muscles of the organization have not been exercised, have not been seen as important, or have not even existed at all.

Communities of practice offer a solution to this problem. Successful collaboration requires the development of new capabilities—of skills, mindsets, organizational processes, and tools. And communities of practice are perfect structures to help organizations flex these muscles because communities are based on collaboration across functional areas.

ENVIRONMENTAL TRENDS	IMPLICATIONS FOR THE ORGANIZATION
Customer requirement for integrated solutions	Greater requirement for interdependence
Increasing complexity and speed of work	
Consolidation—merger and acquisition activity	Increasing need for cross-functional work
Proliferation of alliances and partnerships	
Thinly distributed expertise on a global scale (downsizing)	More geographically dispersed people and capabilities
Greater reluctance toward mobility—relocation and travel	

Table 3.1.
Factors Driving the Need for Collaboration

With the knowledge-driven business environment imposing the need for an unprecedented level of partnership through networks, the capability to collaborate in order to create integrated solutions can create significant value in an organization. You can't partner and collaborate externally within multiple participant value creation networks if you don't collaborate and partner internally. Whenever an organization tries to be a participant in a network, it needs to have collaboration in its DNA (see Table 3.1).

The case for collaboration is made from two perspectives that address customer needs. *Internal collaboration* will be required to draw on the expertise that resides across functional areas and business segments in order to create an integrated solution for the customer. As well, *external collaboration* facilitates an organization's participation in networks that capitalize on each organization's strengths in a value creation network that creates integrated solutions at another level for the customer.

Communities of Practice in the Context of an Enterprise-Wide Knowledge and Learning Strategy

Communities of practice cannot function in isolation. They must be part of a wider strategy that provides the socio-technical platform they require to flourish. An enterprise-wide knowledge and learning strategy forms the basis for creating communities of practice that span the entire organization. If you really want communities of practice to work, they have to be part of a larger strategy that provides direction for the creation of individual and organizational capabilities and then leverages what the organization and the people know.

It's also very important that the strategies that support communities are enterprise-wide. If you don't have the enterprise-wide approach and leverage your technology infrastructure, communities of practice will begin to form along functional or geographic lines. You will then lose your opportunity to develop the ability to collaborate across the organization, which produces the richness you need to create innovative, integrated solutions. And without the enterprise-wide approach, you will continue to support the creation of silos and hoarding of knowledge.

There are two key components to a comprehensive knowledge strategy: knowledge access (accessed from the knowledge repository located on the corporate intranet) and knowledge exchange (carried out through communities of practice). We define knowledge as the ability to take effective

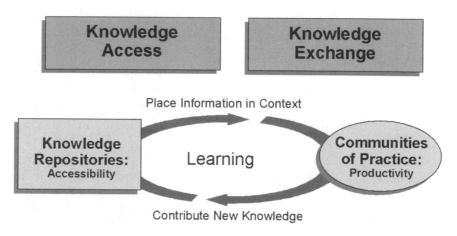

Figure 3.3.
Components of the Knowledge Strategy—The Knowledge Architecture

action (see Figure 3.3). Knowledge is information that has been placed into context and validated by others who have credibility. Information is turned into knowledge and inserted into one's practice through learning.

The purpose of the knowledge access component of this architecture is to put the full knowledge base of the organization at the disposal of every employee. The collective knowledge of the organization is stored here. It is made accessible to everyone without the impediment of organizational boundaries. A mistake that organizations can make is to segment their knowledge access by functions within the organization, which is counter-productive to fostering collaboration across functional areas or business segments. Knowledge exchange makes use of the knowledge that resides in the organization's knowledge base and in the experience of its employees—the exchange of explicit and tacit knowledge. Communities of practice play a significant role in both components. Communities draw from and contribute to knowledge repositories, taking codified knowledge and validating it with their members' experience. They are also a primary structure for exchanging knowledge through the collaborative use of productive inquiry.

Communities of practice are closely tied to action in the workplace. The information that is accessed and exchanged through communities of practice is readily applied to practice (i.e., the work of an individual or a team) because it has been validated by peers and shared in an open forum where members discuss the applicability of the information to the real world. Communities of practice are based on the mutual exercise of personal responsibility. All members share the responsibility to ensure that the information that is passed on is validated according to their own experience. By placing the information in the context of actual experience and validating it, members transform information into knowledge. The knowledge a member shares has his or her "stamp" on it. With some collaborative tools, this means that a photo is attached to a contribution, and a member profile that outlines experience and helps establish credibility may be just a click away.

On the other hand, the corporate intranet is anonymous. As a compilation of forms, procedures, policies, and other materials needed to accomplish work, an intranet for the most part provides information that individual users need to validate for themselves. By this we don't mean that the information on the intranet is incorrect—we mean that it hasn't been presented in a way that the users can readily apply it.

Types of Knowledge

Before we go much further, we should take a minute and make the distinction between how we use the terms explicit and tacit knowledge. *Explicit knowledge* is articulated or codified—the words we speak, the books we read, the reports we write, the data we compile. The deeper level of meaning in an organization, however, can be found in *tacit knowledge*—the unarticulated knowledge that resides in the intuition, perspectives, beliefs, and values that we form as a result of our experiences. Out of the beliefs and assumptions in our individual mindsets, we make decisions and develop patterns of behavior for everything we do. Our mindsets feed on themselves both positively and negatively. We believe what we see, and we see what we believe.

At the individual level, tacit knowledge forms a mental grid—a unique set of beliefs and assumptions through which we filter and interpret what we see and do. The grid guides our "auto-pilot" and our behavior. It acts like a lens that filters our interpretation and understanding of our personal experiences and communication and places boundaries around our behavior. In this way it delimits our performance and thus our results.

Data to Information to Knowledge

It's important in this context to understand how knowledge is formed and how people and organizations learn to use knowledge wisely. Let's look at the process of converting data into knowledge. Pieces of data arrive in our lives and on our desks as separate elements. Only when we compile these data into a meaningful pattern do we have information. As information is converted into a validated basis for effective action, it becomes knowledge. When individuals and organizations move through these levels from data to information to knowledge, the depth of meaning increases and interpretations shift from being highly explicit at the data stage to equal parts of tacit and explicit at the beginning of the knowledge state (see Figure 3.4).

Communities of practice are particularly effective at turning information into knowledge because they deal with information on the basis of experience. Tacit knowledge stems from someone's experience. In a community, members give greater meaning to information by applying their tacit knowledge. This is why communities of practice are so effective at engendering learning. They give significant richness to learning by adding tacit knowledge to explicit knowledge that couldn't otherwise be internalized—how would it be possible to read information (explicit knowledge) about something that someone really isn't totally aware of (tacit knowledge)?

Some people make the distinction between tacit and explicit knowledge by saying that tacit resides in someone's brain and explicit has been written down somewhere. We don't espouse this rather simplistic view. Plenty of explicit knowledge resides in people's brains. If you memorize a poem that was written down, is your knowledge tacit or explicit simply because it now resides in your head?

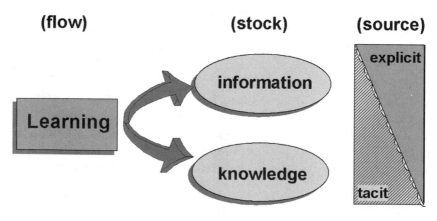

Figure 3.4.
Information to Knowledge

In our experience, people may not even be aware of the tacit knowledge they possess. How do master craftspeople or connoisseurs explain exactly how something is done or the extent of their knowledge? They may not be able to express what it is they actually do to complete an action. Harvesting tacit knowledge becomes quite a challenge for an organization. The best way that we have found to access tacit knowledge is through productive inquiry, getting to the core of an experience and understanding the many facets and nuances based on a need situated in the practice. We've seen many organization embark on projects to try and codify tacit knowledge, an effort that is at best fruitless. If you put communities of practice in place, tacit knowledge will surface naturally and be shared with the people who really need to know it. Next to the medieval guild structure of master and apprentice, a multigenerational community is the best way of getting at the richness of tacit knowledge.

Knowledge Access in Communities

Communities of practice best leverage and heavily rely on the knowledge access component of the architecture. When community members respond to a productive inquiry, they can refer to information made available from a knowledge repository of some sort—perhaps on the corporate intranet. For example, in response to a query on how to qualify a potential lead, a community member might say, "There is a collection of case studies on qualifying leads in the sales force's toolkit. Go have a look." The access to this information is a starting point, but the real value comes when another member adds, "And in my experience, the first stage that is outlined in the case on referrals doesn't work all that well. I've had more success by doing . . .." By providing the validation situated in experience and outlining a possible context for its use, the knowledge is further reinforced by a peer.

But as communities of practice evolve, their interactions often get cluttered by information that no longer needs to be discussed—it has been internalized by members and has been crystallized as part of their practice. It's then important to move this knowledge to a container in order to make it available to everyone in the organization, including the community members who shaped the knowledge in the first place. Information and knowledge that come from communities of practice are relevant by definition, otherwise community members would not have invested their time and energy in developing it.

The systematic development of communities of practice has to take place over time as part of a carefully designed approach. The core proposition of the community has to reflect the business priorities of the organization. In other words, the issues and problems addressed by these communities must be relevant to the strategic challenges of the organization. How can communities become more strategic? Let's look at the case for building communities of practice.

The Business Case for Communities of Practice

Communities of practice become key to capability development as the pace of the market environment keeps increasing and as highly capable people become more difficult to attract to an organization. We've identified four key areas that can be used to build the case for developing communities:

- Avoids the feeling of isolation.
- Promotes innovation.
- Increases the speed at which an organization can deliver new solutions.
- Readies the organization to participate in value creation networks.

Communities Address Isolation

As organizations have had to streamline and work in a multi-site configuration, they have found themselves with widely dispersed and often thin layers of expertise that do not have the critical mass or the depth required for capability development or knowledge exchange through the channels normally found in the workplace (e.g., water cooler, cafeteria, hallway, next office). For example, sales people in an organization that is distributed all over the world can find themselves isolated with no one to learn from or collaborate with on an informal basis.

An online community of practice offers the ideal approach to meeting this challenge. Online or virtual communities of practice allow for synchronous and asynchronous exchanges that transcend both distance and time. Placing communities online provides members with an opportunity to work together.

Communities Address Innovation

As customers continue to insist on integrated solutions, as the complexity of the knowledge required to do work continues to increase, and as the speed at which the organization must react to out pace the competition increases, the need for cross-functional and cross-disciplinary work becomes key to meeting customer needs and maintaining an effective market presence. Having developed the ability to learn in communities of practice, an organization has established a platform where collaborative problem solving and innovation are readily internalized as just the way people do their work.

A key source of innovation is the close interaction with members in a community of practice who have developed the ability to have productive conversations. These dialogues in which assumptions are questioned as a matter of course and people are committed to build on one another's ideas in a high-trust vessel for exchange will contribute significantly to elevating the innovation quotient of an organization.

Some pundits believe that communities of practice can only get better at doing what they are doing within a current set of assumptions. In other words, they don't innovate. Being self-governed means that people often don't confront their own assumptions. Perhaps that's true, but this is where the organization needs to help communities have productive conversations—conversations in which people listen deeply to one another and help those who disagree about something come to a new solution. The result is a synthesis that perhaps represents a new assumption, some new knowledge.

We'll talk more in Chapter 4 about the role of facilitation in communities of practice, but it's important to make the point here that in order to have a healthy level of innovation, a facilitator needs to keep members moving forward to fulfill the community's purpose. If you build this layer in, then your communities of practice will have an innovative effect. If you don't, they may be stuck in only propagating the current state.

Communities Address Speed

Speed has become a strategic imperative for most organizations. The time required for responses to changes in market trends will determine the extent of the competitive advantage achieved by an organization. Increasing the speed to respond to customer needs will in turn shape the durability and the profitability of the relationships with customers. On the other hand, a laggard in the marketplace will experience tension with customers who feel they are left with a product or service of lesser value than what could be obtained from a competitor. When community of practice members encounter a new situation or a new issue they have not seen before, they can get relevant, contextualized, and validated advice that they can readily apply within a relatively short period of time. Instead of having to search endlessly for information, they have immediate access to those who are best qualified to help them—their peers.

Communities Address Network Partnerships

As business networks emerge with the support of new technology, old-style competition is replaced by complex alliances and relationships that link organizations to provide greater value to customers than a simple one-provider/one-customer relationship. The ability to form partnerships and work across boundaries will be key to the choice of partners in the formation of these alliances. Given the strength of these emerging networks, the organization that is left behind will soon experience difficulty in the marketplace. Having extensive experience in building and sustaining cross-functional communities of practice will place organizations at an advantage in the development of these alliances. From this perspective, communities of practice become essential components of the readiness required for competing in the emerging business environment of the knowledge era.

THE STRATEGIC NATURE OF COMMUNITIES AT CLARICA

In this chapter, we've outlined where we see a shift in strategic context and how communities of practice can be leveraged to position an organization with this new strategy. Let's turn then to a validation of this information by looking at four areas where we have been able to realize the new strategic context with communities at Clarica.

- **A tool for alignment in the organization**—providing a common forum for like functions that are distributed across the organization.

- **A forum for problem solving**—creating a space where issues can be resolved with speed and creativity through knowledge exchange.

- **A center for knowledge creation**—bringing people together to accelerate learning and capability building.

- **An organizational infrastructure**—networking across multisite configurations or structures.

A Tool for Alignment in the Organization

As we enhance accountability throughout the organization and emphasize ownership for the profit and loss of a business segment, we adopt an organizational structure that moves away from segmentation by function. For example, the actuaries at Clarica no longer work within an integrated actuarial function. They are distributed in various business units where their skills are required. The advantage of this structure is that we can ensure that our actuaries are clearly attuned to the specific challenges of the business function where they work. The drawback is that we reduce their ability to learn from one another because of the distributed nature of their placement in the organization. They no longer sit next to one another. The casual conversations at the water cooler no longer take place.

As with all approaches to organizational structure, there is a trade-off in distributing professionals who used to have a corporate orientation to business segments. Communities of practice can be strategic in addressing the challenges of distributing professionals across business segments. The community becomes the rallying point, providing a forum for the people who have been distributed to come back together. The community has a strategic purpose because it allows for a systematic approach that can be used across the organization to foster a higher level of performance. The community optimizes alignment so that individuals engaged in similar work, although distributed across an organization, can collectively generate new capabilities that further their practice.

A Forum for Problem Solving

Communities of practice can be a highly effective way to bring together people who have an affinity of purpose and need. With high-caliber facilitation, these communities represent the best way to let people tackle complex tasks with speed and creativity. The multidisciplinary and multi-functional nature of many communities provides a unique vessel for resolving issues in innovative ways. A high-trust environment is created—what Nonaka refers to as "*ba*" (Von Krogh et al., 2000). Within the community, people are not afraid to propose ideas and test their thinking. They are not afraid of being "shot down." Instead, they welcome the suggested refinements or full challenges to their thoughts, knowing that through constructive criticism and collaboration their ideas can be advanced or improved upon in a safe environment.

This community collaboration contributes to the speed with which creative solutions can be developed. Using a community as a forum for problem solving ensures that everyone knows what challenges everyone else is dealing with. People can become engaged as they see the opportunity to contribute from their respective vantage points.

Problem solving, especially regarding business-critical issues, is a highly strategic activity. When Clarica acquired a business from another financial institution, a community of practice was used to inform the due diligence process and support the integration. The project team responsible for the acquisition used the community of practice as a source of expertise to anticipate issues and solve problems.

A Center for Learning and Knowledge Creation

The generation and constant renewal of capability in meeting business challenges is the most important sustainable advantage an organization can have. Yet, in a business context where speed and focus are key elements of success, learning is often neglected as the drive for performance becomes a single-minded preoccupation. Organizations need to transcend the perceived trade-off between learning and performing. Otherwise, the level of performance that is achieved will not be sustainable as the environment continues to change at an unprecedented pace.

A Conference Board of Canada study (2001) showed that managers felt that their employees lacked about 30% of the skills and knowledge they needed to do their current jobs. In itself, this gap represents a significant challenge to increase capabilities through learning. But the more frightening statistic is that these same managers felt that within three years, their employees will lack 76% of the skills and knowledge they'll need to do their jobs in the future.

More than ever, increasing capabilities is a strategic focus. But there is little time any more for setting aside responsibilities in order to engage in learning activities that are separate from work. Learning must be an integral part of work, seamlessly integrated into the routine of the day. In any event, people learn best when striving to achieve in the workplace. Learning must come from meeting challenges and demanding objectives related to work.

The challenge is to approach work in a manner that is conducive to learning. This is where communities of practice provide an unparalleled advantage. Communities lead to the generation of capability by having individuals who trust one another share their experience and put information in a context that is credible and can be used with confidence.

Transforming information into knowledge that leads to effective action requires a level of validation. This confirmation of quality and appropriateness can be best achieved in a community of practice where there is a high level of trust between individuals who are engaged in collaborative problem solving focused on their work.

An Organizational Infrastructure

Organizations of all sizes now operate out of several locations either on a national or global basis. The availability of talent is one of the key drivers in having people collaborate from different sites. The tools that support virtual collaboration allow people to transcend time and distance. It's now possible to collaborate closely with people over a period of time without having face-to-face contact with them. With enhanced bandwidth and the various software tools emerging to support communities of practice, it's possible for members of a community to develop high levels of trust by humanizing the experience. It's possible to weave the organization with these communities in such a way that proximity or the ability to get together frequently is no longer a requirement for effectively working together.

In most of our communities, we have members from across the country. The asynchronous dialogues provide the opportunity for members to discuss items at their convenience. (Canada has five time zones to manage.) Although sometimes a scheduling challenge, we can also facilitate synchronous discussions. The only difference is that our Newfoundland members are thinking about a late lunch while our British Columbia members are contemplating an early breakfast!

The organization that achieves this network of collaboration will have obtained a key strategic advantage not only in terms of cost savings, but also in the ability to attract and retain talent that would otherwise not have been possible.

CONCLUSION

Strategic management gurus Mintzberg et al. (1998) outline ways of looking at strategy. In this chapter, we've addressed three of them:

- **Strategy as pattern**—shows a consistent behavior.
- **Strategy as perspective**—represents the way an organization "does" something.
- **Strategy as ploy**—utilizes a "maneuver" to outwit an opponent or competitor.

By systematically creating communities of practice as a vehicle for increasing individual and organizational capabilities that are actionable, you'll have established a consistent behavior that leverages your knowledge capital, portrays a persona of your organization as a knowledge-driven organization that values its intangible as well as tangible assets, and creates a competitive advantage based on what it knows.

But more important, you will have created a level of organizational readiness that will help you successfully participate in value creation networks that are a result of the new strategic context driven by the marketplace in the knowledge era.

With communities of practice, you have the opportunity to make a significant difference in the quality of your organization's performance and situate it ahead of market demands as an industry leader. A Yukon saying, "The view only changes for the lead dog," speaks volumes to those organizations that are leading the pack!

COMMUNITIES AS A STRATEGIC LEVER— WILL IT PLAY IN PEORIA?

Based on the new strategic context of organizational networks, analyze your organization's position.

1. Is your organization currently participating in any form of value creation network? If so, what does it look like? How many participants are there? What do they each bring to the table?

2. How would you characterize your organization's role in the network?

3. How do you communicate within the network?

4. What capabilities are required to participate in the network? What capabilities did you already possess when you entered the network arrangement? What are you working on now? What needs to be addressed in the future? In other words, what is your learning agenda for increasing your capabilities in order to effectively participate in the network?

5. What is the reaction of your customers? How do they perceive the success of this network that is bringing them an integrated solution?

6. If you aren't currently participating in a value creation network, do you see this structure coming in your marketplace? Where? And how will you be ready to participate?

References

Conference Board of Canada. (2001). "E-learning for the Workplace: Creating Canada's Lifelong Learners." http://www.conferenceboard.ca/elearning/Downloads/CBoC_SFP/e learning_for_the_workplace.pdf

Mintzberg, H., B. Ahlstrand, and J. Lampel. (1998). *Strategy Safari: A Guided Tour through the Wilds of Strategic Management*. New York: The Free Press.

Von Krogh, G., K. Ichijo, and I. Nonaka. (2000). *Enabling Knowledge Creation: How to Unlock the Mystery of Tacit Knowledge and Release the Power of Innovation*. Oxford: Oxford University Press.

Further Reading

Dosi, G., D.J. Teece, and J. Chytry. (Eds.) (1998). *Technology, Organization, and Competitiveness: Perspectives on Industrial and Corporate Change*. Oxford: Oxford University Press.

Hamel, G. and C.K. Prahalad. (1996). *Competing for the Future*. Cambridge, MA: Harvard Business School Press.

Teece, D. J. (2001). *Managing Intellectual Capital: Organizational, Strategic, and Policy Dimensions*. Oxford: Oxford University Press.

Chapter 4

A Blueprint for Building Communities of Practice

Communities of practice in a strategic context are complex organisms that can significantly contribute to an organization's competitive advantage. However, it's not a given that any or all of the communities in an organization will reach a desired level of success or be able to sustain their value over time. In designing a community, careful consideration to the community's architecture and the factors that will support its success can help remove barriers before they challenge the viability and sustainability of the community. Creating a firm foundation for the community is one of the organization's responsibilities. The priority or intensity of these components and factors may vary by organization, but generally speaking, these building blocks are critical to the community's and, therefore, the organization's success.

Creating the Community Environment

In the Strategic Capabilities Unit at Clarica, we have a number of architects attached to each of our teams. Their role is to ensure the success of corporate initiatives. They may have responsibility for outlining resource requirements, identifying capabilities that will be needed and proposing a plan to generate them, or outline the technology that will be integrated into the corporate infrastructure. These building blocks are all important, but the greatest value that an architect brings is establishing the groundwork for the initiative's blueprint—identify a strategy that is linked to the organization's strategic imperatives, articulate the value proposition, and outline the precursors for success. The architect completes the cycle, by identifying how the initiative will be evaluated, the metrics that can measure success.

In this chapter, we assume the role of an architect by sketching the blueprint needed to create the environment for a community of practice. We complete our contextualizing part of the book by laying out the building blocks that are needed to create the community's foundation: the architecture, components, precursors to success, and approach for assessing the benefits.

THE ARCHITECTURE OF A COMMUNITY OF PRACTICE

Though communities of practice have existed for a long time, our experience at Clarica shows that they don't represent an organizational form that people naturally gravitate toward. Informal communities tend to form somewhat spontaneously, but they do not sustain themselves nor do they tend to be systematic in nature. They grow and evolve over time, and there's an attempt to capture their knowledge. But they do not have a significant effect on capability generation.

The fact that these communities exist as informal structures is of interest because they signal an opportunity to leverage a natural pattern that has potential but that hasn't been fully realized. For the most part, sustainable communities of practice need to be assisted in their creation and development. Their evolution has to be purposefully and systematically nurtured.

A case in point is the Learning Community at Clarica. For a number of years, a group of about 45 people, who have responsibility for providing learning in various areas of the corporation, have maintained a Lotus Notes Discussion Database on related topics and met once a month to hear a presentation on a topic of mutual interest—often a case study of a learning approach used in a particular department. While there was value in this community, there wasn't the richness of conversation, the creation of new knowledge, or the ability to move the learning practice at Clarica forward at the pace that was demanded to fully realize the potential of strategic capability generation.

In early 2002, the Learning Community evolved to a new stage. The Knowledge Architect realized the potential that the community had—we could leverage the generative capabilities of learning and collaboration found in these learning stewards and create a model of best practice for

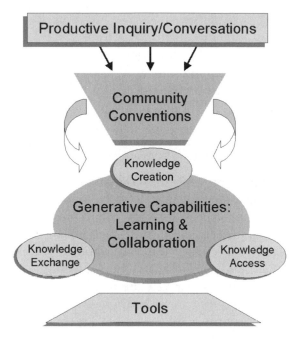

Figure 4.1.
Community of Practice Architecture

the rest of the corporation. The Learning Community was sponsored and funded. An online space using a virtual community tool was created for the whole community with sub-communities created for various special interest groups as well as the Steering Group. With this shift to a strategic context, the community has begun to have a significant effect on how learning opportunities are presented across the corporation at a critical time in Clarica's history.

Situating the Learning Community in a strategic context meant that a more formal architecture would be put in place and resourced to support the community's evolution from a sponsored to a structured community, based on a model used in other successful communities. We'll talk in depth about this process in Chapters 5–7.

The community architecture (see Figure 4.1) consists of four key components:

- **Productive inquiry**—the catalyst that drives capability generation; the need to know posted to the community in the form of questions that result in conversations.

- **Community conventions**—the community guidelines and norms.

- **Generative capabilities**—through learning and collaboration, the generation of capabilities based on knowledge objects that are created, accessed, and exchanged.

- **Tools and technology infrastructure**—the computer and tele-communications infrastructure that supports the community's conversations.

These four components create the community's framework. The need to know is the catalyst for a member to create a question that results in a conversation that is filtered through the community's norms. The community's knowledge objects are accessed and exchanged, and often new objects are created as a result of the conversations. The entire process is supported by the use of collaborative tools—a blend of approaches that facilitates the conversations, harvests the new or newly validated knowledge, and manages the community's knowledge stores.

Productive Inquiry

In Chapter 3, we talked about the information taxonomy—data, information, and knowledge. (There's a fourth layer, wisdom, but we're not quite ready to tackle that plane yet!) Knowledge is information that has been validated by the individual and has been inserted into one's practice as the way to do something. Knowledge is of higher value than information because it has been contextualized, validated, and situated in practice. Knowledge provides people with the ability to take effective action and is directly related to an employee's ability to perform. Communities of practice provide a mechanism for the transformation of information into knowledge. And the key catalyst for this transformation process is productive inquiry.

For example, a community member encounters an issue or a situation he/she has never experienced. He/she turns to other members of the community for advice by asking, "Have you ever seen one of these before?" The productive inquiry is not satisfied by *information*—a simple yes or no isn't going to address the depth of need. Instead, the response, or more likely responses, are offered from a position of experience with the subject matter. While there may be a straightforward reply, chances are a conversation builds in which advice, opinions, and information are offered, again situated in practice. And new knowledge may result from synthesis of member responses.

Productive inquiry initiates the actions of knowledge access, knowledge exchange, and knowledge creation. Knowledge creation is what makes communities of practice much more than a vehicle for sharing information alone. Information is like the grist that is brought to the mill. The community of practice turns it into something meaningful that can be applied to the problem in practice. As a result, a knowledge object is codified, made persistent, and contributed to the community's knowledge repository.

Productive inquiries spark discussion and can be seen as the engine of the validation process within the community of practice. Examples of productive inquiries include:

- How do I do this . . .? Are there particular segments that I should be aware of . . .?
- Has anyone seen something like this situation in the past . . .?
- Who else does this . . .? What can you tell me about it . . .?
- What can I do about this . . .?
- What is this all about . . .? What does it mean for us . . .?
- What am I missing here . . .?

The reliance on productive inquiries within a community is a pivotal point for interaction because it fosters the generation of useful knowledge. The knowledge needed is triggered by a real situation connected to the workplace. Communities are the most efficient and effective way for an organization to generate knowledge because they co-opt what members know. In our experience, the hard way to build knowledge is to say to someone, "Go and create an intranet and harvest everything we know." That approach is very labour intensive, and the value of the knowledge that will be included is determined in someone else's mind—someone who may not even be connected with the practice.

A more valuable knowledge store is created by the people who need to know something. And communities of practice, through their use of productive inquiry, are purpose-built for knowledge identification and creation. The role of the organization isn't to generate the knowledge, it's to provide the opportunity for the community members themselves to build the knowledge that's most valuable to their practice.

Community Conventions

The community's conventions serve as guideposts for how the community meets its purpose. A productive inquiry will be tested against the norms, guidelines, and practices that have been established by the community before it's acted upon. If the question is inappropriate in the first place, the community will let the member know that the community forum is not the place to discuss this particular topic. We've seen this filter work in subtle and not so subtle ways. More often than not it's new members, who haven't quite learned "the ropes," who quickly see the filter in action.

However, a large percentage of the productive inquiries pass through the community convention filters—perhaps because most members are keenly aware of the community's purpose and the benefits of participation. Their time is valuable, so they cut to the heart of the inquiry and immediately begin the collaborative problem-solving process.

Conventions will vary by community, but a pattern usually develops based on the culture and norms of the organization. Governance structures, membership selection criteria, code of conduct, expectations of participation, roles and responsibilities outlines, guidelines to contribute resources and create new knowledge objects, and protocols for online presentations are examples of the types of conventions that shape community-building activities over time.

Generative Capabilities: Learning and Collaboration

Here's where the real work of the community takes place and the real value is generated. Productive inquiries that have passed through the convention filters are acted upon by the members. Probably the best way to outline this process is with an illustration from Clarica's Agent Network

A member posted a query entitled "A Tricky but Basic Case," asking for advice on how to approach a young couple who had recently received a substantial cash gift from their parents. An outline of the couple's financial situation and goals was included. (This productive inquiry not only begins with a question, but also provides some context information that is required to guide the conversation that will develop.)

The discussion develops as members add their ideas almost in the form of a debate about the pros and cons of what should go into the customer proposal—term or universal life insurance, mortgage insurance, and money market options. To the product discussion, members contribute other factors to be considered such as the tax implications and the pressures of purchasing a first home plus tips on how to approach the sales process.

Later in the discussion, the member "reports back" on the progress and, in the end, summarizes the results: two new life policies, an increase in an existing policy, two registered retirement savings contributions, a term deposit, and a financial plan. With the help of community members, this agent was able to analyze options and present a plan that best fit the needs of the customers.

Because dialogues are archived, the conversation was captured as a knowledge object in the community's repository, but to make it more valuable, the facilitator synthesized the discussion and produced a case study. Community members can access the full discussion and see how the threads developed and who contributed what statements. Or they can read the case study. Not only is the knowledge made persistent, it is accessible in multiple formats.

A full cycle is completed based on the community's architecture: a productive inquiry is posted and filtered through the community's conventions, the knowledge assets of the community are accessed and exchanged, and a new knowledge object is created, enabled by the technology tools and infrastructure. The individual's need is met and the community's knowledge assets are increased for all to benefit from.

Tools and Technology Infrastructure

The foundation of the community's architecture is the technology infrastructure that supports collaboration and learning. Current demands on most organizations mean that a community's collaborative space must be accessed via multiple channels. The virtual space needs to be complimented by opportunities to meet face-to-face, on the telephone, and by e-mail. To support the many different kinds of conversations that will take place, the organization needs to provide the community with a variety of tools and approaches to maximize the opportunity for knowledge creation, access, and exchange. Given a geographically dispersed membership and the demands on schedules, online capabilities will make a difference in the value proposition for most communities.

The tools that are used to support the community should be fairly standard across the organization. The objective is to have people become familiar with a tool so that, when they encounter it again, they know how to use it. Creating a level of computer literacy within the community helps create greater readiness across the organization for the adoption of new technology. You don't have to have sophisticated tools to support the community, but the architecture must reflect the need to use multiple channels to develop and sustain interest in the community's discussions.

The key challenge for technology that supports communities is incorporating the social aspects of community at the lowest possible bandwidth. At this point in time because of the disparities in bandwidth across a large geographic space, community members may be limited in their level of participation if the technology incorporates a high degree of multimedia. The community vessel must be equally accessible by all members, otherwise an imbalance occurs and participation will be limited to the "haves" and exclude the "have nots."

Vendors of community technology tools have spent considerable time researching the needs of communities, and a new level of sophistication can be seen in this growing industry. Based on our experience, we suggest that there are four key components to consider in evaluating a technology solution to support communities that are situated in a strategic context. These categories reflect the architecture of the community and, in particular, the process of productive inquiry, application of community conventions, and interaction for collaborating and learning.

1. Facilitates rich conversations.

   Central to achieving the community's purpose is the ability to have quality conversations. With productive inquiry as a catalyst for generating and validating new knowledge, conversations drive the value proposition of the community as the members pursue their "need to know" and their "need to share."

   Functionality that supports conversations includes the ability to:

   - **Support the full cycle of productive inquiry** from posing the question to finding possible solutions, accessing relevant information, validating the information, and creating new knowledge.

   - **Create a tension that challenges the responses to a productive inquiry in order to refine the knowledge**—the ability of a group of individuals to offer varying opinions that develop a more appropriate version of a solution, refining and validating the new knowledge that has been created from a combination of information and members' tacit and explicit knowledge.

- **Sustain threaded dialogue**—a nonlinear representation of conversation that follows the thread of a discussion rather than placing multiple comments on various topics in a purely linear sequence (i.e., chronologically displayed as items are entered).

- **Facilitate the development of the solution**—the ability for an intermediary to enter the discussion, draw in varying opinions and external resources, and move the discussion toward resolution.

- **Keep members in the conversation**—draw in expertise as it is needed, soliciting knowledge through an alert system and tracking refinements to past conversations.

- **Hold conversations in a variety of ways**—the support of synchronous and asynchronous conversations in multiple channels: town hall meetings, informal chats, real-time meetings, small and large group forums, polling and voting, brainstorming, presentations, private discussions, instant messages, and visual and audio in addition to text representations.

2. Encourages participation.

   Establishing trust is the greatest challenge and the most significant reward in creating a sense of community that generates value for the individual, the community, and the organization. Trust is built through participation. Members may initially participate with some hesitation—like sticking your toe in the lake to "test the waters." But once members have had their contribution validated by the community (e.g., recognized for a thoughtful and/or thorough response, an innovative perspective, a contribution to solving a problem, a challenge to norms that moves the practice ahead), their trust level increases to a point where they feel safe in saying, "I don't know . . . or I need to learn . . .."

   Characteristics of the technology that will encourage participation include:

- **Ease of use**—intuitive functionality.

- **A "human face"**—a warm and friendly environment.

- **Convenient, integrated access that is immediate**—simple, straightforward, and engaging access that gives the member the opportunity for just-in-time contribution, integrated into the daily work routines and accessible from any location.

- **Self-service mentality**—I can do this on my own without a great deal of coaching, support, or intervention by other members or community support personnel.

- **Membership directory**—profiles that outline member's personal and professional traits, accomplishments, and values. Links to photos that "put a face to a name."

- **Feedback mechanisms**—the ability to provide as well as receive feedback on the value of contributions, to gauge the mood of the community—its appetite for pushing the envelop or raising the bar.

- **Sustainable involvement**—stimulates the member's curiosity, keeps people interested in participating and coming back to the community—the "eyeball glue" that is sought by so many Web sites.

- **Branded with values**—reflects the organization's, community's, and individual's values; I can see myself and recognize the values that I hold.

- **Multitasking**—the ability for a variety of purposes to be met with one interaction, such as: a contribution is made to a discussion while placing an item in the knowledge repository, booking an event, or broadcasting a request to a selected group of members.

- **Community conventions stated**—quick access to community norms, guidelines, purpose statements, and other references that help me make decisions on my participation.

- **Notification**—reminders that gain the attention of the members in an unobtrusive manner.

- **Additional features**—home page synthesis of community activities, notification of who's online, calendar of events, bulletin board and announcements, synchronous and asynchronous options to participate.

3. Supports knowledge access.

   While conversations are the catalyst for productive inquiry, communities add value over the long term because of the knowledge they generate. The need to access internal and external information as the first level of satisfying a productive inquiry relies on access to the community's knowledge objects. Following the full cycle of information management, the community needs a repository that supports the creation, management, and use of information and knowledge objects.

The technology features that support knowledge access include:

- **Integration with organization's tools and resources**—seamless connection to the tools and resources used in the course of work.

- **Internal and external resources**—access to databases, information sources, and news feeds that can provide overviews, annotations, and a synthesis of relevant information.

- **Straightforward method of contributing**—simple templates for providing pertinent data (e.g., item description, content annotation, meta-data, statement of responsibility).

- **Powerful search capabilities**—ability to locate resources using keywords, natural language, and full-text searching.

- **Various object formats**—ability to store information in any format or document type.

- **Collaborative tools to create new objects**—jointly develop, publish, distribute, archive, update, and expand or renew resources.

- **Evaluate value**—the ability to rank materials, comment on quality or priority, provide statistics of use, and discard when dated or no longer relevant.

4. Provides flexibility of structure.

We noted in Chapter 2 that community is one of the most difficult words to define—an exercise that can consume pages in sociology textbooks. It stands to reason that communities in organizations will take many shapes and need the flexibility to group and regroup, shape and reshape, or adapt and modify their structure to meet the current needs of the membership. The challenge for technology is to facilitate this constant need to evolve.

The functionality to support a flexible community structure includes the ability to accommodate:

- **Self-organizing groups and subcommunities**—the ability of members to group along lines of interest or need that require a distance from the community but also contributes back to the collective knowledge of the community—the ability to group and regroup spontaneously.

- **Secure and open spaces**—creation of different types of spaces for self-reflection and subgroups as well as the community as a whole that honors the privacy of the community and the individual while providing for the flexibility to introduce broad representation as appropriate.

- **Differentiated levels of entry**—provides the ability to engage people beyond the membership, both internally and externally, to participate at various levels in conversations and to contribute to the community's knowledge repository.

- **Networking of multiple communities**—the linkages necessary to share knowledge and collaborate across communities when appropriate, while contributing to the value of each individual community or participant.

- **Firewall restrictions**—management of the value and the limitation of the security of the organization based on the need to work in front and in back of the firewall.

- **Scalability**—to meet the demands of a growing community where increases in membership don't affect performance.

- **Low administrative burden**—the need for a simple and straightforward method of changing the community structure without complex profiling and de-profiling processes.

From the list of features that should be included in a technology used to support communities, we change our perspective to outline the qualities that should be included:

- Humanizes the virtual experience.

- Creates a space in which people can build and sustain trust.

- Offers a range of functionality to facilitate various forms of knowledge access and exchange in pursuit of creating value.

- Wraps a membrane around the community, creating a sense of place while allowing access to and input from external sources.

- Provides barrier-free access that responds to immediate needs.

No matter what technology infrastructure is chosen to support the community, there is a learning curve, a period of time required to reach a certain comfort level with the functionality. Perhaps the greatest challenge for the technology is to incorporate the sophistication needed to reflect the organization's culture and effectively support the community in its efforts while providing a seamlessly integrated tool that encourages contribution and sustains the value of the community to its members.

Blending Approaches

Technology has the ability to increase the value proposition of communities that are geographically dispersed or otherwise challenged to meet face-to-face. It's important to recognize that a community needs to function at several levels, managing a variety of media and taking the best that each has to offer. Figure 4.2 illustrates the combination of channels that support community conversations. Fundamentally what we're saying is that there are choices for how the community can collaborate—and the best possible approach is to blend the three, using the various channels as appropriate.

In the early stages of development, face-to-face meetings help lay the foundations of the community. People meet each other and share stories,

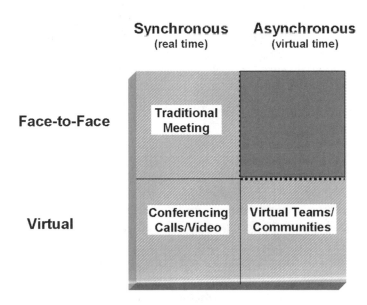

Figure 4.2.
Approaches to Community Collaboration

making connections, and finding common ground. Trust builds quickly and is reinforced with subsequent face-to-face meetings. There may be times when the community wishes to get together to celebrate an event—a significant accomplishment, anniversary, or contribution by individual members. In situations where certain mindsets (i.e., beliefs, values, attitudes) may need to be addressed to debunk misconceptions or misunderstandings, you need a rich dialogue that may not be conveyed effectively in a virtual mode. Or there may be a significant level of energy needed to address an issue that also needs the personal contact.

A virtual, synchronous channel could facilitate the collaboration between two groups such as a regional event that clusters members and then links to another cluster or draws in individuals who couldn't join a larger group. The possibilities are endless, and the lines become somewhat blurred as meeting notes are taken online and distributed at the end of the discussion and dialogues are started with the intent to later add to threads individually in an asynchronous manner.

A blended approach allows us to leverage the technology without losing the value of bringing people together—it extends the community's ability to collaborate in a variety of ways that not only suit the particular conversation but also meet the individual needs of members.

(Please note that the diagram doesn't quite work for the top right quadrant—but we had a bit of fun with it suggesting that in fact one could have an asynchronous face-to-face meeting where people had the time wrong and arrived at 30 minute-intervals, just missing one another . . .!)

The Roles and Responsibilities for Community Architecture

Designing and implementing the architecture to support a community that we outlined above requires a fair amount of effort. The responsibility for the development, continued support, and enhancement of a community's architecture is shared by the three layers involved in the community: the organization, the community, and the individual community members. The collaborative effort that is required is another way of building meta-capabilities into the organization. The very act of developing communities provides the organization with value, as it requires that sponsors, designers, implementers, and early community members become the first frame of reference for the value of collaboration and learning. They set a standard, model an approach, and add to the organization's knowledge about community building.

Components of Communities in a Strategic Context

To get under the skin of a community situated in a strategic context, we can dissect it into components to see the layers at work. We'll use Choo's framework once again to help organize our points. (See Chapter 1 for an explanation of the framework as it applies to the field of knowledge management.) With this approach we show how the framework can be adapted to identify key elements of the community for planning purposes. We've tried to use action-oriented terms to reflect our belief that knowledge is best defined as the capability to take effective action.

The framework helps organize our thoughts about characteristics of a community in a strategic context. But it may paint too simplistic a picture—perhaps one that's even too rosy! Often there is a great deal at stake in creating a community—there's a lot of pressure to succeed and then to sustain that success. Let's broaden the view of communities beyond components and characteristics.

Another way to look at communities in a strategic context is to talk about the opportunities and challenges that they present and the issues related to developing and maintaining these dynamic structures. We'll use the framework's vertical axis to organize the topics. And perhaps raise more questions than we'll answer (see Table 4.1).

Vision and Strategy

Given the community's close link with the organization's strategic imperatives, there is a need to clearly articulate the statements of vision and purpose. A plan to achieve this vision in the various phases of the community's development should be outlined.

Strategic Purpose

We've identified a number of categories that illustrate the type of strategic purpose a community of practice might meet:

- **Strategic theme**—a community purpose that is directly aligned with a theme that is articulated in the organization's strategic imperatives. For example, two communities were developed at Clarica to support the organization's stated goals. The Innovation

	KNOWLEDGE CREATION	KNOWLEDGE SHARING	KNOWLEDGE USE
VISION STRATEGY	Link to strategic imperatives: Identify individual capabilities required Build community vision	Link to strategic imperatives: Identify organizational capabilities required State community vision	Develop partnerships of purpose Establish trust between members and the corporation Communicate value
ROLES STRUCTURES	Include multi-generational members Identify subject experts Create sub-groups by interest or purpose	Use knowledge architects to outline plan for accessing knowledge Create advisory or steering group Provide expert facilitation	Members Stakeholders Sponsors Champions Advisory Group Facilitator
PROCESS PRACTICE	Contribute expertise Reflect on lessons learned Encourage innovation	Improve on approaches to practice Identify new products or enhancements Evaluate approach and benefits Harvest knowledge	Relate to value proposition Motivate participation Reinforce sponsor support Develop community building capabilities
TOOLS PLATFORMS	Provide community dialogue space Provide collaborative tools	Create knowledge repositories	Leverage technology investment Create e-business mindset

Table 4.1.
Community Components

for Growth Network was created to spark conversations around innovation, one of Clarica's six strategic imperatives for 2002. And, earlier when we introduced our commitment to creating a strong brand presence in the market place, a community to support the introduction of an enterprise-wide initiative on the use of plain language was developed to increase our capabilities to delivery *clarity through dialogue* as one of our brand promises.

- **Core organizational competency**—a community purpose that is focused on increasing a core competency through collaboration and learning. For example, due to the cross-functional groups that were being created to meet customer demands for integrated products, we identified the need to establish a standardized approach to project management—an approach that would be used throughout the organization so that as teams came together they would know what is expected, what process would be followed to manage the projects. Under the leadership of project management experts, a community was formed to help identify the standard as well as to increase the capabilities of individual members in the practice of project management.

- **Common development needs**—a community purpose that supports the development of competencies in a specific area that may be used in a number of areas of an organization. For example, due to the complexity of providing customer service on a wide range of insurance and financial products that are sold to individuals and to groups, we have a number of specialized customer call centers. The customer service representatives have a common set of competencies that are required plus a specialized content area. A community of practice was created for people who train customer service representatives with the purpose of standardizing approaches based on best practice that existed within the separate units.

- **Distributed functional expertise**—a community purpose that supports a space for people who have a common functional expertise but are distributed across the organization. For example, our actuaries used to work within a single corporate unit. They sat next to each other, could engage in informal conversation, and could collaborate on problem solving over the tops of cubicles or in the hallways. Once the actuaries were dispersed into business units, they lost their physical proximity and needed a structure to facilitate their conversations. A community of practice was formed to support this purpose.

- **Cross-generational exchange of knowledge**—a community purpose to meet the realities of our aging demographics. One of biggest challenges is to provide opportunities for our experienced employees to pass on their expertise to less experienced people. While we haven't developed a "knowledge ready to walk out the door when someone retires" community, we have made a conscious effort to encourage cross-generational participation in all our communities. Learning from a peer, passing validated knowledge that is situated in practice is our most effective way of collecting the knowledge we need to hold as an organization that otherwise may reside only within an individual. This factor was key to the creation of the Agent Network—we systematically invited experienced and developing agents to promote mentoring across generations.

Convergence of Purpose

While a strategic purpose can be identified from the perspective of the organization, chances are that same purpose may not be seen as critical to either the individual member or the community as a whole. Members are likely to have different rationales for their participation at the outset.

However, it's extremely important that there is a convergence of purpose as seen by the different perspectives of sponsors, the organization, the community, and the individual members. There must be a strong level of coherence around a central purpose in order to maximize the value proposition for each of the stakeholders—a key group being the members themselves.

Roles and Responsibilities

Like the communities in which we live, the people supporting and participating in a community of practice have a variety of roles that help set-up, develop, nurture, and sustain it. In Chapter 2 we looked at the various types of people involved in a community according to their behavior or participation. From our work with communities at Clarica, we've identified these roles from a point of view of responsibility for the community's health and well-being.

Organization's Role

As we noted earlier, the role of the organization isn't to generate knowledge, its role is to provide the leadership and the resources necessary for knowledge to be identified, created, and accessed by the people who need to use that knowledge in the course of their practice. Specifically, the role of the organization in the community architecture is to:

- **Endorse the community approach**—provide a level of leadership and support that values the community's contribution.

- **Provide effective technology infrastructure**—ensure that the community has the collaborative tools it needs to support conversations, store and access knowledge objects, and realize other community activities.

- **Nurture the community's evolution**—encourage the community to continue to develop and evolve to meet its and the organization's purpose.

- **Engender the spawning of communities across the organization**—encourage the creation of communities and support their development in line with strategic imperatives.

- **Steward the implementation of the knowledge strategy**—ensure that communities are central in the strategy's knowledge map.

- **Model community principles of behavior**—provide leadership on the development of meta-capabilities and individual capabilities inherent in an effective community.

When we look at the organization as a network of communities, the responsibility of the organization is to weave communities together. Communities then compliment the boxes and lines that denote the organizational structure. Communities don't detract in any way from this more traditional structure. Instead, they add flexibility to what the organization can do, increase the speed at which goals can be achieved, and provide the capabilities for the integrated solution approach that is required by customers in the knowledge era.

Community's Role

As a self-governed organizational form, communities of practice have a key responsibility in designing and managing the community's architecture. Specifically, the community provides direction, administration, and development for:

- **Governance mechanisms**—as self-governed entities, communities take ownership of the guidelines necessary to keep the community moving forward toward its goals.

- **Conventions and norms**—members look to the community to help outline the components of its culture and practice that guide the community's activities.

- **Knowledge object creation and access**—communities are responsible for managing their knowledge, outlining approaches for creating, storing, and accessing their knowledge objects.

- **Maintenance of the community space**—in order to leverage the tools and technology that enable the community's activities, the community ensures that its members are familiar with the collaborative tools and that the space is well utilized.

- **Sub-communities and the connections between them**—as the community evolves, themes within the overall practice start to appear and the community is responsible for self-organizing how they want to develop their conversations and maintain the connections between the main community and its segments.

- **Alignment with corporate strategy**—as part of the "bigger picture," the community needs to understand where it fits in the organization's network of communities, its relationship to the knowledge strategy and to the organization's governing strategy.

- **Advancement of the practice**—while there is emphasis on the support for each member to increase capabilities, the community's primary purpose is to move the practice ahead, which in turn improves the organization's ability to perform and helps create its competitive advantage.

The self-governing nature of the community places a great deal of responsibility on the community to manage the resources that are provided by the organization and to ensure that the community is constantly moving toward its purpose. A steering or advisory group, the facilitator, and community leaders may play a more prominent or visible role. But in the end, it's the community members who will make the difference. The community will not sustain its value if all the responsibility is left to a handful of organizers.

Individual Member's Role

Membership in an informal community tends to be less permanent than in a structured community—people tend to come and go depending on their level of interest at the time. When the community is aligned with a strategic purpose, the members see a direct effect on their ability to perform because of their involvement in the community, so they stay involved. Their level of participation may vary, again based on interest and time availability, but their commitment level remains high and they have a feeling of responsibility to keep the community alive. Individual community members, then, have a responsibility to:

- **Bring problems of practice to the community**—keep the community active in pursuing ways to address problems in the practice.

- **Participate in the productive inquiry conversations**—provide expertise, advice, and opinion to help solve the problems presented.

- **Develop community conventions**—participate in shaping the guidelines and norms that govern the community.

- **Establish links with other communities**—support the creation of a knowledge network across the organization by making connections between the various communities in which they are members.

- **Engage in personal and professional development**—continue to increase individual capabilities that in turn will challenge the community to keep the practice moving forward.

Although they have the shortest list of responsibilities compared with those of the organization or the community, the members play the most important role. Without the commitment of individual members to quality participation, the community's value is not sustainable, and, within a relatively short period of time, the community will cease to exist.

Along with these roles come some tensions:

- If membership has its privileges, will we create an exclusionary group? Are we building a gated-community mentality that keeps people out rather than lets them in?

- Working on work-related issues sounds like a glorified team to many. How will you distinguish the community from other organizational structures? How will you show its unique characteristics and create support for the role a community plays in the organization?

- The organization's role is to provide support for the community, but it may not be invited to participate in the community itself.

Can management provide resources with no strings attached? How can the community build the trust that is necessary to assure management that the community that is funded by the organization is focused on achieving its purpose, not on creating an undercurrent that moves against management directions?

- Where does the facilitator report? If paid by the organization, but guided by the advisory group, where is his/her accountability? Is the facilitator one of us or one of them? What are the boundaries of the facilitator's liaison role? How are sensitive issues kept confidential?

- As in all forms of human interactions, there are bound to be tensions—between community members, between members and the facilitator, and between sponsors and the community. How are these tensions resolved? What responsibility does each participant in the community development process have to keep the tensions productive—as catalysts for improvement rather than a deterrent to progress?

Policies and Procedures

Policies and procedures support the community in accomplishing its purpose. We talked earlier about how the community filters the productive inquiries posted by the members through a series of community conventions. We'll talk more about our experience with putting guidelines in place in Chapter 7. In this section we'd like to look at the mechanics of the community—how the pieces of the architecture work together to facilitate the community's conversations and capability generation.

Accessing Information vs. Exchanging Knowledge

There's no question that people need a lot of information to do their work. With the rapid changes in the marketplace, there is a steady stream of new information coming down the pipe faster than it can be ingested. "Drinking from a firehose" and "drowning in information" are popular analogies that typify the situation for many employees. The community offers the ability to move beyond information overload to meaningful knowledge exchange.

Corporate intranets and document repositories provide access to a wealth of codified information—a place where people go to find basic information for answering questions or solving problems. But often the single dimension or static nature of information doesn't provide the level of meaning that the individual requires to take effective action. Within a community, knowledge exchange provides access to people's experience in a given situation. When people who have had a similar situation can talk about their experience, they can outline what worked and what didn't work and how their experience can be applied to another situation. They can say, "Here are some things that you need to think about, things you need to be careful about." When this information comes to the members with meaning, they are able to take action. The new knowledge becomes an inherent part of practice—it's not just lying out there unattached to real situations. Community members can internalize it, make it theirs, and assimilate it into how work is done. It's the difference between simply accessing and reading information and having it given meaning through the experience other people who work in similar situations.

Knowledge is the precursor to effective action. Communities play an essential role in providing opportunities to learn—not just to access information. This is how communities contribute to generating the capabilities that will serve to realize business objectives.

Infrastructure—Tools and Platforms

Given the current work environment, chances are the community will have some form of technology available to support its collaboration. Once considered the tail wagging the dog, technology as an enabler has year after year increased productivity. Organizations now have a better handle on leveraging the infrastructure in which they so heavily invested during the past decade.

Technology's Development Cycle

We've seen technology move through an amazing maturation process (see Figure 4.3). When first introduced, technology was used to automate business processes—to make them less labor intensive, less manual. Data processing centers of the 1960s and 1970s came of age when huge computer systems were created to store and manipulate data that previously had been relegated to paper and microfilm. Appropriately named for its ability to "compute," this new technology had a significant effect on selected areas of the organization.

From a focus on collecting and storing data, technology advanced to be able to interact with data, to order and compile it in a systematic way to

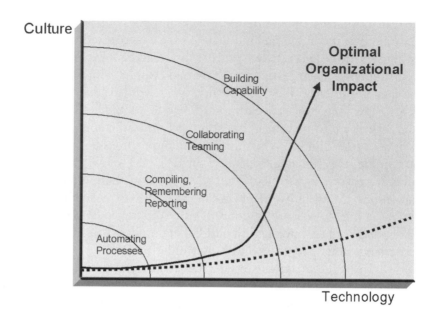

Figure 4.3.
Stages of Technology Development

generate reports and produce information on transactions. Legacy systems that competently handled transactions were replaced with systems that could yield and remember data about these transactions. Computers as information management systems had a more significant effect on the organization as a tool for making decisions from an informed position.

What we're seeing now is a new level of technology development—the ability to support collaboration across functions, disciplines, and organizations. With advancements in telecommunications and computer technology, organizations now have the ability to collaborate across functions and disciplines, between selected individuals as well as between large groups of individuals that may be locally situated or geographically dispersed. Technology tools are now part of most processes within an organization, integrated into the daily routine of employees as well as supporting all functional or operational areas that support the organization's business.

The ability to telecommute, collaborate with colleagues around the world in real time, and bring just-in-time learning to the desk top are just a few indicators of technology's next stage of development. We talk about this next phase and how it furthers the work of communities in Chapter 11.

Changing Business Approaches—Leveraging Technology

In an interview about our work with communities, we were asked about the effect of the terrorist attacks of September 11th on the way we do business. Was there an increased emphasis on establishing online communities in light of heightened security and restrictions in ease of travel? Given our geographically dispersed company, there's no question that those attacks have affected the way we do business. But we see the events of September 11th more as a catalyst for accelerating a change that was already underway than as a particular incident that caused a change in our approach.

In most instances, travel was the preferred method of doing business. Bringing staff to the head office or another central location for a myriad of reasons meant that we could interact with our agents and employees in a meaningful way. But we were seeing the toll that travel took on our employees—the effect of travel on personal lives and a growing negative effect on commitment to the corporation. In addition, the costs of travel were continuing to increase. To bring 50 agents from across Canada together for a meeting represented a significant investment on the part of the corporation and the agents—an investment that might be necessary, but was perhaps not the best use of both time and money.

At the same time, bandwidth is increasing and becoming more affordable. We now have more opportunities to rely on virtual means to do our business. As technology tools are enhanced and bandwidth increases, opportunities for quality interactions via technology also increase and may go a long way in addressing a need to physically be present in a given situation. The performance of the organization has a lot to do with the quality of conversations both internally and with customers. So, talking with one another—entering into dialogues where we are really listening to each other—to build on one another's capabilities helps us achieve more. And advancements in technology provide us with an opportunity to have these conversations in a way that has not been available until now.

Partnering with Community Technology Infrastructure Vendors

Advances in technology have provided organizations with options that continually transform the way they do business. The level of sophistication that is available brings with it a corresponding level of complexity that challenges organizations to understand the implications and take advantage of all that is available, while trying to provide employees with intuitive, integrated solutions.

As outlined in the previous section, the challenges in providing effective software solutions that support communities of practice are significant. While collaborative tools exist that will support the basic interchange, software has a substantial challenge in providing solutions that can be fully harmonized with the organization's culture and maximize the community experience. This challenge can only be met through a partnership approach between the organization and the vendor—a collaborative effort that brings together the extensive knowledge base surrounding technology's efficacy and the intimate understanding of the organization's culture.

Communities are an integral part of an organization, and the technology that is used to foster community development is so embedded in the way the community functions that a disconnect between the technology and the community would be extremely harmful to all the efforts spent in helping the community succeed. When choosing a vendor to support your communities, the capability to partner should be a key criterion.

No magic pill, plug-and-play, or shrink-wrapped solution exists that can meet the complex challenge of merging culture and technology to the level needed to create a high-trust collaborative environment for communities. Although we recognize the value of standardization and purchasing "off the rack" products whenever possible, when it comes to creating a community vessel, customization will be required. The key challenge is to produce the right blend of the social and cultural requirements of the organization with the capabilities of technology that will continue to evolve as the organization evolves and the technology advances.

In our opinion, a partnership with the vendor is the only way to achieve the level of customization required. The option to develop in-house is not viable. A community needs an extremely rich level of functionality that continues to evolve—an expensive proposition if carried out alone. Rather, we need to spread the core investment across as broad a customer base as possible to reduce the basic costs of ownership and shift the resource dollars to satisfy the requirements for customization.

Partnering with vendors models the principles of the value creation network that we talked about in Chapter 3. Each participant brings to the table its expertise—the customer with a knowledge of its culture and community requirements; the vendor with an understanding of the technology and the experience gained working with other customers. This might be too simplistic a view, but it serves to illustrate the basis of the collaboration—the ability to provide a product that an organization needs that in turn informs the vendor's research and development of the product for the rest of the market.

The customer/technology vendor partnership can be explored from a variety of perspectives:

- **Collaborative development:**

    To fully integrate an organization's culture and a company's technology solution, the technology vendor must become sufficiently engaged to understand the organization's social and cultural requirements. This understanding can't be established in advance of an agreement to buy. It must be built over time with significant input from the organization and a genuine commitment from the vendor to knowing the customer.

- **Continued product evolution:**

    With markets driving change at an increasing rate, organizations must continue to evolve their interaction with the marketplace— to move from a make-and-sell mentality to a sense-and-respond approach that more closely meets the needs of the marketplace. A vendor/customer partnership creates an understanding that all participants have a stake in the continued development of the product—that needs will be met according to a jointly agreed upon schedule set by the pace of market demands rather than by fixed development cycles.

    The product also needs to be enriched on a gradual basis. As the technology becomes embedded in the day-to-day routines of the community, a significant change in how the tool functions can impede the continued development of the community. Enhancements should be introduced in degrees, based on community priorities. A partnership approach ensures that the customer has meaningful input on the product's evolution. If the customer isn't involved and the vendor heads in a significantly different direction, the community's development trajectory could be altered.

- **Complement to internal resources:**

    Partly due to the sophistication of technology solutions, vendors have adopted a new business model in which the majority of their revenue stems from consultative services to the customer, not from the sale of a software package or computer system. If an organization doesn't have appropriate internal resources or expertise, the vendor can assume a closer relationship with the customer in order to integrate the solution. However, the consultant resources, like the technology solution, must first understand the organization's culture as a context for the consulting. Vendors who don't invest in doing so will find that their consulting services along with their technology solution will not achieve a satisfactory level of acceptance by the organization.

- **Alignment of purpose:**

  As vendors realize the effect of culture on the use of technology tools, customer/vendor partnerships will deepen. Although different objectives are identified for each participant in the partnership, an alignment of purpose is achieved through the recognition that these tools are not culture neutral—that the shrink-wrapped solution can not be unceremoniously dumped into a workplace and be readily accepted. To achieve success, the tool must be tailored to the needs of the culture—a state that requires a deep understanding of the organization's values and mindsets.

- **Long-term view:**

  The vendor/customer relationship should be a creative partnership that is innovative over the longer term. As communities are spawned across the organization, the need for a standardized tool that supports various communities becomes a significant factor. The goal is to have an organization that is based on a network of communities. If there isn't a common platform, the community effort becomes segmented, and the value of a seamless network of communities is lost. People can't easily move from one community to the next and the knowledge assets remain inaccessible to the broader organization.

There's no question that the type of relationship we're discussing here is more complex than a straightforward contract. You have to maintain an ongoing relationship to create value for one another. All partners must be able to see the value that each participant brings to the relationship and maintain an open and honest dialogue on the challenges.

Clear expectations need to be stated. The vendor has to be willing to marry the social aspects of the organization to the software. If they have a shrink-wrapped view of the world, it's unlikely that they'll satisfy your community needs.

Precursors for Building Effective Communities of Practice

Whether you call them critical success factors, barriers to success, issues and challenges, or "must haves," there are elements that are precursors to success. It's a given that we do not intentionally set ourselves up for failure. But we can be blindsided if we don't pay attention to the factors that can challenge our success. We need to mitigate as many risks as possible to clear the path for the community. It will have enough challenges as it gets going, but there are things that we can do to provide a fertile ground to give it the greatest chance for early successes that will fuel its development.

Communities of practice become a highly leveraged tool for organizations that want to systematically cultivate and enhance learning and collaborating as meta-capabilities. You can have communities of practice that you don't leverage. In fact, we'll wager that you have multiple communities at work in your organizations right now that are not contributing to the organization's success at a level they could be because you aren't maximizing their potential systematically across the organization. Communities of practice require rich soil in which to grow and develop the ability to contribute to the overall success of the organization.

McDermott (2000) outlines the critical success factors of communities of practice in terms of management, community, technical, and personal challenges. We found that the precursors for building effective communities at Clarica cross the layers of organization, community, and individual members that we've used to organize other discussions in this book. In fact, you can see an element of all three layers in each of the seven critical success factors that we've identified. Often there is shared responsibility for ensuring that these situations are addressed before the community's launch or throughout its development. In the end, you want to ensure that you've done everything you can to establish the right conditions and keep nurturing your communities.

To create the best situation possible for communities of practice to succeed, we suggest that an organization in partnership with the community and its members address the following factors:

- Shared sense of purpose and ownership.

- Self-initiated view of learning and a readiness to learn from each other.
- Overall climate of trust and involvement.
- Partnering mindset and corresponding skills.
- Strong technology platform.
- Supportive context and leadership endorsement.
- Realistic expectations on return on investment.

Shared Sense of Purpose and Ownership

People across the organization and communities must identify with a shared sense of purpose for communities. They must share in the ownership of the organization's strategy to leverage communities as part of a broader commitment to the value of a knowledge strategy and to develop meta-capabilities. Without a shared sense of purpose and ownership, people will wonder why they should participate in a community, why they should support its development, or how a community can possibly make a difference in any success.

Through a shared sense of purpose and ownership, we model the generative capability of collaboration. We recognize that our involvement in community development at any number of levels makes us individually successful as we help other colleagues become successful. Communities of practice cannot function without a high level of interdependence both within the community and in the environment that surrounds it.

Self-Initiated View of Learning and a Readiness to Learn from Each Other

Communities of practice will thrive in organizations that place priority on capability development. Learning must be considered an integral part of the work individuals do as well as the work of the organization as a whole. People in the organization must assume responsibility for their own learning, which only comes once people have assumed full ownership for their performance. In other words, people must be actively engage in learning in order to fulfill performance commitments. And there must be agreement in the organization that learning is essential to sustain high levels of performance.

A focus on learning is sometimes seen as admitting that you don't know everything you need to know or even should know. For communities to thrive, the members must accept that no one has all of the answers to resolve issues, to respond to customers, and to create new solutions. It has to be okay to say, "I don't know how to do this . . .."

The level of expertise required in an organization is well beyond what any single person can mastered. People must be ready to learn from one another. They must be willing to ask questions that will draw on the experience, the knowledge, and the insights of their colleagues. They must be willing to admit that they don't know something. And the community must be willing to support them in admitting a need and increasing their capabilities. Communities succeed, in part, because collaborative learning is an integral part of the culture—an organizational norm.

Overall Climate of Trust and Involvement

People have to believe that their active involvement in communities of practice will serve to achieve worthwhile objectives. They must trust that their contribution will make a difference and will be recognized. It would be extremely difficult to create communities of practice in an organization where little trust has been established—where individuals feel that their managers and colleagues only have an interest in their own success; where people feel that there is more interest in their demise than their success. Without this level of trust, people will question the value of participating in a community and may avoid participating at all costs because they aren't sure of the underlying motives of the organization or management.

Learning and acquiring capability stem from asking questions, which may signal a sense of vulnerability (e.g., admitting that you don't know something). The community has to be safe place where members can be honest and admit that they don't know something. Communities of practice can be conducive to learning and innovation if there is a willingness to ask questions, engage in productive conversations, and contribute honest answers. In order for creative thinking to permeate a community of practice, participants must be ready to engage in a dialogue robust enough to test one another's assumptions. They must be willing to explore issues, to build on one another's ideas in a constructive manner, and to collaborate on creating new viewpoints. None of this can happen without a climate of trust.

Partnering Mindset and Corresponding Skills

Effective partnering means that people are ready to give up control and trust that others will accept responsibility for their role in the partnership, including the outcomes. The ability to let go is based, for the most part, on the belief that people will do the right thing, given half a chance.

For communities to succeed, the organization has to be oriented to partnering, seeing the need to build the meta-capability of collaboration into its DNA. The organization must support the notion that through partnering, we can increase synergy. And in the end, the organization and its employees must collectively believe that the whole is greater than that proverbial sum of its parts.

Strong interpersonal skills are essential to partnering. These skills also contribute to productive conversations, to effective dialogues, and to the resolution of conflicts as they emerge, which if you watch a community, you will discover are the cornerstones of its activities.

Strong Technology Platform

Supportive technology is necessary for building effective communities of practice in any organization. Although in the past, communities of practice have flourished in organizations without technology platforms to support them, our experience tells us that this is no longer realistic. The asynchronous nature of the online environment represents a key require-ment for speed and immediacy. It can take several months to bring a sig-nificant number of people together for exchange. By the time meetings actually take place, the discussion planned has probably lost all relevance. The exchange has to be made timely and convenient. The discussion must be sustained and yet not place unnecessary strain on a member's time or ease of participation. Technology can enable this form of communication.

The technology must be based on socio-technical principles. It must provide an electronic vessel that is conducive to building trust among members. It must keep friction costs to a minimum. This vessel must be hospitable and support productive conversations online. An effective ves-sel can provide for a surprising level of candor and genuine exchange as people become used to a new way of having conversations.

Supportive Context and Leadership Endorsement

Communities of practice must be actively endorsed by an organization. Leaders must recognize communities as a strategic resource, providing a legitimate platform for learning, collaborating, and creating customer value. The leadership of the organization must invest in the infrastructure that will support the development of communities and articulate a strategy to integrate communities into the way the organization works. With appropriate support, communities can yield a high level of value.

Leadership support takes the form of commitment, investment in a technology infrastructure, guidance on process, and provision of other required resources. Without a high level of support, communities will be left vulnerable because they will lack the legitimacy they need to be sustainable over time as an integrated element of the organization's fabric. One way to strengthen communities of practice is to provide them with official sponsors from the ranks of senior leaders.

The support provided by leaders must be facilitative in nature and must focus on ensuring that the communities they sponsor have the right level of resources and support from other managers. Senior leaders must be prepared to invest time and money in building and sustaining communities.

Even with a strong corporate knowledge strategy, introducing communities into an organization requires the application of change management principles. In fact, creating one or many communities in an organization represents a major intervention in the way the organization functions. In other words, the formation of a community of practice is not without implications for the organization and the established managerial order.

Territorial issues or other obstacles are prone to crop up as communities interact with the formal accountability structure of the organization. In this context, sponsors can make a particularly important contribution in terms of "boundary management." For example, there may come a time when the sponsor will have to intervene in order to ensure that technology support for the communities is given the right level of priority. Other boundary management issues might include modifying the organizational policies and processes that pose barriers to active participation in a community. Again, senior leaders will be required to span these boundaries on behalf of the community.

With communities of practice, we are establishing another dimension in which things get done in an organization. A new structure often ends up in competition with existing structures if it isn't fully endorsed at the senior level. It's fair to say that you won't get everyone onside. You shouldn't wait until you do because that may NEVER happen. Make sure you have the support of key people and continue to build that support.

For the most part, people who speak out against establishing communities are not speaking from experience. Instead, they may have some theoretical objection to communities or fear of change. Our best advice is to introduce a community well positioned for success and start working through the leadership challenges that may exist.

While leadership support is imperative to a community's success, a controlling presence by a senior manager can be toxic. It's crucial that sponsors do not prescribe the community format, activities, or outcomes. Instead, they must work with internal community leaders to provide resources, coordination, and advice, lending support and legitimacy to the community's development.

Realistic Expectations of Return on Investment

Putting an infrastructure in place to support community building can represent a significant investment in time and resources. The extent of need for new infrastructure will depend on what the organization already has in place in its people, strategy, culture, and technology infrastructure. The financial contribution from communities of practice to the organization's bottom line may not be readily quantifiable.

Leaders have to consider the cost-benefit ratio of this investment in organizational and strategic terms and make a managerial judgement based on less quantifiable information. It is important to have a realistic view of the possibilities and limitations of communities of practice. Although they enhance organizational performance through the resolution of specific organizational issues, they do not represent a panacea for all organizational ills.

Without a realistic view, communities of practice will be left vulnerable, lack legitimacy, and their sustainability will be questioned. We'll talk more about metrics towards the end of this chapter. But it's important to note, that while the knowledge era will bring new ways of doing business, perhaps the most significant change will be in how we measure or count value. There's an enormous amount of discussion about how to value knowledge assets, moving employees from the debit side to the credit side of the ledger and assigning value to knowledge assets that are intangible.

As communities are more pervasively valued across the economy, we believe measures and methods of valuation will be adopted so that decisions that are not primarily based on leaps of faith will no longer present a challenge to creating communities. In the meantime, it will be important for business leaders to not assume that the effect of communities of practice can be readily assessed in terms of dollars and sense.

Creating the right environment to foster community success requires a great deal of attention to fundamentals that can also benefit the organization in other areas. The seven critical success factors we've outlined above can support any organizational initiative, but in particular, they will pave the way to success for communities of practice that are situated in a strategic context.

COMMUNITY SUCCESS CRITERIA

How do we know that a community is successful? What value is it contributing to the organization, the community, or the individual member? From what or whose perspective will success be measured?

It's appropriate to begin this section with a series of questions because that's essentially what measurement is all about—finding answers to questions. The challenge becomes deciding on the right questions! We'll talk more in Chapter 8 about our particular approach to assessing the value of a specific community at Clarica, but to complement the discussion of critical success factors, we'll identify items that we believe are useful in determining whether or not the community is working well. We've grouped the statements by where we see the value creation points of the community:

- **Community building**—Is the community meeting the needs of its members? Are the members participating and contributing at a level that is valuable?
- **Community acceptance and support**—Does the community's value extend beyond its own borders? Do other people see the value of a particular community and communities in general?
- **Community mechanics**—Does the community work? Are the right tools and processes in place? Is the infrastructure supporting the community?

Community Building

- Members have the confidence that their questions will be answered. They know that they will get support from the community when they need it.

- Members are passionate about the theme that represents the focus of the conversation in the community.

- Members share in the ownership of the community and exercise leadership as required to ensure its effectiveness. They are committed to making it work because they see it as a worthwhile investment of their time and efforts. They make sure that the community realizes its purpose.

- The community is actively developing knowledge objects. The pace and quality of these objects become leading indicators of the community's vibrancy and value.

- Although the community constantly evolves, members are clear on its purpose and how it should function. They are committed to making it work. They have clear and realistic expectations for the participation of other members. When issues emerge around expectations, members can confidently engage in a process that will lead to redefining a joint set of expectations.

- The quality of the dialogue is preserved through tensions between advocacy and listening. When different viewpoints emerge on a given discussion, attention is centered on managing differences in mindsets and assumptions, with the recognition that alignment is important to the effective management of interdependence in the community.

- The inevitable disagreements and conflicts are dealt with in a respectful and timely fashion—dealt with productively rather than punitively. Issues and challenges are positioned as learning opportunities that strengthen the community.

- Members are able to debate and discuss things together without losing sight of the collaborative context in which their work must take place. They respect each other's opinions. Discussions don't become unnecessarily polarized without an overriding commitment to finding solutions acceptable to all concerned.

- Members feel that the community offers an environment where they can be honest and where they feel safe in asking questions about what they don't know. They are not afraid to speak up or put forward a more creative idea that may not be part of the accepted wisdom of the practice.

- Members feel the support and endorsement of the organization's leadership for their participation in communities. They are confident that their contribution to communities will be recognized as important and worthwhile.

- Members feel that their participation in the community has made a difference to their performance and capability as well as to others. Members feel that their time is well spent.
- The membership community is multi-generational. Members at different stages of their careers find relevance in the exchanges and are recognized for their contribution.

Community Acceptance and Support

- Managers who are not members of the community accept the self-organized nature of the community because they have confidence in the benefits the community brings to the organization. They no longer feel the need to exercise their authority or control over the activities of the community.
- Communities are an accepted form of organizational structure and identified as a strategic resource.
- Managers are predisposed to the community concept. They recommend creating communities when they identify a situation where a community could best fill a need for capability generation, collaboration, and problem solving.
- Communities and their members are recognized for their contribution to the organization's success.
- The language of community building is the language of the organization.

Community Mechanics

- The community functions on an efficient basis. It has the right procedures and processes in place. If any components need to be modified, the will is there to make changes to improve the community's infrastructure.
- The community tools are straightforward to use, and support is available to address any technology issues.
- Technology enables the community's work, increasing members' abilities to communicate in multiple channels.

- Facilitation keeps the community focused and moving ahead toward achieving its purpose.

- Members at varying levels of technology and Web literacy find support in enhancing their capabilities.

COMMUNITY EVOLUTION

In Chapter 2, we introduced a community development cycle that was identified by Wenger, McDermott, and Snyder (2002) (see Figure 2.1). As with all organic forms, a cycle of growth can be discussed. However, we can also look at changes as part of an evolutionary process. We can look at the evolution of communities in terms of a maturity model—how a particular community moves from its infancy to expanding into sub-communities and networks with other communities, increasing its generative capabilities as well as its value to the members, practice, and organization. We can also look at the maturity model from the point of view of the organization, plotting its growth from creating a pilot community to becoming an organization made-up of a network of communities that wrap around the organizational spine, filling the gaps between the boxes and lines. We'll look at these models in more detail in Chapter 11.

As we discussed earlier, the community development strategy should sit within a larger organizational knowledge strategy that focuses efforts on creating then leveraging knowledge assets within the community. An approach should be defined that outlines the stages of development of the community, the roles of supporters and participants in the community's development, and the resources needed to support the development of this strategic resource.

We're not at a level of maturity at Clarica where we can say that we are first and foremost an organization of networked communities. We have the building blocks in place. We now need the advantage of time to permeate the organization and extend the network to include communities of customers and external partners.

CONCLUSION

The strategic nature of communities of practice stems from their ability to systematically enhance the performance of the organization. In this context, these communities are no longer a tool to deal with a specific issue, but become an integral element of the fabric of a high-performance organization.

A community of practice is a complex structure. Think about the analogies that people use to describe communities of practice—the human body, a beehive, the agricultural cycle, the medieval guild system, or the physical form of communities in which we live and work (villages, towns, cities). Any way you look at communities, the multiple layers, varying perspectives, mosaic of members—the richness of possibilities is extensive (see Figure 4.4).

This graphical representation attempts to peel back the layers of a community of practice to reveal the dynamic interchange of people (based on their expertise and their needs) learning and collaborating to increase their capabilities and generate new knowledge that extends the performance of the individuals, and therefore, the organization. The figure shows how we need to focus on the community's value to members to fuel its development. In its essence, the community co-ops the individual capabilities of its members to create value for all members.

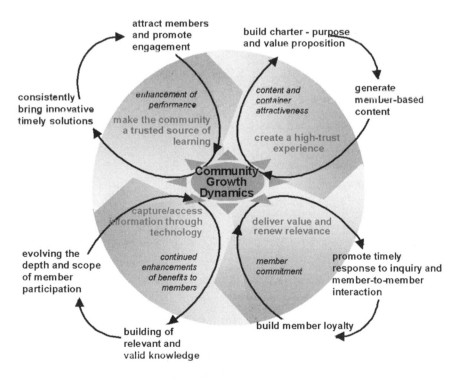

Figure 4.4.
Community Growth Dynamic

The figure shows how we need to focus on the community's value to members to fuel its development. In its essence, the community co-ops the individual capabilities of its members to create value for all members.

The ability to form different kinds of communities that are highly effective at using virtual tools to collaborate and overcome business challenges can enhance any organization's capabilities—not just organizations that are geographically dispersed. With increasing demands on face-to-face meeting time, the ability to collaborate asynchronously can make a significant contribution to getting work done. People can collaborate on problem solving at their convenience rather than waiting to coordinate meeting and travel schedules.

Not every community necessarily has a *strategic* purpose in and of itself. But every community of practice contributes to the organization's fabric, weaving a cohesive network in an unbureaucratic manner that contributes to building an overall capability to collaborate and learn. While a single community adds value, a network of communities gives an organization a decisive competitive advantage.

With a careful plan that puts the right elements in place, communities have the potential to transform the organization and make it viable as we move squarely into the knowledge era in which business rules, and therefore its models, will need to change.

CREATING THE FOUNDATION—WILL IT PLAY IN PEORIA?

1. Components of the architecture we outline in this chapter may already be in place in your organization. Identify the components that you have.

   - Means for asking questions. How do people participate in productive inquiries?

   - Collaborative technology. What tools do you use to connect people?

   - Learning. What is your learning strategy?

   - Collaboration. How do people work together to solve problem? What are the structures and norms?

2. How could you link your existing building blocks in support of developing communities?

3. What kinds of relationships do you have with your technology vendors? Could you rate any of them as a "partnership?" If so, what are the characteristics? If not, what is preventing you from establishing partnerships with any one of them?

4. What level of trust exists in your organization? If you were to suggest the development of a community, would possible participants question your intentions or gladly welcome the idea? Is it safe in your organization to admit that you don't know something?

References

McDermott, R. (2000). "Knowing in Community: Ten Critical Success Factors in Building Communities of Practice." *IHRIM Journal*, 4 (1), pp. 19–26.

O'Dell, C. and C.J. Grayson. (1998). *If Only We Knew What We Know: The Transfer of Internal Knowledge and Best Practice*. New York: The Free Press.

Wenger, E., R. McDermott, and W.M. Snyder (2002). *Cultivating Communities of Pratice: A Guide to Managing Knowledge*. Cambridge, MA: Harvard Business School Press.

Part II

Building Communities of Practice in a Strategic Context

In Part II, we set the stage for community building by looking at the core concepts of capability generation through a comprehensive knowledge strategy. We also discussed communities as a strategic resource and what factors needed to be in place to support their successful development. We now move to the middle portion of our framework—a look at a tactical approach for building communities. In the next four chapters, we outline how we put the theory into practice to design, implement, and assess a community of practice situated in a strategic context.

By illustrating the process and discussing the lessons learned modelling the process, we validate the information we acquired—what other researchers and practitioners have contributed to the conversation about communities—and present it as new knowledge that we created from our own experience.

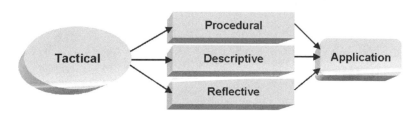

Figure PII.1.
Tactical Framework

In this part of the book, we complete the shift from an overview of communities in general to a description of how we developed a community of practice in a strategic context—the Agent Network, a virtual community of practice for Clarica agents located across Canada. We move from a discussion of conceptual elements to an illustration of actual practice.

Chapter 5

COMMUNITY DEVELOPMENT PROCESS MODEL OVERVIEW

After a brief overview of Clarica and the key characteristics that support our knowledge work, this chapter tells the story of how a community of practice for Clarica agents was started. We explain the need for a process model by first talking about failed attempts to put communities of practice in place and then discussing why a formal process made a significant contribution to the success of the community development. As an overview of the process model, this chapter covers the key elements. The details of the design and launch phase are in Chapter 6 and the implementation and growth phase follow in Chapter 7.

A BIT ABOUT CLARICA

For many of you, Clarica may not be a household name. So we should take a moment to explain a bit about the company. We've chosen to highlight elements that form a foundation for supporting communities of practice:

- Business environment
- Culture
- Knowledge management approach

- Technology infrastructure
- Strategic imperatives, our business aspirations.

Clarica Life Insurance Company has provided customers with insurance and investment solutions for 130 years. In addition to individual retail and group insurance, Clarica provides a full range of wealth management products. In July 1999, Clarica became a publicly traded company and introduced a powerful new brand with a promise of *clarity through dialogue*. With offices across Canada, Clarica serves nearly 3 million customers in Canada and 225,000 in the United States through 8,000 agents, staff, financial planners, and group representatives. Headquartered in Waterloo, Ontario (about 75 miles south west of Toronto) and with over 100 agencies and offices across Canada, Clarica has been named one of the top 20 knowledge management companies worldwide.

The following quick facts help situate Clarica in the financial services industry:

- Canada's first and oldest mutual insurance company
- Insures one in ten Canadians
- First in retail life insurance in force in the Canadian market
- Second in Canadian market share of retail insurance (based on income from premiums)
- Largest provider of corporate loans among life-insurance-based financial institutions
- First Canadian mutual life insurance company to demutualize
- IPO of more than $860 million was second largest ever on the Toronto Stock Exchange

Like most companies, Clarica has seen a fair amount of change. Through acquisition, Clarica has entered new markets and successfully integrated new staff (e.g., Canadian business of Prudential of England, MetLife Canada, Sun Life's life retrocession and financial reinsurance business, and Canadian Group Retirement Services business of Royal Trust). With demutalization, Clarica policy holders became shareholders, changing the business focus to creating shareholder value and strengthening customer relations with a new name and brand promise. And as of the writing of this book, Clarica is working toward a merger with Sun Life Financial in which Clarica will be a wholly-owned subsidiary and the center for Canadian Operations for both companies.

CHARACTERISTICS OF A KNOWLEDGE-SHARING ORGANIZATION

From its inception, community and collaboration have been fundamental components of Clarica's fabric. In the agriculture belt of southwestern Ontario, communities supported each other not only in barn raising and quilting bees. They came together and pooled their financial resources in case of unexpected hardships through death or other tragedy that could challenge the viability of a family farm.

The Ontario Mutual Life Assurance Company was formed to manage these pooled financial resources. The first 500 policies were issued from a second floor office above Moses Springer's general store in Waterloo, a small town in southern Ontario. Over the evolution of the company, a community focus remained central to the business philosophy.

What makes Clarica different from other financial services companies? Without digressing into a pitch to buy stock, purchase a policy, or seek employment, we'd like to profile the characteristics that distinguish Clarica as a knowledge-sharing organization. Our business approach, culture, and values create a knowledge-sharing persona and form the foundation for creating vibrant communities— a key factor in our ability to continuously increase capabilities.

Guiding Principles

Clarica has always seen the benefit of involving employees in establishing the cornerstones of its business values. People across the organization contribute to developing key messages, and Clarica actively communicates these cornerstones to shareholders, customers, business partners, the community, and, of course, to the agents and employees.

- **Mission:** To help our customers achieve financial security and, in doing so, create maximum value for our shareholders.
- **Vision:** To be the clear first choice of customers, shareholders, members, and communities.
- **Values:** To make choices guided by our values: stewardship, partnerships, and innovation. We will make these choices live through our actions in all we do.

In addition to these mission, vision, and values statements, Clarica has articulated an extensive list of commitments to its stakeholders (customers, shareholders, employees, and the community) explaining how Clarica will "live by" its cornerstone statements. Two commitments to employees, in particular, support the community of practice work:

- To provide opportunities for developing an indvidual's capabilities through continuous learning.
- To foster an environment that fulfills our values through open dialogue, collaboration, teamwork, and trust.

Strategic Imperatives

To focus business efforts, the strategic imperatives provide the foundation for all corporate and business unit plans. All actions must be directly linked to one of the strategic imperatives. Communities with a strategic purpose, then, must be closely tied with as many imperatives as possible, showing how the community will contribute to achieving these goals:

- Enhance financial performance
- Grow through acquisition
- Grow through innovation
- Achieve industry-leading e-business capability
- Accelerate development of Clarica's brand
- Increase our speed of action

Strategic Capabilities Focus

With a focus on accelerating the generation of capabilities in the organization so that we can achieve our business imperatives, Clarica moved away from a traditional human resources management structure to a model that focuses on strategic capabilities. Just as organizations have tended to focus on products rather than customers, the traditional human resources function tends to focus on its tools (e.g., compensation, training and development, recruitment, staffing) rather than on the capabilities of the employees. This compartmentalized approach does not meet the needs of a knowledge-driven organization.

The strategic capabilities model provides an approach and supporting structure that ensures that knowledge and learning become an inherent part of effective business leadership throughout the organization. Specifically, a strategic capabilities model:

- Ensures the development of an organizational context geared to self-initiative and interdependence.

- Provides the platform for accelerating learning at the individual, team, and organizational levels.

- Ensures that the organization has the capabilities that allow it to develop customer relationships targeted at a strategic level.

The main benefit of this new organizational approach is that the strategic capabilities structure acts as a catalyst to move faster with coherence and clear purpose.

At Clarica, the Strategic Capabilities Unit's mandate is to partner with business colleagues to ensure that all employees are ready, willing, and able to support increased profitability and meet business challenges. The Unit accomplishes this mandate with a team of practice leaders, consultants, architects, and project managers. (See the earlier discussion in Chapter 1, Figure 1.8, and Table 1.1.)

Brand

Clarica used to be called "The Mutual Group." With demutualization in 1999, it was obvious that another name would need to be chosen and a new brand established. Clarica invested significant resources in researching a name and creating a new identity for the company. The brand promise, *clarity through dialogue*, is perhaps best illustrated by a recent television commercial. Confused couples on a dance floor look up to a person calling out square dance instructions. Due to the string of unfamiliar terms delivered in a rapid monotone, no one knows what to do. They are unable to act. (Move to a close-up of people standing still and looking bewildered.) A Clarica agent comes to the stage and "translates" the instructions into plain language. With a nod of understanding, the couples begin to work through the intricate steps—smiling faces all around. Strengthening the Clarica brand is a high priority for Clarica, one of its strategic imperatives.

The brand effort is managed by two teams within the Strategic Capabilities Unit—one with an internal focus (brand experience), the other with an external focus (brand expression). Clarica believes that you can't have an authentic brand on the "outside" if you aren't living it on the "inside" as well.

Commitment to Communities

"Clarica's Contribution" is a corporate citizen program launched in October 2000. With a commitment to making communities better places in which to live and work, Clarica matches all United Way donations from employees and agents, dollar for dollar. Donations to other charities are also matched up to $500 per employee and Clarica donates 1% of pre-tax domestic profits to charity. Through an extensive volunteer program, Clarica agents, employees, and executives logged over 30,000 hours in the community in a six-month period. People at all levels, including the CEO, volunteer in every walk of the community—from arts to recreation to shut-in services. And among its many programs, Clarica provides ten houses adjacent to corporate headquarters at no charge to charitable and not-for-profit organizations for use in support of their programs and services. For example, Big Sisters, Cystic Fibrosis, and the World Wide Opportunities for Women operate out of Clarica facilities.

Technology Infrastructure

One of the pillars of Clarica's Knowledge Strategy is our technology infrastructure. Like most companies, we've invested heavily over the last decade in enterprise-wide access to tools and applications that increase our productivity and link our people and resources with a just-in-time approach. The technology architecture supports the acquisition and integration of applications to ensure consistent quality and enterprise-wide availability. Over 90% of our business transactions are performed online.

All agents are equipped with a laptop with automated forms, product information, and client profiles. In 2001, we converted over 7,500 desktops to a new standard image—an initiative that provided agent and employee with the tools needed to access information, facilitate collaboration, and increase productivity. A key application that supports knowledge access is *Clarica Connects*, the corporate intranet that was launched in 1999. *Clarica Connects* acts as both a portal and a content repository with over 80,000 items managed by content providers who publish 80–100 new documents daily.

Clarica's Exclusive Sales Force

Because Clarica's sales force is the focus of the community of practice that we're highlighting, we should take a closer look at this group of people who form the agent practice. With a history that goes back over 100 years, the sales force has evolved to meet the challenges of practicing in a unique environment.

Working exclusively for Clarica, agents are restricted to selling Clarica-developed products or products from other companies with whom Clarica has a partnership or referral relationship. For the most part, agents have access to a comprehensive range of services, and Clarica continues to develop new products to meet market demands.

Unlike most financial services companies, Clarica's agents are self-employed. They are independent business people, not Clarica employees. Most agents run their operations as a sole-proprietorship. Some are incorporated and have their own limited company. Some have combined their levels of expertise with other agents and created multiagent corporations. In addition, there are semiformal partnerships, agent alliances, and situations where agents simply work together without any formal agreement. Some agents work out of a branch or agency office (occupant agents); others have either a storefront operation or work from home (nonoccupant agents).

Commissions are based on a revenue-sharing system. Every time the company receives income, so does the agent. There are no upfront or "heaped" payments. Instead, there is a leveling that takes a great deal of pressure off the sales cycle. When an agent retires or leaves the business after being fully vested (approximately eight years), the agent receives a Commission On Release (CORe) from the guaranteed sale of the agent's block of business.

Agents tend to function at a fairly high emotional level because that's how they sell to their customers. They bring to the present a possible future that has a great deal of emotional meaning to people. They function with great commitment. Many agents form lasting relationships with their customers due to their involvement with client life-events—the cycle that often drives insurance purchase. It's not unusual to see agents attending a first birthday party or paying their respects at a funeral.

With requirements for credentials and continuing education, the agents are continually increasing and renewing their capabilities. They possess a high degree of computer literacy and are considered some of the most technology-enabled in the industry. Increasing technology-related capabilities has been a priority because of the way Clarica does business. Over 90% of all transactions are completed on a personal commuter and transmitted to company mainframes. A large percentage of insurance applications are underwritten on the basis of computer analysis, and many investment transactions are paperless. The only visible evidence of the transactions is a signature page, and that will likely disappear in the near future.

THE AGENT NETWORK—DEVELOPING A COMMUNITY WITH A STRATEGIC PURPOSE

With over 3,000 independent agents working in agencies, branches, and offices (often in their own homes) across the second largest landmass on earth, Clarica saw the advantage of supporting a virtual forum where agents could discuss their businesses. Given the strategic role that the agents play in the organization, they were chosen as the focus of a community of practice development project—the creation of the Agent Network.

In the pilot phase, 150 agents from across Canada were invited to join the community. They represented a wide range of years of experience, areas of product or service expertise, and markets served. The goal was to have a wide cross-section of participation. In order to create a confidential space for discussions, membership in the community was restricted to agents. Sales force support staff and management were not given access to the community's collaborative tool, nor were project sponsors.

Initial efforts by the Steering Group (two agents, two agent-development staff members, and two members of the Knowledge Team) helped the community take shape. They worked to establish a vision of what the community might look like, creating a persona that would engage the invited members and piquing potential members' curiosity by outlining some of the possibilities. To give form and function to the vision, a starting point that would later be tailored by the members as they came together as a community, the Steering Group drafted a purpose statement for the Agent Network:

To support the growth and productivity of Clarica's sales force with a three-tiered approach:

- *Developing agents (less than five years of experience) can obtain support.*

- *Experienced agents (five or more years of experience) are continually renewed.*

- *All agents can network to grow personally, professionally, and technically, leading to innovations in sales strategies.*

Aligned with the purpose, objectives for the agent community included:

- Support the career growth of developing agents in order to improve career satisfaction, productivity, and retention.
- Support the renewal and continued professional development of experienced agents. The community will be a means to step experienced agents to their next range of professional potential.
- Provide opportunities for agent networking that will lead to greater sales innovation and professional cohesiveness and strength.

The Steering Group thought that while these points were extremely important statements to help guide the community development, they were more appropriate for a strategic plan than for communicating with the Agent Network members or the agent community at large. There needed to be other words, a more concise phrase that would draw the members together and give them focus. An accessible statement needed to be developed to represent the agent's commitment to the community and provide direction for the community's activities. In the end, the purpose statement was refined so that it could be used on the community bulletin board, newsletters, and other communication spaces:

To develop and share our personal, professional, and technical expertise, leading to innovative strategies and growth of our business.

Because this was a sales-oriented group, the Steering Group felt that we needed a slogan—a mantra that would be the rallying point, something they could put on a button or a T-shirt. They chose: *For Agents, By Agents.* We found that these four words spoke volumes. The phrase clearly stated who constituted the community membership and where the responsibility of ownership lay.

The first phase of the pilot was focused on designing and launching the community, assessing the community's progress, and making recommendations for next steps. Due to previous failed attempts at establishing a community for agents, we took our time with this project and carefully rolled out the community with a great deal of attention to the details that would help ensure success.

KEY ACTIVITY	TIME-FRAME	RESPONSIBILITY
Design community	4 weeks	Steering Group
Identify Phase I participants	4 weeks	Steering Group, Sponsors
Prelaunch introduction	2 weeks	Facilitator
Launch the online community	2 weeks	Facilitator
Develop the community	12 weeks	Steering Group, Facilitator Members
Assess value of Phase I	4 weeks	Steering Group, Facilitator, Members
Prepare recommendations	2 weeks	Steering Group, Facilitator
Identify the process model	2 weeks	Facilitator
Make decision on recommendations	1 week	Sponsors

Table 5.1.
Community Development Process Milestones

Table 5.1 outlines the key activities that encompassed an eight-month pilot project timeline for designing, launching, implementing, and evaluating a community of practice with a strategic purpose.

As we moved toward our launch date, the day that the community would go live, we encountered the usual stumbling blocks—some minor and some mountainous. But by then, the community had taken shape, it had already established a life of its own. The Agent Network shot out of the starting gate, for the greater part under its own momentum, and hasn't looked back since!

In Chapters 6 and 7, we continue the story of the Agent Network with a closer look at all the elements that came together to develop this community. But before we move into the details, we'll outline the approach we used to help us succeed in putting this community in place.

THREE STRIKES AND YOU'RE OUT:
LEARNING AND KNOWING

Based on our focus of generating capabilities, Clarica may well be identified as a *learning organization*—a term popularized by Senge (1990).

Although the study of *organizational learning* has a longer history, both concepts are directly related to an organization's ability to increase capabilities and to innovate through a focus on the learning process.

It's no surprise that multiple definitions for the learning organization exist, each with an emphasis on a particular aspect of a complex concept. We favor Garvin's (1993) definition because it more closely aligns with our efforts to be proactive, to focus on the action-oriented persona of a learning organization:

> *A learning organization is an organization skilled at creating, acquiring, and transferring knowledge, and at modifying its behavior to reflect new knowledge and insights (pg. 4).*

Five key activities characterize a learning organization:

- **Uses systematic problem solving**—makes decisions based on data rather than on assumptions and uses problem-solving techniques in learning approaches.

- **Experiments with new approaches**—searches for and tests new knowledge in an ongoing program of small experiments.

- **Learns from own experience and history**—takes the time to reflect on successes and failures. Analyzes them systematically, codifies the lessons learned, and provides access to this knowledge.

- **Learns from the experiences and best practice of others**—benchmarks best practice in the industry through environmental scanning.

- **Transfers knowledge quickly and efficiently throughout the organization**—shares ideas broadly, providing access to knowledge and collaborative tools (Garvin, 1993, pp. 5–12).

Senge (1990) would argue that no organization can ever truly call itself a learning organization because ". . . the more you learn, the more acutely aware you become of your ignorance" (pg. 11). So, we stand corrected and make the slightly modified statement that Clarica is an organization that continuously strives to increase individual and organizational capabilities through learning. In other words, Clarica is committed to "learning about learning," trying new ways to improve on our practice of learning as a process that creates new knowledge.

The early 1990s focus on learning as a process that increases capabilities has now shifted to what an organization DOES with what it has learned, how it leverages its existing and newly created or acquired knowledge. While the term *learning organization* is still used, the emphasis is now on the next level of the information taxonomy (data, information, knowledge, wisdom)—on creating knowledge-driven organizations. Learning for the sake of learning is not the end goal; rather learning as the process of turning information into knowledge leading to effective action is the new focus of the knowledge era.

The business literature and press are full of knowledge words—the knowledge-based economy, knowledge-enabled workers, knowledge-driven organization. The process of creating new knowledge (i.e., learning) is still a key factor, but what distinguishes an organization is its ability to recognize its knowledge assets and its capability to capitalize on them—what the Special Library Association has coined: *Putting Knowledge to Work*.

Choo (1999) defines a knowing organization as one ". . . that links up the three strategic information processes of sense making, knowledge creating and decision making into a continuous cycle of learning and adaptation" (p. 18).

In a nutshell: based on experience, a knowing organization strives to make sense of information and apply it in order to create new knowledge

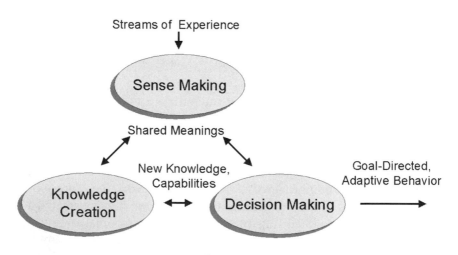

Figure 5.1.
The Knowing Cycle

and/or capabilities that are then used to make informed decisions that will direct behavior, thus leading to achieving one's goals.

Before we get lost in a debate about exactly what kind of organization we're striving to create, let's move to our experience with implementing communities of practice that have strategic importance to the organization. Our experience illustrates characteristics of a learning organization (the encouragement to take risks and the acceptance of failure) and a knowing organization (the ability to leverage actionable knowledge through creating meaning, innovating, and making decisions).

While there is a great deal of encouragement to innovate and tolerance for trial and error at Clarica, there comes a point when results are expected or a decision to abandon and move on needs to be made. After two rather spectacular failures at establishing a community for agents, we were fast approaching the end of our proverbial "nine lives." Rather than sweep the cracked and broken pieces under the carpet and just start again, we stopped to analyze what went wrong. What were the lessons learned and the mistakes to be avoided? What new knowledge did we possess? In other words, we took the time to stop and reflect on our experience and plan an approach based on our new knowledge.

Implementing a Project Management Approach

We turned to a more structured project management approach to guide the design and implementation of a community of practice with a strategic context. A pilot project was identified and sponsored by the vice president of strategic capabilities in partnership with the vice president of sales force operations. The project groundwork was laid by the Knowledge Team, a group of knowledge architects and consultants who draw on the expertise of specialists from the information technology solutions department, another group who works with business units to design technological approaches tailored to individual needs.

The project was managed by a member of the Knowledge Team in cooperation with a Steering Group, consisting of two practicing agents, two members of the sales force development business unit, and Clarica's Knowledge Architect. Much attention was paid to details to ensure the project's success. We spent time exploring the nature of communities and understanding the agent environment. In the end, we designed a community with the potential to maximize value for its members and Clarica. The focus was to renew and increase individual and organizational capabilities as they relate to building strong customer relationships through the provision of Clarica products and services.

The purpose of the community development pilot project was twofold. First, Clarica wanted to put in place a vibrant community of practice for its independent sales agents. Second, a best practice process model would be identified. By documenting the approach and the key lessons learned, Clarica would have a process that it could replicate when developing other communities to support strategic imperatives.

What was different about our new approach to establishing this community? In our third attempt, we:

- Established a pilot project with cross-functional sponsorship from stakeholders at the executive level.

- Defined the strategic nature of the community: purpose, projected benefits, and alignment with strategic imperatives and business unit priorities.

- Engaged a team of people and obtained input from the larger body of stakeholders

- Articulated principles of the community approach.

- Laid a foundation of understanding about the nature of communities and how they could contribute to increasing capabilities.

- Provided resources (people, tools, materials) to the community.

- Selectively communicated the pilot project's progress.

- Created a parallel project to identify a process for designing and implementing a community.

In addition to these factors, we had perhaps the most significant advantage—experience! The past two failures, our continued study of communities, and our collaboration with an experienced vendor of community tools had increased our capabilities. In other words, we were taking advantage of key components of our knowledge management strategy—we leveraged our new knowledge, our architecture and technology infrastructure, and the unique culture of our agents.

We made a conscious effort to formalize our processes, documenting our ideas and providing statements of direction. Because we had a dual purpose for developing this community (i.e., a purpose from Clarica's perspective and a purpose from the agents' perspective), we identified objectives for the pilot project from a strategic point of view that complemented the community's purpose. While these two perspectives are closely aligned, they are nevertheless coming from two directions: bottom up from the agents and top down from the corporate sponsors. But they did converge. While the corporation was looking for increased productivity from the sales force, the agent was looking for an increase in his/her own business. Fundamentally we're talking about increasing the bottom line—for Clarica and for the independent agent.

Corporate objectives for the community development pilot project included:

1. Support sales force objectives: Grow the sales force (e.g., hire new agents, retain existing agents) and increase sales force productivity.

2. Create an online "space" for a community using Clarica's technology infrastructure.

3. Identify an approach to sustain community value: for Clarica, for the agent members.

4. Increase agents' computer literacy with a focus on increasing awareness of the Internet in support of e-commerce initiatives at Clarica.

5. Evaluate the use of a Web-based application for community development.

6. Identify a process model of best practice for community development.

From these objectives, you can see a definite technology theme. There's no question that Clarica wanted to use the community experience as a way to increase the technology capabilities of the agents—especially their Internet skills. As we pointed out in our overview of Clarica's agents, we have automated most processes around the sales cycle, and many agents are reasonably comfortable with their PCs. However, our corporate focus on achieving industry-leading e-business capability meant that we needed to increase agents' capabilities to integrate Internet-based tools into their practice and saw participation in the community as one approach to achieving this objective.

Rather than train agents on Internet use as a specific skill, we gave them an Internet-based tool as a means of learning from each other. We provided them with a "real life" use of the Internet rather than a set of modules from which they would learn in isolation from their "real work." They learned the use of the Internet through their use of the community forum. This approach is consistent with our understanding of adult learning principles, that adults learn best in the context of their work, where the learning is practical and the application of new skills is immediate.

Although technology is extremely important to our business, it isn't going to replace Clarica agents. Our e-business strategy firmly places the agent at the heart of the sales process as the customer relationship manager. While our customers value technology as a way to access information or complete a transaction, they have delivered a strong message that their relationship with their agent should be kept front and center. Technology remains an enabler, a tool used by agents and employees to increase capabilities and support relationships—key factors in achieving our strategic imperatives.

A PROCESS MODEL FOR DEVELOPING COMMUNITIES WITHIN A STRATEGIC CONTEXT

At the end of eight months, we completed an evaluation of our efforts in establishing the Agent Network and turned to analyzing the approach we used, with the goal of identifying a process model of community development.

The process model wasn't developed in isolation. We had input from the Knowledge Team, including the Knowledge Architect, the Knowledge Exchange Architect, and the Community Facilitator. The process model was developed from a synthesis of experience that would form the basis of best practice.

The community development process model (see Figure 5.2) is intended as a guide to key activities and their relationships—the main steps needed to develop a community of practice. The danger of a process model is that it can appear to be a step-by-step technical manual—a cookbook full of recipes for success. However, the objective of the model is to highlight key points for consideration and for adapting to individual situations.

While a process model tends to portray a linear pattern that moves from beginning to end, the actual process is usually anything but linear. Instead, there is a constant cycling, an exchange of information among the various phases or steps that occurs throughout the process. Often actions accomplished in one step are modified or improved upon in subsequent steps—new knowledge then influencing the process. And some actions, such as communicating with stakeholders or planning community development activities with the members, are not confined to a particular step or phase—they happen at various, if not all, steps in the process.

Rather than simply present a two-dimensional map of our approach, we structured the discussion of the process model around three perspectives of our experience:

- *Procedural*—a figure that graphically represents the processes or steps that are taken to meet the objectives. The actions or activities that are necessary to put an infrastructure in place to support the development and growth of a community of practice aligned with a strategic purpose.

- *Descriptive*—a narrative that tells the story and describes the resources (human and material) that are required to accomplish the process steps and produce the deliverables (the explicit or tangible outcomes and the documents).

- *Reflective*—a discussion of key issues, lessons learned, and best practices that are identified through an analysis of the process of community development in the pilot project.

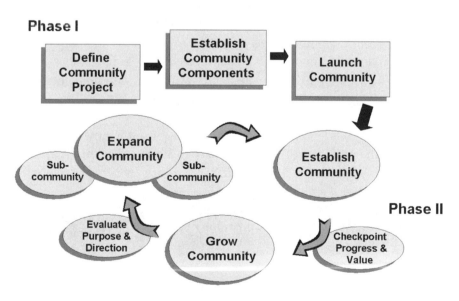

Figure 5.2.
Community Development Process Model

The printed page poses some restrictions on conveying the process of community development. It's difficult to represent the depth and complexity of this process in a two-dimensional drawing. The multidirectional arrows we're tempted to insert would only complicate the illustration and confuse the reader. To provide the extra layers of perspective without producing diagrams that long to leap off the page, Chapters 6 and 7 outline the details from all three perspectives (procedural, descriptive, and reflective). But for the purpose of getting the process model on the table, we'll begin by looking at a diagram of how we developed the community pilot project in two phases: Phase I—Community Design and Launch and Phase II—Community Implementation and Growth.

Community Development Phases

In Phase I (see Figure 5.3), preparing for the community's implementation took place in three main steps with the active involvement of a project manager, the Steering Group, and a team of resource people from a wide range of functions/disciplines:

1. *Define community project.* The community development project is planned—the elements of the community are identified (setting the context) and the project is outlined.

2. *Establish community components.* The project tasks are identified (often in the form of issues to be resolved) and completed.

3. *Launch community.* The online community is now accessible to the members using a Web-based application.

In Phase II (see Figure 5.4), the community itself is now the process driver, not the project plan as was the case in Phase I. During this phase,

Figure 5.3.
Phase I—Community Design and Launch

the community matures through a continuous cycle of development, evaluation, and growth with the support of a facilitator.

1. *Establish the community.* A sense of community is developed through knowledge creation and exchange in member discussions, shared resources, and related activities.

2. *Checkpoint—assess progress and value.* The community's value to its members and sponsors as well as the development approach are informally assessed.

3. *Grow the community.* Directions are identified for increasing the community's value through community building, knowledge creation and sharing, and knowledge navigation approaches.

4. *Evaluate purpose and direction.* A formal review of the community's progress and its value to its members and sponsors plus a look at the direction it wishes to move in as the community expands to meet the identified needs of the community and the organization.

5. *Expand the community.* Take the community beyond its initial implementation, expanding in membership and scope, increasing its value, and situating the community in the larger community network.

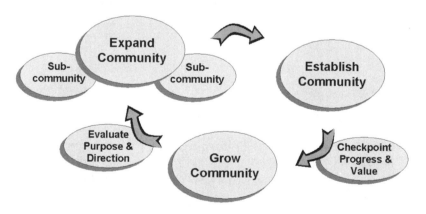

Figure 5.4.
Phase II—Community Implementation and Growth

The context was identified and the project defined, including the resources that would be required, the infrastructure that would support the community's exchange, and the approach that would guide the process. Key objectives and actions included:

- Create a steering group to guide the community development.
- Hire a project manager and establish a project approach, including the roles of steering group, facilitator, and sponsors; creating working documents; and establishing a corporate liaison.
- Identify the network of corporate resources needed to put the community infrastructure in place.
- Draft the project plan with milestones and timeframe.

Why a pilot project? We've learned over time that, when introducing an approach with the high level of sensitivity and anticipated success that was attached to this community (not to mention the history of previous failures), the wise choice is to begin with a defined pilot project. At Clarica "pilots" are part of our approach to innovation—a place where new ideas can be tried out and then modified or adjusted before being rolled out to the entire organization. Ironing out the wrinkles before engaging our entire agent population seemed the way to go, especially considering that we were using a new form of technology, a leading-edge but fairly untried application, and a new form of facilitation. To mitigate the risks, the pilot project status gave us some breathing room.

The Five C's

With the pilot project underway, we soon identified common characteristics of a community of practice:

- **Conversations**—the key to learning. The process of productive inquiry where people ask questions and continue with conversations that lead to solving a problem, increasing capabilities, creating new knowledge, and moving our practice and business forward.
- **Collaboration**—the interdependency model that reflects our belief that we don't learn in isolation. We engage our colleagues to help us find solutions to the challenges of our practice.

- **Commitment**—our promise to participate in realizing the community's purpose and furthering its goals. Our willingness to commit time to the community reflects our belief that our contribution will make a difference.
- **Connectivity**—the ability to work in a virtual environment, creating networks of people and their expertise that would not have been available in a "just-in-time" fashion without the aid of the technology infrastructure that connects us.
- **Capabilities**—the link between strategy and performance—what it takes to achieve our goals. The skills, attitudes, beliefs, mindsets, and knowledge sets plus the policies, procedures, and other resources that we bring to our practice as the bridge between what is strategically important and how we achieve our successes.

We'll come back to these five characteristics later when we talk about assessing progress and creating value for the many layers of interests involved in a community.

CONCLUSION

When strategic imperatives are driving a process, flying by the seat of your pants, from all we've learned, is definitely NOT the way to go! Strategy in itself suggests a focus on direction and application of efforts in a consistent, aligned manner. We're not suggesting that our first two attempts at developing communities of practice were totally unorganized, ad hoc efforts. But in our third attempt, we applied the rigors of strategy development and project management to achieve an unqualified success. We have to believe that this approach made a significant difference.

Guided by the action-oriented characteristics of a learning organization with a solid knowledge-sharing culture in place, we reflected on our past experience, analyzed what lessons could be learned, gained new knowledge, and applied our capabilities to design an approach that would produce a sustainable success.

STRATEGY AND PROCESS—WILL IT PLAY IN PEORIA?

1. **Reflection.** One of the grandfathers of modern educational theory, John Dewey (1933), suggested that we learn more from

reflecting on experience than from the actual experience. Engineer and sociologist Donald Schon (1983) popularized the notion of the reflective practitioner—stopping to think about what you're doing along the way to improve your decision making. What experience have you had in doing a "postmortem" on a project? What typically happens at the end of a project in your organization? Do you have a formal or informal process to stop and take the pulse of a project before it's completed? Is there appetite in your organization for learning from previous mistakes—or just from successes?

2. **A culture conducive to sharing.** Can you quickly lay your hands on your organization's vision, mission, and/or values statements? Do you have an outline of your strategic imperatives, business objectives, or other expressions of purpose? Can you list characteristics of your organization that lay the foundation for communities of practice—for creating new and sharing existing knowledge?

3. **Managing projects.** Do you have a standardized approach to project management? Do you know of an expert or mentor who could help you learn how projects are typically managed in your organization? Do you have resources that could help you increase your project management skills?

References

Choo, C.W. (1999). *The Knowing Organization: How Organizations Use Information to Construct Meaning, Create Knowledge, and Make Decisions.* New York: Oxford University Press.

Dewey, J. (1933). *How We Think: A Restatement of the Relation of Reflective Thinking to the Educative Process.* Boston: D.C. Heath and Company.

Garvin, D.A. (1993). "Building a Learning Organization." *Harvard Business Review,* 71 (4). pp. 78–91.

Schon, D.A. (1983). *The Reflective Practitioner: How Professionals Think in Action.* New York: Basic Books.

Senge, P. (1990). *The Fifth Discipline: The Art & Practice of the Learning Organization.* New York: Doubleday.

Chapter 6

Phase I:
Community Design and Launch

The first phase in the development of a community is described (define community project, establish community components, launch community). During this phase, the focus is on the logistics—putting all the pieces of the puzzle in place to create the community vessel. Process is highlighted as the steps are outlined, but time is spent discussing key issues that surfaced at each step and the best practice that was identified through lessons learned in the design and implementation of the Agent Network.

Overview

As noted in Chapter 5, we took a structured project management approach to designing and implementing the Agent Network. We couldn't afford another failure, especially in a community with this level of strategic importance where the stakes were high. We strongly believed in the value of communities of practice as a vehicle for increasing capabilities, as a way to promote learning. We knew that they could make a significant contribution to achieving our strategic imperatives. But we didn't have a viable approach for establishing a community in a strategic context—for creating a foundation from which a community could develop and then sustain its value to the individual members, the community at large, and the organization.

In this chapter, we explain how we designed the community from the perspectives of the process model (steps that we took to put the community in place), describe our actions (objectives for each of the process steps), and reflect on what worked well and what needed to be reconsidered in subsequent community development projects (key issues and the lessons learned). Examples of tools and approaches used to accomplish the process steps are outlined in Chapter 9.

As we work through the community development process, keep in mind that this is not a lock-step process. We talk about items in a specific sequence, but realistically, there's an awful lot of two-stepping going on. Have you ever seen a dance pattern—the black footprints stepping through the intricacies of a dance? While we strive to present a straightforward fox-trot, the reality is that we're often dealing with a merengue moving at warp speed! As with most projects, there isn't a clean hand-off from step to step. The constant cycling that we talked about before continues throughout the process. However, there are discrete steps and a critical path that can be followed to set up a successful launch of the community.

The first phase of the Community Development Model takes us from initial design through the point of launch (see Figure 6.1). It focuses on the design and implementation of the logistics or project phase of com-

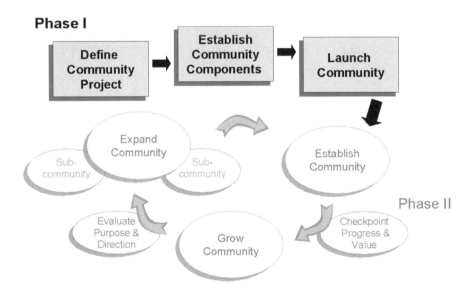

Figure 6.1.
Community Design and Launch

munity development—putting the foundation pieces in place on which the community will be built. Using a residential community as a comparison, this first phase is the time that the land is staked out (i.e., boundaries, what's included and what isn't), the infrastructure is put in place (e.g., sewers, roads, electricity), the buildings are framed (e.g., houses, schools, stores), and the residents are attracted to the community as a good place to live. Sounds simple? If you've ever built a house, let alone a sub-division, you'll have an appreciation of the complexity!

Borrowing from the art and science of engineering, we approached the community development project in terms of a problem in design—the need to outline the project from the perspectives of context, content, and form. Our three-step approach to design included:

- **Define the Community Project**—set the context, outline the project approach, identify the resource requirements, define the deliverables.

- **Establish Community Components**—put in place governance, membership, infrastructure, user support, content, learning, facilitation, and communication.

- **Launch the Community**—obtain sponsor sign-off, provide access to community site, provide member log in and site information, and establish community personality.

Before the project actually started (although work with sponsors, key community members, and a community software vendor had already begun when we formulated the go/no go decision), a project manager was selected and given the responsibility for designing and implementing an approach for completing the community groundwork and then getting the community up and running. The project manager coordinated the efforts of a team of people and was the primary liaison with sponsors and other key stakeholders.

For each step in the process, we provide an overview of the activities completed followed by an illustration of the deliverables, identification of key issues, and a discussion of best practice based on the lessons learned through reflection.

Step 1—Define the Community Project

To put some boundaries around the project, we began by defining the community development project (see Figure 6.2). At Clarica, we have a

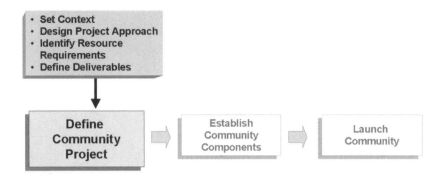

Figure 6.2.
Define Community Project

fairly rigorous process for managing projects that is guided by a charter developed for each project. (The charters follow the Project Management Book of Knowledge structure. See example in Chapter 9.) The charter guides the project, keeps it on track, and most important, provides a clear description of what's in and what's out. In the first step toward establishing the community, the foundation is laid:

- **Set the context**—identify the business environment and strategic imperatives, understand the community members' and sponsors' environment; characterize the knowledge-sharing culture; and define what is meant by a community of practice.

- **Design the project approach**—create a steering group; establish project management approach; identify roles and responsibilities; choose community application; create project strategy and action plan.

- **Identify resource requirements**—list people and materials required to complete the project.

- **Define the deliverables**—identify the tangible outcomes.

Set Context

We talk a lot about *context* at Clarica. It's key to our Knowledge Strategy and the first component of our e-Learning Model. Without context, we're missing an understanding of our environment—the ability to explain why we're heading in a particular direction or why we need to increase certain capabilities by acquiring new knowledge. By spending time up front on understanding context, we're more likely to succeed because people understand:

- **Purpose**—why it's important to do something, what is the need.

- **Relevance of the initiative**—the relationship to other strategies or initiatives and the value proposition.

- **Environmental factors**—what's contributing to the need and what influences are in play in the business environment from a corporate and individual perspective.

- **Culture**—what's the appetite for learning and sharing knowledge and what do people believe about the value of collaboration and innovation.

- **Definition of a community of practice within a strategic context**—what do we mean by community and how is the community positioned strategically.

- **Expectations**—what can we expect to see as a result and what can someone interacting with the project expect from their involvement?

In other words, setting the context helps to create shared meaning (see Figure 5.1), an understanding of what is proposed, how it is positioned, and what is expected. It's also a time when developers can gain a better understanding of the issues and opportunities related to the community.

Researching Environmental Factors

When identifying the context for the community, the primary activity is learning—researching the environment by talking with people and reviewing related materials, understanding the needs of the people involved in the practice, identifying the links to other strategies and initiatives that could strengthen your community project. Even if the community developers have been involved in the business and have extensive experience in the specific field that is related to the community, they need to peel back the layers of the onion to learn what is at the core of the practice—what are the drivers, the influencing factors, the issues, and the opportunities?

This research has a dual benefit. Not only will you gain important knowledge about the prospective community members, you've started the public relations and marketing efforts by getting people thinking about the community—how they may want to be involved, what the benefits will be, how the community can extend their practice.

Define Communities of Practice

In Chapter 2 we noted that communities of practice have existed for centuries, but that the term is only a little over a decade old. When identifying context, a key step in outlining the community project is to define what you mean by a *community of practice*. People may not be familiar with knowledge management principles and vocabulary, let alone what you mean by establishing a community of practice with a strategic purpose. With a clear definition, you help people understand the concept—it creates meaning for them and starts them thinking about the value of being involved in a community. This questioning is the beginning of productive inquiry—the catalyst for conversations

Let's look again at Wenger et al.'s (2002) definition of a community of practice:

> *Groups of people who share a concern, a set of problems, or a passion about a topic, and who deepen their understanding and knowledge of this area by interacting on an ongoing basis (p. 4).*

We've learned the hard way. By providing clear definitions, you can go a long way in avoiding confusion and helping people create meaning—they know what's being talked about. With clear definitions we have a better chance of "singing from the same song sheet." Our message to sponsors, invited community members, and the rest of the organization is crystal clear. This shared meaning helps increase our agility and the speed with which we can attain our goals.

In Chapter 9, we'll take a closer look at various interpretations of the term *communities of practice* and the need to establish a definition that reflects your own situation.

Design the Project Approach

Once the context has been identified, you can start designing the project. We found that by putting a formal project management structure in place, we were able to keep track of the many details that needed to be attended to in order to build the community infrastructure. When it came time to launch, we had established an extremely professional persona for the community, and we credit this early success to our project design.

Under the direction of the project manager, the project approach was outlined:

- A Steering Group was created to guide project development and evaluate progress. This group consisted of two agents who participated as founding community members, two sales force development staff, and two members of the Knowledge Team (architecture and implementation).

- Roles and responsibilities were defined for the Steering Group and sponsors. With the combination of agents (community members) and corporate executives and staff, we had to ensure that people knew what their roles would be: where their responsibilities lay, what expectations were for their participation, and how the various roles would relate.

- A Web-based tool was chosen. Because the community membership was dispersed across the country, we needed a mechanism for putting the community online. We selected a tool and started negotiations with the vendor.

- A project strategy and plan were developed. In keeping with a project management approach, a project charter and action plan with milestones, resource requirements, and deliverables were outlined.

Identify Resource Requirements

People with expertise in various areas were the key resource requirement. We learned early in the community development process that "it takes a team to build a community." By involving people from a variety of areas, we not only gained the expertise we needed, we continued to build interest in communities across the organization. The work was a collaborative effort, and its success depended on our ability to bring together the right team.

In addition to the Steering Group, we had a working group that consisted of people from: information technology, security and user support, sales force development and training, sales force technical support, graphics services, corporate communications, and legal services. These people lent their expertise in planning the technology architecture and delivery of the community infrastructure as well as building community elements.

At another level, we continued to work with sales force management and other executives in the organization. Once again the purpose for engaging senior management was not only to create a solid foundation for the Agent Network, but to reinforce the value of knowledge sharing and capability generation through community participation. Gaining the support of key stakeholders also increased the awareness and buy-in for the importance of communities tied to strategic imperatives as a means of creating shareholder value and strengthening customer relationships.

In addition to people resources, we outlined the technical and material resources that would be required to support the community infrastructure. A budget for equipment and telecommunications was outlined. We also relied heavily on our community software vendor. With their experience in creating communities, they provided us with direction on how to lay the proper groundwork, what obstacles to expect, and how to mitigate risks.

Define Deliverables

For each step of the community development process, deliverables were identified—tangible indications that we had met our project milestones. The deliverables for this step all relate to the project definition, including:

- **Governance documents**—project charter and purpose statement.
- **Project plan**—the outline of the project strategy and approach.
- **Working documents**—the discussion documents that directed the required course of action around specific tasks.
- **Presentations**—a comprehensive outline of the community development approach that could be tailored for different audiences.

Examples of these deliverables are provided in Chapter 9.

Reflection

Building the Agent Network was the primary objective of the pilot project, but we also wanted to identify a process for establishing communities that could be replicated with other communities. So, we took our time and carefully planned our approach. In total, the timeframe from conception of the idea to create a community for independent agents to its launch was about five months. This first step of defining the project took about a month from when the project manager was hired.

As part of setting the context and defining the terms, we spent a great deal of time outlining our key messages. Specifically, we looked for answers to these questions:

- How do we create value in the community that justifies corporate investment in developing and supporting the community and justifies the members' time commitment to knowledge sharing?

- If wildly successful, popularity can create havoc. Are we ready to handle possible growth-related scenarios? Can we anticipate the issues and challenges that might arise?

- How can trust be established within the community? How can we help create an environment where members feel safe contributing and sharing knowledge?

- How can we earn the trust of senior executives—trust that the discussions in the community are constructive, that the stated purpose is achieved, that the community is not seen as an exclusionary tool to obviate management and other stakeholders?

We also faced some operational issues that could have derailed the project:

- How do we position the project with no French language option? Without the language capability, we exclude a significant portion of our agent community.

- How do we address compensation for the time spent by agents participating in the Steering Group? As independent business people, agents have performance expectations that do not consider time spent away from selling, even if the time is contributing to the greater good of the organization.

- How do we meet the technology challenges—cost and connectivity? With a virtual community, how do we ensure equity of access to all members?

Best Practice

As part of our reflection, we also identified best practice principles—lessons learned from our experiences in defining the project. Key to our commitment of building a successful community was the age-old expression, "You only have one chance to make a good first impression." We put significant effort and resources into the community design to pave the way for a quality experience. We wanted to ensure that the first impression of the community was positive and would set the stage for success. Specifically we learned:

- The opportunity exists—don't over strategize or fall into analysis paralysis. Take the risk!
- Work hard NOT to create a corporate image for the community. Let the community develop its own persona.
- A diverse steering group membership helps to identify a wide range of community development elements. The varying perspectives and past experiences of an eclectic membership can help identify issues that will need to be addressed or dimensions that will need to be explored to facilitate the community's development.
- Broad representation of the membership in the steering group is important to ensure that the community, not the organization, is driving the process.
- It's not easy to find experts on specific topics. The complexities of business often mean that there are no easy answers to be found in one place (e.g., document or manual) or in one person. A team approach to creating the community foundation can provide the range of expertise needed to put all of the various pieces in place.
- Sponsors or champions can model trust by empowering a steering group to create a community environment where members can openly share their challenges and opportunities without the involvement of management. It takes a great deal of courage for an organization to provide resources with few strings attached!
- In a competitive sales environment, the limits to sharing knowledge are surprisingly few. The agents were incredibly open in sharing their expertise within the community. Our initial concern that members would be reluctant to share their "tricks of the trade" was unfounded.

- There's a distinct difference between knowledge and information. Knowledge sharing provides the context for "advice" and discusses the application of knowledge (the "how to" of an idea). Information sharing provides the resource background. Both activities are needed in a successful community of practice. One role of the facilitator is to acknowledge the importance of information sharing, but to continuously raise the bar to promote the more valuable sharing of knowledge.

- In addition to sponsor support, executive management support is critical. Keep senior management informed of the developments and seek their advice. Draw them in on successes, not only for problem solving.

Step 2—Establish Community Components

The project management approach has been established and the context for the community has been identified. Now it's time to roll up your sleeves and get the community development moving forward. In this second step before the community is launched, the bulk of the infrastructure work is completed (see Figure 6.3).

At this point, you're making some educated guesses. There's no way to predict exactly what will happen once the community is launched, but you can plan for a range of situations. Your project management skills are in high gear as you coordinate the efforts of the steering group and working

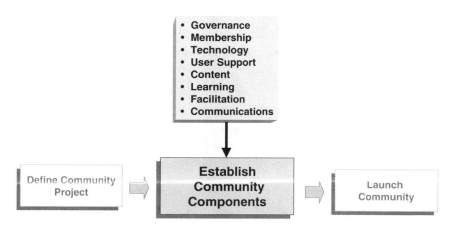

Figure 6.3.
Establish Community Components

groups in order to accomplish the tasks you outlined in the project plan. The juggling of details, emotions, and egos while marching toward a launch date for the community makes life interesting. But with each completed action, the community takes shape and its personality begins to emerge.

The greatest effort in the design phase is putting all of the components of the community in place. We identified eight components that group the logistics, the functional aspects of the community's development:

- **Governance**—the structures needed to guide policy and process development—to make decisions about the community's purpose, directions, and approaches.

- **Membership**—the selection criteria and invitation process.

- **Technology Infrastructure**—the computer application or software chosen to support community development and knowledge sharing; the collaborative tool used to support the virtual community.

- **User Support**—the help desk issues and solutions or approaches needed to ensure access to the community and usability of the application.

- **Content**—the personal data for member profiles and seed content that will populate the community at launch and during the initial community development stages.

- **Learning**—the materials and resources to familiarize community members with accessing and using the computer application.

- **Facilitation**—the moderator, guide, cheerleader, and traffic cop who ensures the smooth exchange of ideas, nurtures community building, and provides liaison with stakeholders, the application vendor, and other interested parties.

- **Communications**—the public relations activities to promote the use of the community as well as to keep sponsors, senior management, community members, and Clarica members informed of the community's development process.

These components form the community's foundation. They provide the infrastructure, the tools, processes, and procedures that facilitate the work of the community. They create the space where discussions and community activities take place. They organize and make accessible the community's knowledge. The logistics that support the members' creation and exchange of knowledge in a community with a strategic purpose play an important role in the community's success and value creation for the organization.

While the logistics for a less structured community may not be as sophisticated as in the community that we're profiling, to gain maximum value for strategic purposes, the logistics for this type of community must be focused on achieving success.

In the appendix, we provide a toolkit for the many details that need to be addressed in creating a community.

Outline Governance and Community Structures

For communities situated in a strategic context, the governance and community structures are highly developed in order to meet specific goals. Unlike an informal community where learning is encouraged but no specific objectives have been set, this strategically situated community has articulated a commitment to improving practice, has identified targeted outcomes, and is guided by a value proposition in its purpose statement.

One of our Steering Group members compared the Agent Network to the Rotary Club. No one had to join, but those who did believed in the value of the organization and were committed to a code of participation and followed rules of conduct. General guidelines were developed as draft statements by the Steering Group. The intent was that once the community was established, the membership would finalize more comprehensive statements concerning rules of conduct and participation.

Not all governance issues were addressed during this step. For example, several key governance elements (e.g., creating the Steering Group and defining the roles and relationships of stakeholders, sponsors, and members) were defined in the first step of the community development process. However, the bulk of the governance work was accomplished at this step:

- **Statement of community purpose**—the reason the community exists from the perspective of its members.

- **Membership criteria**—a profile of membership and an overview of the selection and invitation process.

- **Guidelines for participation**—the code of conduct for members.

- **Statement on security, privacy, and liability issues**—processes to ensure confidentiality and rights to privacy not only for members, but for their customers who may be referenced in discussions.

- **Statement on language**—in a bilingual country, measures to ensure that both official languages are supported.

- **Outline of community development**—a broad plan of action to grow the community.

- **Collaborative processes**—the tools necessary to work with the members and the Steering Group.

Establish Membership

Once the membership criteria and process were identified, the Steering Group began inviting people to participate in the community. Coordinated by the project manager, the Steering Group developed the following materials and processes:

- **Invitation process**—the approach (including a script) to invite participation.

- **Invitation list**—the candidates and their contact information.

- **Invitations**—a cover letter from the sponsors and formal invitation that was created with the help of Graphics Services.

- **Follow-up process**—telephone script and e-mail draft to solicit responses from candidates who hadn't confirmed their participation after the printed invitation was sent and to find out why those who declined were not interested in participation (i.e., what were the barriers to community membership?).

Obtain Technology Infrastructure

In the design step, we started the process of contracting with a vendor to supply the software that would support the community's activities and provide access to content that was generated. In the case of the Agent Network, we selected Communispace—a Web-based application that provided a full range of community development capabilities. (See Chapter 4 for more information on this process.) During the infrastructure development phase we:

- **Completed the service agreement**—technology purchase process including reference checks.

- **Branded the site**—customized the software with Clarica "look and feel" wherever possible.

- **Customized features**—selected options to modify the software's basic functionality as appropriate to the community's needs and Clarica's technology standards.

Address Technical Issues and Outline User Support

Without a doubt, working out the technology infrastructure was the most time-consuming activity in establishing the community's infrastructure due to the complexity of putting a community online. We addressed this issue in the critical success factors outlined in Chapter 4, but it is important to note that establishing a virtual community requires the concerted efforts of all those involved with the community development in partnership with your information technology or systems people.

At Clarica, we have a team of technology experts who work with business units to select, implement, and upgrade applications that support business processes. These consultants drove the process of putting the technology in place—a crucial role that coordinated the requirements of sales force technology, integrated technologies (the corporate group), the software vendor, and the business partner (in this case the Knowledge Team).

To put the technology in place, with the help of our internal technology consultants we:

- Mapped the technology infrastructure needs—application and access.

- Identified firewall/network security issues—requirements to supply software using an application service provider (ASP) model, where the software resides on third-party systems rather than on our own systems.

- Completed a corporate security audit.

- Identified support needs and outlined a process for support of members in accessing the application.

- Created a quick link from the corporate intranet to the Web-based software.

Prepare Content

The software that supports our virtual community provides a blend of synchronous and asynchronous tools to facilitate community knowledge creation and sharing. To set the stage for community activities and highlight the software's functionality, we outlined an approach to populate the site with some content. We wanted to have items available that would show the value of participating in the community—that would make the members want to come back for more and encourage them to contribute their own ideas and materials.

To put a human face on the virtual community, we stocked the user profiles with member contact information and photos. Our technology support group automated the data selection process and preloaded selected fields to save the members time in completing their profiles. Simple contact information was extracted from internal databases and photos were available from an earlier project to create agent Websites. Members could then put a face to a name and learn a little bit about a member's background and credentials, which was extremely important for building relationships. We also developed an update routine to keep the profile information current.

To stimulate conversations and model productive inquiry, we initiated five discussions in the threaded dialogue section of the collaborative tool. The rather straightforward topics were chosen to get the members talking and trying out the software. And a sample chat was started to give members, who, unlike their preschool-aged children, had never experienced an online chat before.

To kick-start the knowledge exchange process, we prepopulated the knowledge repository—a library of materials that members could use to refine their business approaches. But before actually loading the materials, we had to:

- **Establish selection criteria**—characteristics of materials to be included.
- **Outline a format for submissions**—standard information to be used in the descriptive paragraph (e.g., originator/author, purpose and history of use, file format, client response to materials).
- **Identify key words**—terms to be assigned to the material for subject access.

- **Solicit contributions**—contact selected members for materials.
- **Identify materials to be included** (based on selection criteria).

And to further highlight the community's knowledge-sharing possibilities, we put up an exhibit of photos in the "gallery"—a place for digital snapshots. We chose photos that showed the Steering Group hard at work on behalf of the community and a frazzled facilitator trying to keep an unruly bunch in line.

Learning to Use the Community Technology Infrastructure

The initial learning effort was focused on introducing members to the basic functionality of the community software, which was accessed via the Internet or the corporate intranet and looked very much like a Website. As noted earlier, the vendor's training materials basically consisted of a drop-down help menu that needed to be accessed online. In itself, this help support was quite good for someone with basic Web literacy. But we needed to provide a more substantial tutorial for the members who had either little or no experience with a Web-based application.

We developed three paper-based learning resources that were later made available online within the comunity:

- **Community user's guide**—a technical manual that focused on *using* the functionality, not just describing what a particular button "did."
- **Day-one scenario guide**—a suggested approach for walking through the key sections of the site on a member's first visit to the community.
- **Reference card**—quick tips for using the community site.

Clarica has a comprehensive sales force development unit where corporate programs are designed and often delivered at the local agency level by specialized personnel who provide technology coaching to agents. We realized that these people could be a valuable asset in helping agents use the community application, which supported a sales force objective of increasing the Web capabilities of agents. We offered agency coaches a guest pass that was governed by a principles-of-use statement. These passes were readily available during the first month of the community launch. At the end of the initial launch period, agency coaches could con-tinue to access the community to help members navigate the community site, but the passes needed to be signed out from the facilitator. The pass-word control to guests was monitored for the sake of the community's pri-vacy and security.

No formal training course was offered on the use of the community site, but members had a number of options:

- Consult the paper guides (also available online in the commu-nity's library).
- Get help from an agency coach.
- Contact the community facilitator who would walk through var-ious aspects of using the application.

During the ramp-up period, the facilitator was ever-present in the community and would practice with whoever might be online and stumped or just want to try out various collaborative functions. There were surprisingly few panic calls, smoking computer terminals, or disen-franchised members, and there was a general willingness to roll with the punches that technology might throw. Within a short while, the members were supporting each other in how to use the site.

Currently we're revamping the learning approach by developing online tutorials that will be available on the corporate intranet. These online learning solutions will be generic in their approach in order to support a number of communities that are all using the same software.

Clarify Role and Responsibilities of the Facilitator

The Agent Network has had a dedicated facilitator since its online launch—someone to keep discussions moving forward, remove barriers, help members avoid pitfalls, and act as traffic cop and liaison officer, coach, and guide. The literature on communities of practice is clear that facilitation is key to a community's success. In informal communities, there is someone who volunteers to organize the community. In formal communities, facilitation helps leverage the knowledge creation and shar-ing, encouraging the members to push the envelop on building capabili-ties and applying new knowledge to the business situation.

Because of facilitation's integral role, we've taken a more in-depth look at its attributes and approaches in Chapter 4 in our discussion of critical success factors. In addition, we've included a number of the tools used for facilitation in Chapter 10. But to contribute to the discussion of infrastructure components in the design phase of community development, we'll highlight the objectives for establishing the facilitation role.

During the infrastructure development step, the Steering Group:

- Established the role of the facilitator—acknowledged the need for a facilitator and suggested how the facilitator would interact with the community.
- Provided guidance on the agent environment and coached the facilitator on how to interact with the membership.
- Advised on the liaison role between the confidential community and the corporation.

At the same time, the facilitator was increasing her skill level by:

- Taking an online course on online facilitation.
- Researching the fundamentals of facilitation.
- Participating in a community of practice for online facilitators.
- Learning the community site member and administrator functionality.

Because our facilitator had the dual role of project manager and facilitator, she had a broad knowledge of the community development process and managed many aspects of our partnership with the community software vendor.

Establish Communications Plan

Leading up to the community launch and during the first three months of the pilot phase, we did not widely communicate our community-building efforts. Instead our communication efforts were focused on the community membership and stakeholders. We made numerous presentations prior to the launch about communities and their contribution to increasing individual and organizational capabilities—learning vehicles that make a significant difference to an agent's business performance. These presentations were intended to gain support from stakeholders and would be stepped up once we evaluated the pilot phase and made recommendations to expand the community to the larger agent population.

While infrastructure was being created, a communication plan was drafted, and we provided:

- Updates for helpdesk staff on the community's progress.
- Summaries for sponsors and corporate executives on community developments.
- Corporation-wide communiqués via online newsletters.
- Information on the project posted on the corporate intranet.

The communication activities increased in Phase II when we began to grow the community and create increasing value for its members and Clarica.

The tasks undertaken to meet the objectives in these eight areas of building the community infrastructure are further outlined in Chapter 9. A table with the objectives for each step and an illustration of how they were accomplished can be used as a basis for formulating your own approach to creating a formal community infrastructure in your organization. As well, there are examples of documents that describe these various infrastructure elements as they applied to the development of the Agent Network at Clarica.

Reflection

Because we had started some of the infrastructure building while we were designing the project, the timeframe to complete the components in this second step of community development was approximately six weeks.

The launch date for the community was set as December 15th, and we worked diligently toward meeting that target. We chose this date because the two-week ramp-up period would fall over the holiday season when we thought our members might not be as focused on customer-related activities as they would be at other times of the year. Over the holidays, their customers were usually otherwise engaged—buying insurance policies as stocking stuffers or Hanukkah gifts wasn't a high priority, so agents might have some extra time to familiarize themselves with the community site.

If we missed this two-week window, we would be into the registered retirement savings plan purchase season (in Canada from January 1st through the end of February). Due to the focused efforts of agents during these first two months of the year, Clarica has a moratorium on introducing new tools, products, or services to agents. If we missed the December 15th date, our launch would have to be postponed until March—an unacceptable two-month delay. So there was a great deal of incentive for getting the infrastructure pieces in place in order to launch the community on time.

For the second step in designing this community, we found the key issue was keeping the community membership, not the logistics, at the forefront of our efforts. In identifying the community context, we heard loud and clear that agents needed a private space to discuss their practice, and the motto "For Agents, By Agents" provided a very clear message about the community's purpose and focus.

Our efforts needed to be centered on issues surrounding community membership and participation. At the same time, we had to address the logistics and infrastructure—a catch 22 of sorts. Losing track of the forest for the trees meant that we might end up with a beautiful community infrastructure with no one willing to participate. On the other hand, if we didn't pay attention to details of the community vessel, we would more than likely not be able to either attract or retain interested members.

At the same time, we needed to ensure that corporate interests were not abandoned. But without a doubt, the community was up front and the members were center stage.

Key issues at this point included:

- **Limitations of community member technology platform, equitable access, and cost of access.** As independent agents, the community members had applied Clarica technology standards in some not-so-standard ways. The agents also pay a flat rate to access Clarica resources, and with the differences in Internet service provision across the country, we had communication challenges.

- **Limitation of participation to agents.** Many agents have assistants whom they employ to support their businesses—often to support their use of technology. Governance issues arose regarding prospective members' desire to have their assistants access the community on their behalf because their own keyboarding and computer literacy levels could hamper their participation. Questions of confidentiality and trust were raised.

- **Clarica limitation of liability statement.** At the eleventh hour, we realized that we hadn't sufficiently addressed corporate legal concerns. We needed to limit Clarica's liability and formalize members' participation with a signed statement. We addressed this need with an assumed-acceptance-of-terms approach similar to that used with shrink-wrapped software. If you break the seal and use the product, you agree to the conditions.

- **Security of agent data and community conversations.** Because our vendor would be hosting the Web-based application on its own servers, we didn't have the protection of our firewall. You can imagine the issues! Data about our agents as well as the conversations held within the community needed to be secure. As a result, we had to comply with secure socket-layer standards and pass a security audit.

- **Compliance and branding.** Because our business is highly regulated, we have a comprehensive compliance layer that limits our liability. The community would house agent-generated materials, items that would not have been passed through compliance or brand scrutiny. Guidelines would need to be put in place, and a link to the liability statement would need to be made.

Best Practice

We knew that a team approach was necessary to accomplish all the tasks that we had outlined. The Steering Group provided excellent guidance, but they were not able to assume responsibility for much further involvement. Once we were in the throes of establishing the community infrastructure, we gained an even greater appreciation of the wide range of expertise that was needed to put the community in place. In particular we learned:

- Community membership should reflect the diversity of the group. A wide range of expertise, market experiences, geographic location, years experience, agent organization structures, and technology expertise should be encouraged. Such diversity provides a rich base for knowledge transfer, establishes a country-wide network, and creates coach/mentor relationships.

- A team approach shortens the development time, increases the quality of the launch, and provides a natural communication/ public relations network throughout the organization. The project management role coordinates the network of resources required.

- Wherever possible, use existing infrastructures to support the community (e.g., agency coaches, help desk personnel, agent assistants). Capitalize on the familiar user support mechanisms for community members. Avoid reinventing the wheel where costs are duplicated, users are confused, and community participation is seen as separate from normal routines.

■ User education should focus on use or application of the functionality rather than the functionality alone. The training approach available from the vendor at the time of our launch was very functionality focused—telling the user what the various buttons were for, but not how to apply the features. We developed two additional learning aids: a day-one scenario— what to do to get up and running in the community—and an application-oriented user's guide that explained functionality in the context of how the member would actually use it to participate in the community.

STEP 3—LAUNCH THE COMMUNITY

The community members have been identified, the software has been customized, the learning tools and support resources have been distributed, the sponsors have signed-off on the launch, and the community members are waiting for the community's doors to open. In Step 3 of the community development process, the Web-based software that supports the community's online activity is made available to the members during a facilitated ramp-up period where members are encouraged to edit their profiles and familiarize themselves with the software functionality.

At this point, the project manager's role diminishes and the facilitator's role increases as the community members are greeted at the door and the

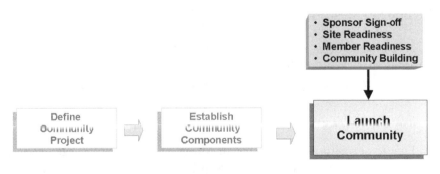

Figure 6.4.
Launch the Community

tone for the community is established. As the community goes live, several key actions need to be completed:

- **Sponsor sign-off**—obtain permission to proceed with the community launch.
- **Site readiness**—ensure that the technology is in place, profiles are loaded, and the community is populated with an appropriate amount of content.
- **Member readiness**—set up the members for success in using the community application and provide support trainers with appropriate information and access.
- **Community building**—begin facilitated activities: welcome members, reinforce use and contributions, begin to gather usage statistics, and encourage broad participation.

Would that the launch were as simple as flipping a switch and cracking a bottle of champagne over a computer screen! Even with all the planning efforts that preceded the launch, we experienced eleventh-hour barriers that jeopardized going live with the online community, but they were, in the end, resolved in time. We launched the community after the following sequence of events:

Obtain Sponsor Sign-off

The corporate sponsors shouldered the risk for the community. Before we launched the community, the sponsors signed off on the project, signaling the "all clear" for sending the log in information to the members.

Ensure Site Readiness

A final test of the community site by the facilitator and Steering Group ensured that the technology was in place, the access point was clearly labeled from the corporate intranet, and content was populated.

Ensure Member Readiness

Due to security issues, the log in information had to be sent via our corporate e-mail system, which sits inside our firewall. At the same time, we couldn't distribute the learning guides via the e-mail system due to limitations in bandwidth available to agents and some agency branches and corporate policy that restricted file attachments to e-mail messages sent to agents.

Our plan had been to send log in and training information electronically, modeling life in the online world. But we had to opt for a dual approach—log in information via e-mail and learning information, day-one guides, and the reference card distributed through the corporate mail system. This extra mail distribution step produced a time lag, especially for community members who weren't resident in a branch office. Their materials had to be forwarded from the agency office to their home office.

At the same time, agency trainers were provided with a guest pass for log in and the same paper-based tutorial materials. In addition to paper copies, the tutorial materials were available in the community's online library. An excellent approach if you could figure out how to get INTO the library, but a bit of a challenge for community members who may not have been able to work out the steps of accessing the community site let alone the library within!

It wasn't the best approach, but in the end, members got their materials and were able to log on with varying degrees of success. The two-week ramp-up period provided enough time for most people to become comfortable with the site's functionality.

The log in information was distributed on the evening of December 14th and the site was officially launched the following morning.

Begin Community Building

The site had been prepopulated with content—dialogues to begin discussions, member profiles seeded with basic contact information and photos, and a sampling of documents in the library and photos in the gallery.

As members ventured into the community, the facilitator welcomed them at the door, e-mailed congratulations on successfully contributing to the community, and reported on the progress of the launch to all members.

During the ramp-up period, no formal activities were planned, as the Steering Group thought that members would want to take their time getting used to this new approach to sharing knowledge. We underestimated the isolation many members operate within and soon saw that meaningful participation began on day one. No need for icebreakers and party games for this group. They rolled up their sleeves and got down to business. By the end of the ramp-up period, all of the facilitator-initiated dialogues were closed off and over ten work-related discussions were underway on how to improve business approaches.

Statistics were gathered in a facilitator's log and via system administration—the number of questions posed regarding functionality, changes in user profiles, and site contributions. Establishing benchmarks from day one helped to show the growth of the community and provide qualitative as well as quantitative measures of impact.

Reflection

We've built it. Will they come? Can they jump the hurdles that we thought might be there, let alone the ones we hadn't anticipate?

The Agent Network launch coincided with the launch of a new version of the software we were using to create our virtual community space. Due to inconsistencies in the new software release, the community facilitator spent considerable time resolving a significant number of software bugs. This unanticipated challenge meant that facilitation was focused more on software problem resolution than community building. In the end, the members were incredibly understanding about the time and effort required to work out the technical kinks. In fact, the technology challenges served to bring the group together—to collectively tackle the beast and find ways to make the community hum.

(Please note—we DO NOT recommend that you deliberately plan significant technology challenges as a community-building activity. However, should technology stand in the way, seize the opportunity to turn these challenges into learning opportunities that make your community stronger!)

During the two-week launch period, technology was the central issue, creating challenges at all levels of communication, distribution of materials, and member use of the community software. We stretched our resources to address internal technology issues, agent-related issues, and issues with our community software vendor. For a company with a reasonable level of techno-savvy, we still made assumptions that led to false starts and, in the end, a significant amount of extra work. But we ironed out the technology kinks and chalked up experience as follows:

- Due to limitations in distributing files via the e-mail system to agents, support information for the community application (e.g., user's guide, day one scenario, reference cards) had to be provided in paper form. Cost of production and distribution plus the time needed to distribute the information by traditional mail methods were increased.

- For security reasons, distribution of log in information had to be done via e-mail, making the distribution of materials needed to launch the community a two-step process where paper information was sent via corporate mail and log in information was sent via e-mail.

- Remembering passwords became an issue, especially with infrequent users. Because the passwords had to be maintained by the facilitator (the corporate help desk could not access the site), the facilitator had to be accessible beyond the normal workday.

- Computer and telecommunication technology presented challenges for the agent desktop image and the community software. Project management and facilitation efforts were focused on resolving more technical problems associated with the virtual nature of the community than anticipated. Technology support resources from corporate IT were required well beyond the design step.

Best Practice

The launch period generated a great deal of excitement. Members were meeting each other, swapping stories, renewing old acquaintances, and learning how to use the application. Even with the holidays at hand, we had a high log in rate, and enthusiasm was building for the official start of community activities in January. The two-week ramp-up period helped resolve technical issues, familiarize the members with the online application, and kick-start the community-building process. A few lessons learned from this period include:

- Much of the pre-launch work is administrative. Depending on the number of members, plan for adequate administrative resources to support the pre-launch activities.

- At launch, the focus is entirely on the community members. The facilitator's role is key at this point, encouraging members to participate and helping them to become comfortable with the community application. Out-welcome the welcome wagon!

- Right from the beginning, start gathering usage statistics that are crucial to designing assessment tools and establishing a benchmark for future community development. In assessing how far you've advanced, it's good to know where you started.

- Manage user expectations of technology. We hadn't anticipated the problems that we would experience with the technology. We erred on the side of not giving more attention to possible technology hurdles and fell on our faces. Members should be aware of possible pitfalls with technology, and adequate support and work-arounds should be in place.

- Don't over-plan the community. The facilitator is there to keep the momentum going, but the drive for community development should come from within. We had thought that we would need to prepopulate the community with information and materials that the members would find valuable enough to keep coming back. We learned that the community would take the responsibility for creating value. The five dialogues that we started (recommended by the Steering Group) were outdistanced by member-initiated conversations within the two-week ramp-up period! It was worth having something there for the members to see as a model, but we pulled facilitator-led discussions quickly once we realized that the community wanted to set the tone and direction for conversations.

CONCLUSION

As we look back on the five months that it took to get all the pieces of the puzzle in place to launch the Agent Network community, we have to admit that this was the least enjoyable part of community development. We realize that it was necessary and credit much of the success of the community to the quality infrastructure that was put in place. The attention to details, the thoroughness of the planning, and the collaboration of a network of experts helped us accomplish our goals of creating a vibrant, healthy community and identifying a process that could be replicated for other community development projects.

The process stood us in good stead with both the community members and our sponsors. The messages were clear that this community could make a significant contribution to our strategic imperatives, that the members could easily increase their capabilities through the high caliber

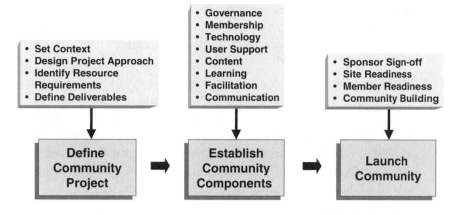

Figure 6.5.
Phase I—Community Design and Launch

of conversation and knowledge. Early in the development of the Agent Network, we could see that this community was:

- An important initiative that has the potential to contribute to superior performance of the organization.
- Carefully planned and fully resourced to facilitate success.
- Created with a handpicked membership, but will become self-selecting through the individual levels of participation as the community develops.
- Living up to its slogan: For Agents, By Agents.

From the rigors of community design and project management, we move to the wilds of community development and growth, where the challenge shifts from pushing a string uphill to herding cats!

DESIGN AND LAUNCH—WILL IT PLAY IN PEORIA?

1. **The team approach.** Early in the process, we learned that it takes a team to develop a virtual community. The complexities of balancing community building, technology infrastructure and support, and corporate interest in communities with a strategic purpose cannot be successfully addressed without the combined effort of a team. What resources would you need to bring

together to build a community in your organization? How would you identify the expertise and create a cohesive group? What structure exists or needs to be created to support the team in their efforts?

2. **Technology.** A virtual community relies heavily on a solid technology infrastructure. What technology would you need to support your virtual community? What's currently in place? What needs to be acquired? Who will manage the technology aspects? How will the new technology (or software) be introduced to the community members? Who will coordinate the ongoing technology needs? Is your community ready to "go virtual?"

3. **Vendor relationships.** The software works hand-in-hand with the technology infrastructure to create the virtual space for the community. What kind of collaborative tool would best meet the needs of your community? Do you have a software evaluation and selection process to guide your choice? What is your organization's approach to vendor partnerships? Can you work cooperatively, relying on the expertise of your vendor to help guide the community development process—or would you rather not have input past the purchase/lease of the software? How can you leverage the knowledge of your vendor?

4. **Hurdles.** We approached the community development process a bit naively, missing some of the key issues that needed to be addressed. What's the appetite in your organization for begging forgiveness when you didn't have the foresight to seek permission? What issues could impede the community's creation? Does your organization have concerns about security, liability, privacy, and confidentiality that need to be addressed?

References

Wenger, E., R. McDermott, and W.M. Snyder (2002). *Cultivating Communities of Practice: A Guide to Managing Knowledge.* Cambridge, MA: Harvard Business School Press.

Chapter 7

Phase II:
Community Implementation
and Growth

Following the community project design and launch phase, we move to implementing and growing the community. The graphical representation of the process is supplemented with narrative to tell the story of how the Agent Network took shape. The process is a lot less definable, less controlled in this phase. It's the time when the community takes responsibility for itself—setting its own directions that are supported by a facilitator, but not controlled by a project manager. The successes aren't measured in terms of project plan milestones, but rather as endorsements from community members who are seeing value from their participation in the community and from corporate sponsors who see the community's purpose being realized.

Overview

The community components were put in place and members had a two-week period to "kick the tires" of the community site—a time to get to know each other and become comfortable with the functionality of the Web-based application. In Phase I, we worked in three parallel streams:

- **Membership**—the groundwork of bringing people together, selling them on the benefits of sharing knowledge in a community.

- **Logistics**—the project management aspect of getting all the components together to create a community infrastructure, a place for the community to call home.

- **Corporate support**—keeping the sponsors and stakeholders "in the loop" of community development without directly involving them.

In Phase II of the community development process, we move from a focus on creating the community vessel to a focus on the workings of the community itself. In this chapter, we look at the community from two perspectives—the collective voice of the group and the individual contributions of the members.

THE COMMUNITY MEMBERS

We hand-picked people to be the founding members of the community. Working with regional vice presidents, we selected agents who would be keen to try something new and predisposed to sharing their expertise. We also selected members on the basis of geographic, gender, and age distribution, identifying people with a range of customer types, product mixes, and levels of experience.

Our goal was to start the community with 150 members. The invitation list included just under 150 names. Our expectations were that approximately 50% would accept. Each of these 75 agents would then ask another agent to join the community—the rationale being that the buddy system would help establish community sharing because each member would know at least one other member. We'd also hoped to have a balance of experienced (over seven years) and developing agents (under three years) so that mentoring would happen naturally.

To our surprise, we had a 95% acceptance rate in the first round of calls after the invitations were distributed! We had to stop asking people to bring along a buddy, otherwise, we would have doubled the size of our target population. We wanted a manageable number of members for the pilot phase and were concerned that volume might affect the community's effectiveness.

This high rate of acceptance was an early indicator of the community's probable success. There was a great deal of interest in learning from one another, of creating a network of agents who could share their problems and their triumphs. As we noted earlier, agents learn best from one another. They come together in a very realistic, pragmatic business-grounded form of learning. In the eyes of an agent, no one else has more credibility than another agent in a similar situation. They care for each other. They deeply understand each other, and that sense of support engenders a great deal of learning, increasing capabilities and extending the quality of their practice.

COMMUNITY IMPLEMENTATION AND GROWTH

The implementation of this community of practice was designated as a pilot project, which meant that there was a fixed time period in which to study:

- An approach to community development.
- The assumptions concerning the benefits of community participation from the perspective of the membership and the corporation.
- The resources required to support a community's development.

Following the community's launch, we started a three-month implementation and growth pilot phase. Members were aware that we would base our assessment of the value of pursuing this community on their feedback at the end of the pilot phase.

Phase II of the community implementation process and growth (see Figure 7.1) is focused on creating a sense of community and creating value for the members, the community, and the organization. At this point, the process moves away from the linear structure that we saw in Phase I to a cyclical process where development, evaluation, and growth interact in a dynamic way. As new ideas or situations are presented in the community, they are evaluated, accepted as is, or modified, discarded, or expanded upon. A collective voice begins to form as the community's personality emerges.

In Phase II, the community members took responsibility for the community. This shift in responsibility was palpable. In Phase I, the majority of the decisions were made by a handful of people, and the process of putting the infrastructure in place was tightly controlled by the project manager. Now, the community members were in the driver's seat. A core of community leaders and champions emerged, and a rhythm of participation was established. Facilitation kept the community moving forward, but the direction was definitely in the hands of the community membership.

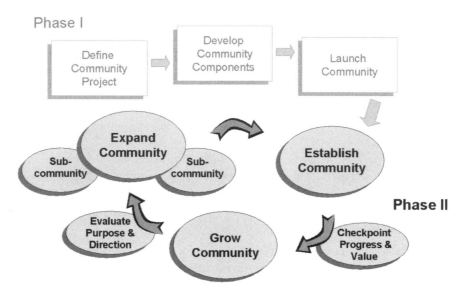

Figure 7.1.
Phase II—Community Implementation and Growth

STEP 4—ESTABLISH THE COMMUNITY

After the launch and the ramp-up period, the community began to take shape. A sense of community, which actually started in the project planning steps, took hold. Although some community members had been with the organization for years and knew agents from across the country, they had never had the opportunity to engage in conversations in this manner before. Instead of picking up the phone and talking to an individual (or more likely leaving a voice mail message), sending an e-mail to a few colleagues, or attending a sales conference or agency meeting to touch base with their peers, they were able to pose a question in a dialogue and have 149 responses without leaving the office or picking up the phone.

A sense of the community's value also began to emerge as members assessed their participation from a "what's in it for me" perspective that soon balanced with a "what's in it for the community" perspective. Expectations began to be met or missed as conversations struck a chord, met a need, identified a possible new direction that hadn't been considered before, or missed the mark. Commitments to participation began to be made with members coaching other members on software use and community involvement. And as people got to know one another, a network of expertise began to build—connecting people with like situations and challenges.

The early days of the community's implementation were spent just getting to know who was in the community and testing out the functionality of the site. Profiles were filled out and members began to find similarities in business situations. Facilitation continued to play a key role in helping members see the benefits of their participation and ensuring that the community site was functioning properly. Key activities included:

- **Complete member profiles**—get to know the members.
- **Assess needs and identify styles**—what do the members need to know? Identify preferences for methods of knowledge exchange. Identify pockets of expertise (what does the community know?) and gaps (what does the community need to know?).
- **Introduce facilitation resource**—establish role and personality of the facilitator.
- **Encourage participation**—contribute to discussions and knowledge repository.
- **Increase community site literacy**—help members become comfortable with the site functionality.

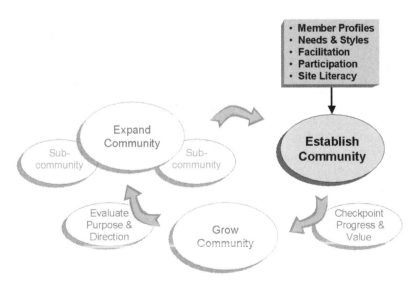

Figure 7.2.
Establish the Community

Not all members had logged in during the ramp-up period, so in addition to getting the community rolling, we also continued to welcome new members to the community and help them become familiar with the community site functionality.

Complete Member Profiles

The Web-based application that we used to host the online community was designed to humanize the online experience. Member profiles were at the core of adding the human touch to the online environment. The profile template had two parts. The first part provided a digital photo of the member and profiled professional information (e.g., years of experience, markets served, areas of expertise, professional designations). The second part of the profile was optional—a set of questions that profiled the personal side (e.g., favorite pastimes, a funny experience, a reason for joining the community) combined with an opportunity to create a digital scrapbook.

The database of profiles provided information about the members, a click away at any point in the community tool. Photos of the members were next to their contributions in dialogues, the home page showed who was currently online in the community by displaying the photos, and whenever a person's name was underlined, there was a direct link to his or her photo and profile.

In our guide to the members' first visit to the community site, we suggested that they begin by filling out their profile. We gave them a head start by loading the profile forms with photos and contact information.

Throughout this step, the facilitator encouraged members to complete their profiles and get to know the other community members by checking out other profiles One of our community leaders was religious about checking new profiles and would send welcome messages highlighting some fact that the new member had chosen to include. We were able to link people with similar interests, business directions, and customer challenges based in part on the profiles.

Our software vendor encouraged us to start off the community profiling with some "fun"—icebreakers designed to help people get to know each other. A suggestion was made to the Steering Group that we host a scavenger hunt through member profiles to get the ball rolling, and we got our first real taste of the persona the community wanted to establish. We heard loud and clear that this was a place for professional exchanges, that games would diminish the credibility of the community, which had come together to improve their practice—not to play parlor games! In no uncertain terms, we were to focus our planned activities and facilitation efforts on creating a professional persona for the community. And so we did.

Assess Needs and Identify Style

Before we launched the community, we established a few ground rules to guide participation. The Steering Group felt strongly that we should not establish a whole slate of rules and policies before we saw what the community needed, how the members would participate, and what situations might arise that would need guidelines to resolve. Instead, we stated that the community would be governed by the standard Clarica code of conduct for agents. But we soon saw that we needed to put a few guidelines in place, particularly around confidentiality and appropriateness of discussion topics.

Early on, a member posed a question about how to approach a customer. Details of the customer's situation were too explicit and the customer's confidentiality was in question. One of the community leaders commented about the inappropriateness of some information that had been presented in the discussion, and the facilitator worked with the member offline (via e-mail) to point out concerns to the contributing member and coaching other members in the common dialogue on how to handle customer confidentiality.

In another instance, a member used the cut and paste function to copy full sections of a discussion that supported an opinion in a controversy and forwarded it to a branch manager. This time the confidentiality of both the contributors to the particular dialogue and the community were breached. And as before, the facilitator coached the individual offline and the community online.

There was no malicious intent in either of these situations, but the follow-up was swift and firm by the facilitator to ensure that the community learned some guidelines of participation and what was acceptable conduct for the conversations.

Introduce Role of the Facilitator

The facilitator continued the ramp-up role of greeting new members at the door and assisting with queries on site functionality, but the role expanded as the community shot past the welcome mat into the meat of their purpose.

Billed as the coach, coordinator, liaison, and traffic cop, the facilitator established her role not through her personal profile (although one was available in the membership directory) but through action. Unlike the overly enthusiastic waiter who approaches a table, pen in hand, ear-to-ear smile plastered across his face, and announces, "Hi. I'm Jason and I'll be your server tonight," our facilitator tried a more subtle approach, working offline (via e-mail or telephone) with individuals and online in the community site through selected contributions to dialogues—always asking permission to proceed (e.g., sounds like we have a bit of confusion about that, shall I check with product marketing and get back to the group?) before inserting a presence in the community.

The facilitator was hired by Clarica, and, although she reported to the Knowledge Architect, she took direction from the Steering Group. As a new employee with no previous experience in the financial services industry but a long history in teaching and private sector business development, the facilitator was on somewhat neutral ground, not seen as a head office lackey or informant. Often compared to a lioness by the sponsors, the facilitator protected her charges but nudged them out into the real world on a regular basis.

Encourage Participation

The conversations between the community champions and the enthusiastic leaders who were emerging quickly were lively, varied, and to the point. To encourage participation, we seeded the dialogue section with five questions to start the community using this asynchronous, threaded discussion portion of the site. One discussion topic asked what the members would like to see happen in the community, what areas would they like to explore? Within the week, the dialogues initiated by the facilitator were left in the dust, and the community sprinted ahead on its own.

Without any coaching, we had a classic case-based problem-solving question posted by one of the members, which we referred to earlier. A relatively new agent started a dialog called "A Tricky but Basic Case," asking for advice on how to approach a young couple who had recently received a substantial cash gift from their parents. The member began by outlining the prospective clients' financial situation and goals. The discussion developed as other members debated the pros and cons of universal life, term, and mortgage insurance and outlined money market options, identifying tax implications and the pressures of purchasing a first home. Later, the member reported back on the progress and summarized results:

two new life policies, an increase in an existing policy, two registered retirement savings plan contributions, a term deposit, and most important—a financial plan. The final comment was, "I walked them down to the local lawyer's office to make an appointment for wills and powers of attorney. I anticipate that they will become star clients."

With the help of members of the Agent Network, the agent was able to analyze options and present a plan that best fit the needs of the clients, laying the foundation for a relationship that will only strengthen over time. Music to the ears of the Steering Group and the sponsors, we had our first example of making a difference to a sale.

While the dialogue section was the focus in the beginning, we were also trying to build content in the knowledge repository. Members began to contribute agent-generated materials—copies of newsletters, marketing materials, financial calculation templates, and stories of successful approaches. Rather than a contest (remember, we couldn't have any FUN in the community), we put out a challenge to increase the contents of the repository to 30 items by the end of the month. The winner was the community, not a particular member. The prize was the shared knowledge, not another pen with *Clarica* embossed in blue and orange.

Increase Community Site Literacy

Introducing the Web-based application that we used to host the Agent Network community proved to be less of a challenge than we expected. While our members had been chosen for their level of technical literacy, we knew that their comfort level with the Web was not as high as with the other Microsoft Windows-based applications on their laptops.

To increase their familiarity with Web conventions, we started by introducing new activities using a different functionality each time. We showed people how to engage in a threaded dialogue instead of a simple sequencing of statements that would in the end be just a long list of unrelated topics. We hosted a "fire-side chat" with the sales force vice president so that the community could learn how to use the synchronized chat facility. We used the voting and polling feature to find out what topic the membership would like to pursue as a continuing education course.

Rather than throw the user's manual at the members, we helped them become familiar with the functionality as they continued their efforts to build the community. We situated their learning in the use of certain community-building activities, not in a description of site functionality.

Reflection

There's no question that establishing value and creating a sense of community is a continuous activity—it goes on throughout the life of the community. But there is a need, especially with a new community, to pay particular attention to these two key components of community from the start. Without a feeling of belonging and making a difference and seeing that the community can make a difference in their practice, the community members will soon lose interest, their commitment will wane, and the community will cease to exist within a relatively short period of time.

The central issue that emerged soon after community members began to interact was the need for selected policy statements and guidelines. As the members began to establish a sense of community and to value their participation and the contribution of others, they also became concerned about what was common ground and where the boundaries were, especially when some members perceived that other members were overstepping those boundaries.

With the help of the Steering Group, we began to establish draft guidelines, taking them to the community for discussion, and having the community decide on the approach. In particular, we needed to address confidentiality:

- Members who were not comfortable with technology and keyboarding had their assistants work in the community on their behalf. Questions were raised regarding the presence of nonmembers, even if they were working on behalf of a member. Could members trust that the conversations would remain confidential?

- At one point, materials were copied by a member from the knowledge repository and distributed to everyone in a branch office without the author's permission. Although the contributing member was pleased that another member found his material useful and wanted to share it with everyone else in the branch, a need for a statement on use of items (materials and dialogue contributions) that originate in the Agent Network was identified.

- Confidential customer information was presented as part of a dialogue conversation on how to approach a sale, prompting coaching on how to present cases. The level of information that could be shared and the details that could be discussed in an anonymous fashion needed to be outlined.

Best Practice

When it comes to developing a sense of community and community value, it's not that the members don't know how to function in a community. Many of the agents were active in their own communities, belonging to various service organizations and groups associated with schools or churches. And, although they were independent business people, there was a connection to Clarica, a branch office, and various financial services industry professional associations. In other words, the members knew the ropes of belonging to a community.

But for many of the members, it was their first involvement in a virtual community that used an online collaborative tool and a corporately sponsored community of practice. The rules of the game were slightly different, and we had to work together to find these boundaries. Remember the corporation's batting average wasn't very high in establishing a community for agents—we had a lot to figure out!

Once the community was up and running, we all learned a great deal about how this entity could take shape. In particular, we learned that:

- Community is about connections. Developing the community through identifying expertise and materials to help solve problems and develop strategies that maximize opportunities results in a network of people and resources who may not have previously been connected.

- The community takes on a life of its own. Facilitation guides the process, but the momentum and character of the community are established by its members.

- In the early stages of community development, facilitation is a key activity. Resources must be dedicated to the role of encouraging members to actively participate in the community and coaching them on the use of the community site.

Step 5—Checkpoint:
Assess Community Progress and Value

Here's where the two-dimensional aspect of a model lets us down. The graphical representation shows that, once you've started to establish a sense of community and community value (which isn't a finite act itself), you then assesses the community's progress and value proposition before moving on. In fact, the community, its leaders, and its related organizational structure should be constantly taking the pulse of the community. Given the nature of community members, chances are you won't have to wait to find out how things are going. People will let you know—positives and negatives, full barrel.

On the advice of our community software vendor, we sought feedback on our progress. Six weeks after launch, we asked the members to contribute their thoughts in a dialogue to obtain anecdotal feedback and analyzed some of the statistics that we'd been collecting about the number of logins, percentage of members who had filled in their profiles, and other quantifiable levels of participation.

This step is here to remind the people who are supporting the community that it's important to stop and take an informal check on the community's health—is the community moving ahead? Are barriers beginning to form? Are the conversations productive, supporting the members and moving their businesses ahead? So far so good?

Rather than waiting for a postmortem on a serious issue that may result in the failure or death of the community, a permanent channel for feedback should be maintained and regular queries (individually or to the entire community) should be instituted. Approaches include:

- Obtain informal feedback on community progress—collect informal comments made in dialogues, sent in e-mails, made in related meetings.
- Consult your steering group and sponsors on issues and opportunities—solicit feedback on perceptions.
- Analyze statistics—establish a baseline for various participation points.
- Provide feedback to community software vendor—keep channels of communication open regarding the status of the application and feedback on member satisfaction.

We could have overdone it. Like our enthusiastic server, Jason, we could have checked too often whether or not the meal was meeting expectations. There was a lot riding on the success of this community project, and the inclination was to be overly anxious about ensuring that everyone thought that this community was the best idea we'd had yet in implementing the Knowledge Strategy.

The checkpoint was a very informal step, but an important one. It helped us calm down a bit because the feedback was positive. For the most part, we were on the right track. It was still early in the community's

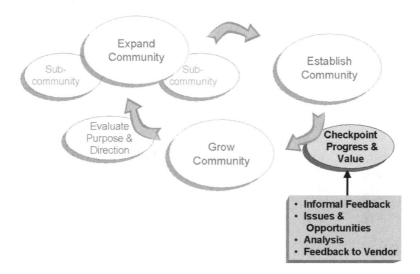

Figure 7.3.
Checkpoint—Assess Community Progress and Value

implementation and members were still finding their way, but they seemed to appreciate that we were checking in with them rather than just barrelling full steam ahead without consulting with the larger community.

Obtain Informal Feedback on Community Progress

The facilitator kept a file of comments that had been made in conversations in the various dialogues and chats within the community site, received in e-mails, or made during Steering Group meetings. At the checkpoint step, the comments were collated and provided to the Steering Group.

Consult Steering Group and Sponsors on Issues and Opportunities

The community brought together three key stakeholder groups: the community membership, the corporate sponsorship, and the sales force executive. As part of the on-going communication effort, these stakeholders were provided with information (qualitative and quantitative) and their feedback was solicited on how the community was progressing— whether or not their expectations were being met. Was the community providing the value in achieving strategic imperatives from their point of view?

Analyze Statistics

As part of the project management and facilitation efforts, quantitative statistics had been gathered on: rate of invitation acceptance; administrative factors such as number of log ins, profile changes, requests for new passwords; participation rates such as number of new dialogues, comments per dialogue, new references, bookstore and gallery items; and application-related issues such as problems with enhancements, features/functionality not working correctly, and error messages. On the qualitative side, we looked at the depth and breadth of conversations, participation in planned activities such as synchronous presentations and chats, and contributions to the knowledge repository, gallery, and bookstore.

Provide Feedback to Community Software Vendor

With a virtual community, the technology is central to creating the space where the community comes together. If it's down, the community can't continue its conversation as a group in a collaborative manner. We talked about the need for a strong partnership with your vendor in the critical success factors in Chapter 4. The partnership relationship is built on communication. So whether at the checkpoint or other formal evaluation step or, in fact, throughout the life of the community, working closely with the software partner is crucial. On an informal basis, the facilitator and account support representative were on the phone daily, if not more often, in the beginning. Formally, we began with weekly phone conferences to track issues, gain input from their experiences with other clients, and plan next steps. The partnership that evolved was key to the success of the virtual community. And, our input as customers to the vendor contributed to improvements in the community software for all of their customers.

Reflection

Due to our enthusiasm for the success of this community, it would have been very easy to just collect the positive feedback that we saw in discussions: "Don't you guys think this is great? What did we ever do before we had the Agent Network? Thanks for helping me change my approach—it made a big difference to the sale."

At this step, we began to think more clearly about how we would measure the value of the agent community. Our community software vendor encouraged us to establish metrics and outline a measurement plan that would not only assess the value to the community members, but would also provide data to address possible management concerns on the return on the investment. For the Agent Network, ROI was not driving the development of the community. We already had the sponsors' support that we needed to sustain the development, a solid commitment that did not expect quantifiable measures of direct effect on bottom-line performance.

Chances are we lost some of our readers with that statement. Due to the economic realities of today, few REAL projects can claim no pressure to acknowledge a positive return on the investment. We can't just push aside our accountability for the expenditure of resources. We'll talk more about our philosophy of measurement within Clarica's Knowledge Capital Initiative in Chapter 8. But thinking back on this particular step of the community's development, we were certainly wrestling with measurement issues:

- **What data should be collected?** Measurement and evaluation experts always advise people to plan their evaluation approach, knowing what it is they're looking for and only collecting data to answer specific questions. In other words, the splatter approach is frowned upon. We plead guilty and admit we didn't have a formal plan. We pretty well kept our eyes open on all fronts to see what patterns were forming. Not knowing what to expect regarding the development of this community linked closely with a strategic intent, we had little to go on. As far as we knew, communities of this nature had not been discussed in the literature or at conferences, so we were exploring new territory.

- **What are the expectations of members, sponsors, and other key stakeholders?** Understand what the various groups need to know in order to gauge success. Value propositions will change from group to group. Ensure that you have the full range covered and target your key messages on the community's progress and value by audience.

Best Practice

When we designed the project, we thought that we would do a formal evaluation at the end of the pilot project phase (approximately three months after launch) with the purpose of assessing the value and making recommendations about next steps. The consultants from our community software vendor strongly encouraged us not to wait that long, to start getting feedback right from the beginning as a way of creating a sense of community, showing that the members had input in the direction right from the start, not just at the end.

Our hesitation was due to our preoccupation with a formal evaluation process. What we learned was that a continuous, informal process allowed us to stay in touch with the opinions of the members—to ensure that the community was living up to its motto: For Agents, By Agents. This approach provided us with continuous suggestions for improvement—small, incremental steps that fine-tuned the approach and contributed to the community's success in a more subtle manner than a major adjustment that might have resulted in too severe a change. Concerning assessment, we learned to:

- **Establish a routine of seeking constant feedback.** Welcome comments throughout the development process, not just at certain points along the way.

- **Keep the channels open, acknowledging positive as well as negative comments.** Be willing to meet concerns head on in order to make the community a better place for its members.

- **Collect statistical data in order to create a baseline.** When venturing into new territory, it's important to establish a baseline from the very beginning for measuring progress. We hadn't predicted how fast the community would take off. If we hadn't put some measurement mechanisms in place from day one, we would have missed or had to reconstruct data that provided valuable information for later comparisons to other communities.

- **Communicate results.** Good news and bad news should be communicated to the various stakeholder groups. Include measures in regular forms of communications such as newsletters, bulletin boards, and announcements. Did you know that . . . ? helps frame the progress of the community on an ongoing basis.

Step 6—Grow the Community

The community had been up and running for a couple of months and the personality that we saw emerging shortly after the launch was well on its way to being established. The members had created a basic level of trust and were willing to put the necessary effort into making the community fly. As they became more comfortable with the technology that supports the community and continued to test the boundaries of the community, the power of their collaborative problem-solving and voice emerged.

The Steering Group and community facilitator continued their efforts to support community building, acting on recommendations from informal feedback from the community members as well as their own observations of participation.

Using Wenger et al.'s agricultural analogy of "cultivating communities," a fertile environment had been prepared, seeds of community development had been planted, care and feeding had been provided through facilitation, and the fruits of the labor begin to show. The community headed toward its goal, creating branches of new knowledge, leafing out through exploration of new ideas or approaches to solving current problems, adding girth with content, and strengthening its roots through a network of relationships within the community and across the organization. Key actions at this step included:

- **Construct community activities based on identified needs**— provide opportunities to explore topics and issues of concern to the members.

- **Familiarize members with community software functionality**— introduce new functionality situated in the topics the community wants to explore in the most appropriate type of activity.

- **Focus communication on the value proposition**—highlight the successes achieved by individual members and the community as a whole.

- **Strengthen the network of expertise**—identify people with various expertise to help solve specific problems.

- **Harvest knowledge**—create a synthesis of dialogue content and presentations for reference.

The community was in high gear. Members were addressing their individual needs, which in turn contributed to the aggregate value of the community as a network of expertise, innovation, and collaboration. Synchronous and asynchronous conversations in the community forum were the primary methods for creating new knowledge, exchanging existing knowledge, and outlining approaches for applying knowledge.

While in the collaboration space, a member working asynchronously could see who else was in the space and could engage them in real-time

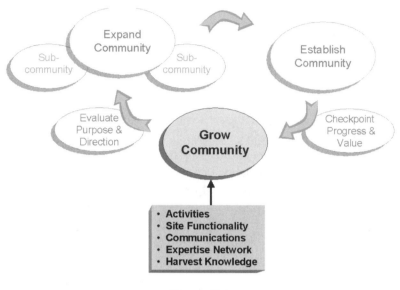

Figure 7.4.
Grow the Community

chats. In this situation, what started out as asynchronous participation became a synchronous conversation.

In addition to the dialogue space, the knowledge repository continued to grow. The members had access to the case studies that were a synthesis of previous conversations. By converting tacit knowledge to explicit knowledge, we were able to provide a permanent record of effective sales and marketing approaches, deepen members' understanding of product features and mixes, and present best case business practices. At the heart of the members' conversations was an increasing understanding of the value of building strong customer relationships.

So, the community was in effect actively contributing to shaping the organization's culture.

Construct Community Activities Based on Member Needs

When we prepared the community for its launch, we seeded the dialogue section with questions that were identified by the Steering Group. As we noted earlier, these discussions were quickly eclipsed with dialogues started by members. By the end of the three-month pilot phase, 45 discussions had been started ranging from queries about product offerings to seeking advice on handling specific client situations or clarification of Clarica policy.

Dialogues that showed a need to further develop a skill or broaden an understanding of a topic prompted the development of online sessions with guest speakers. Using a combination of the community software's functionality (dialogue, chat, polling and voting, and the reference library), we offered synchronous and asynchronous means to further explore a topic, bringing in guest expertise and combining it with the expertise of members to increase the capabilities of all members.

Familiarize Members with Community Tool Functionality— Expectations and Limitations

Given the company's commitment to increasing agents' Web-awareness in order to support e-commerce, we continued to highlight the features of this new type of *Web-based application*. While agents were familiar with accessing Websites, most had no experience with using a Web-based tool. The curiosity about how such a tool worked without being loaded like software on a personal computer was a motivation for participating in the community in the first place. To learn the possibilities continued to be a draw for community involvement.

Managing member expectations about the pros and cons of a Web-based application was woven into the plan of community activities. Opening "new windows" within the application and navigating was one of the biggest challenges—members often didn't know where they were when jumping between hypertext links. Accessing documents that had been stored in the knowledge repository was also a challenge. If an item was created in a particular application (e.g., Microsoft's Excel), they needed some form of spreadsheet software to open the item. It took a while for us to recognize that not everyone was as familiar with his/her desktop image as we had originally thought! And limitations of bandwidth capabilities from local Internet service providers were constantly under review as response time became an issue for some members.

Focus Communication on the Value Proposition

The value proposition was complex. What's in it for me? What's in it for the community and the agent body at large? What's in it for my customers? What's in it for my business partners and staff? What's in it for the project sponsors? What's in it for the Knowledge Team? What's in it for the

Sales Force—management as well as the development and support business units? What's in it for the company? A value proposition could be posed from any number of angles and variations on a theme.

For some of the members, the value proposition was first and foremost directly related to their business—will my participation in this community result in increased sales? For other members, the value of participation came from sharing their knowledge, helping other members (both developing and experienced agents) improve their practices based on the experience of others. For some agents there was a great deal of satisfaction from helping people avoid duplication and reinventing the wheel. Others were quite appreciative of being selected to participate—felt that they had been recognized by management and their peers as people who could help make a difference in the lives of other agents and to Clarica's bottom-line performance.

All of our communications, whether individual e-mails, group notices of community activities, the bi-weekly newsletter, dialogue summaries, or external presentations, focused on the value that was generated by the community in so many ways, at so many levels, and for so many people.

The strategic positioning of the community and the value that resulted from the collaborative effort were key messages within the community, across the organization, and beyond to the financial services industry and the larger population interested in the application of knowledge management principles.

Strengthen the Network of Expertise

Many knowledge management approaches include initiatives that create or strengthen and promote an organization's network of expertise, which is sometimes called the yellow pages. Skills inventories, lists of interests, and links to involvement in specific projects can be used to identify people in a network of expertise. Mentoring, coaching, study groups, buddy systems, and peer tutoring are examples of ways that people link up with other people in their search for a solution to a current challenge.

A community of practice is a perfect place to strengthen an organization's network of expertise. In the past, success in landing a job shifted from "what you know" to "who you know." This shift can also be applied to the work environment. While one's own competencies (attitudes, skills, and knowledge base) provide the foundation for performance, knowing where to find the expertise you need to complement your own expertise is key to successful performance.

Within the virtual community site was a comprehensive profile section. Filling out the template helped other community members see all the people participating in a conversation. The profiles also helped establish the credibility of the person providing the suggestions or comments—their designations, years of experience, types of markets served were all listed. These profiles situated members in the many layers of expertise found within the community.

Given that Clarica's agents are distributed across the country, many somewhat isolated in small, rural communities, the Agent Network provided a place where agents working on their own could link up with agents in like situations, thus reducing the feeling of isolation and creating a resource team to assist in problem solving and increasing individual capabilities.

Harvest Knowledge

With over 45 archived dialogues and 15 current dialogues, each with an average of 15 comments, there was a mountain of material to sort through in the community after only three months. Leave the community for a week, and a member's log-in welcome message could list hundreds of items for review.

In order to make the knowledge exchange accessible, a key role of facilitation was to take dialogues that had been completed and write a summary to be filed in the knowledge repository. Searchable by key words in the title or assigned as meta-data, the summaries provided an important record of the Agent Network's activity and a library of information for members who might not have contributed to the particular dialogue at the time or needed a refresher of the discussion contents at a later date.

Making knowledge persistent, coaxing out the tacit knowledge that often sits below a person's awareness and making it explicit and accessible by other members was a huge value proposition realized by this community.

Reflection

We were on totally new ground with the Agent Network. A Clarica-funded initiative to support a community of independent agents with no Clarica management participation (other than as invited guests) had significant risks. Some agents and Clarica managers believed that the confidential community was bound to increase the divide between the corporation and its independent agents. What if the agents used the space for Clarica-bashing? What if the discussions were used to further an individual rather than the community of agents? What if Clarica policies and practices were the target of criticism? What if wrong information was presented as fact?

Once the community was up and running and we had communicated the high level of member participation to our stakeholders, concern began to grow about the wisdom of the agent-only membership and the lack of involvement of Clarica management in the community. It wasn't that management didn't know that agents spoke with one another, airing concerns on Clarica policy and approaches. The management concern was that Clarica was in fact facilitating these discussions by providing a forum for the conversations to take place!

It was at this point in the community's development that the Agent Network faced its first significant hurdle—a challenge to the corporation's support of a confidential community. The actions of one member regarding a Clarica policy issue resulted in a perception that the Agent Network was being used to further the personal goals of one member—a member who, in the opinion of management, had not gathered all the facts and was inciting other agents to act on partial information.

In the end, a public relations effort and support from the community sponsors addressed the concerns, but the incident highlighted the need for building community on the basis of agreed-upon principles and guidelines, a need to expand the public relations efforts to talk about the benefits of the community, and a need for a channel to voice concerns between the community and the organization.

Regarding confidentiality as the key to building trust, we learned the following:

- The confidentiality of the Agent Network was compromised by a series of e-mails sent outside of the Agent Network to Clarica executives. The need for guidelines regarding confidentiality (e.g., customer names and other pertinent information), relationship between the community and the company, and the important role of the facilitator was confirmed while this incident was being resolved.

- Confidentiality needs to be extended beyond giving facts about a client in order to obtain help from members. There is a need for confidentiality around the topics discussed within the community and the individual contributions. Cutting and pasting dialogue contributions (minus the contributor's name) is also a breach of confidentiality.

- The role of the community facilitator needs to be articulated—especially in light of the liaison role with the company that is providing resources to support the community's development. Members must be able to trust that the facilitator is working in the best interest of both the community as a whole and the individual members, providing supplementary information sources to help move a problem to resolution.

- With the expansion of the Steering Group, we first thought it would be necessary to develop a statement on the group's roles and responsibilities. Drafting the guidelines was a challenge as they became too restrictive. A decision was made to postpone the development until after the pilot phase when a new Steering Group would establish a working relationship with the community.

Best Practice

Membership has its privileges and the select nature of the Agent Network brought with it a level of exclusivity that, not to put too fine a point on it, made some Clarica management very nervous. Communication was key to avoiding misconceptions surrounding the lack of management control and participation of the company in the agent community.

- The tensions that exist in communities that are supported by an organization call for enhanced communications in order to avoid misunderstanding about what is "going on" in the community.

- Successes of the community need to be communicated on a regular basis as a reminder of the continuous value that the community is adding to the business.

- Turn conflict/issue incidents into learning opportunities to help the community grow.

- As the community develops, core members recognize the power of the community, seeing value in a unified voice to discuss issues with management.

- Technology is a great enabler while at the same time a source of frustration. Managing expectations around what the bandwidth will support, how a Web-based application differs from applications found on the desktop, and the technology learning curve are important considerations to address while building community.

STEP 7—EVALUATE PURPOSE AND DIRECTION

A letter of thanks to the founding members of the Agent Network at the end of the first phase of the pilot project started: "We thought it was a good idea. We thought you might be interested in trying out some new technology to share ideas. We thought we had a pretty good plan in place to get the ball rolling . . .."

Clarica embarked on developing this community of practice based on a set of assumptions identified by the corporate sponsors and the Steering Group—assumptions that anticipated success and a significant value proposition linked with strategic imperatives. While informal evaluative comments had been collected throughout the pilot phase, during this step, a formal evaluation was completed to test the value proposition to the community membership, measure success, identify areas for improvement, and make recommendations for expanding the community.

The formal evaluation step followed the standard outline of a research project:

- **Design a data collection tool**—develop an online survey to measure specific points.
- **Gather and analyze data**—create a mechanism to record answers and analyze patterns and trends, providing statistics and qualitative findings to inform recommendations.
- **State findings and make recommendations**—use the findings as a basis for outlining next steps.
- **Communicate results**—provide a summary of the data and recommendations as appropriate to the various audiences: sponsors, community members, the broader community of agents, and the organization.

In order to obtain an unbiased opinion from the members of the community, we used Clarica's marketing research department to manage the formal evaluation of the pilot project. With input from the community facilitator, they designed, administered, and analyzed the findings of an online survey. Their expertise in gathering data from agents via an online

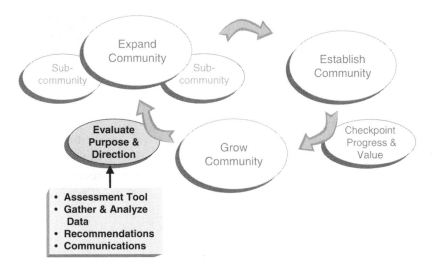

Figure 7.5.
Evaluate Purpose and Direction

tool was a valuable asset to the evaluation phase. And their objectivity lent credibility to the survey process.

Design a Data Collection Tool

To provide a context for the survey, the community facilitator prepared a draft outline of the proposed evaluation process, listing the assumptions and suggesting areas for exploration. A survey questionnaire was drafted and reviewed.

Gather and Analyze Data

The online survey was distributed to all community members via e-mail. Responses were requested within two weeks and were returned directly to the researcher. A rich analysis through qualitative and quantitative perspectives was provided to the facilitator, who distributed it to the Steering Group.

State Findings and Make Recommendations

A full report outlined: the process followed, lessons learned in the community development process, results of the pilot phase evaluation, and recommendations for next steps for expanding the community. The community facilitator also prepared a summary of the findings and an overview of the recommendations.

Communicate Results

A summary of the evaluation was posted in the Agent Network's knowledge repository, highlights were included in the community's newsletter, and a one-page summary was prepared for distribution to the sponsors, community members, the broader community of agents, and the organization.

Reflection

Early in the project, we made a commitment to ongoing assessment. But given the pilot project status of the Agent Network, it was important to put a formal assessment process in place in order to gather data in support of recommendations for next steps. The whole area of assessment was a challenge for us. In the past, Clarica provided resources for communities of practice (e.g., Lotus Notes discussion databases, mail-in e-mail databases, templates), but we had not supported a community of practice to the extent we did with this community (e.g., a Web-based application, facilitation, costs of a Steering Group and project manager).

We'll talk more about measurement and evaluation in Chapter 8, but reflecting on this step sparks a number of questions that we had to address in establishing a more formal evaluation approach.

- What triggers the "evaluation point?" For the Agent Network, it was a timeline (at the end of the pilot project phase I). For other evaluation, when is the right time? Is there a set of indicators— e.g., number of log ins, dialogues, and active participants?
- The formal evaluation was focused on the community members. Are there other audiences that we should have formally surveyed—e.g., sponsors, management, customers?
- The response rate for the e-mail survey was not high. Lack of time and information overload were identified as barriers to participating in the evaluation. Should we consider a multiphased evaluation approach rather than a one-time survey to increase the range of input?

Best Practice

As a pilot, the Agent Network might have ceased to exist after the formal evaluation if the members and/or the sponsors had not seen a value in continuing the community. The formal evaluation is important from several perspectives:

- **Assesses the community development approach**—the process that was followed to get the community up and running (e.g., the invitation process, training, tools, facilitation, resources).
- **Assesses the value**—for the members, the sponsors, stakeholders, and the organization.
- **Identifies growth potential**—the will of the community regarding its purpose, function, and path. Where does the community want to go? How would it like to grow? What does it need to continue or expand on its success?

Initially, we had not planned to use the researchers in the marketing department to design and administer the formal evaluation. The Knowledge Architect suggested the approach in order to complete the evaluation in a relatively short time frame. In the end, it provided us with a higher quality of evaluation than we might have been able to achieve on our own (i.e., developed by the facilitator with the advice of the Steering Group). The lessons that we learned in this step include:

- The use of a third party for formal evaluations helps establish a greater level of trust for the survey respondents and credibility for the findings.
- Evaluation is a springboard to expansion and growth. Recommendations based on evaluation findings establish the foundation for the community's growth and identify the next steps to achieve specific goals.

Step 8—Expand the Community

We started the Agent Network as a pilot project with a selected number of members and a desire to test our assumptions about the value of communities as a forum for increasing capabilities linked to strategic imperatives. We also wanted to test the technology to see how we could leverage

Clarica's technology infrastructure in creating a virtual forum in partnership with an application provider.

With the formal evaluation completed and the contents of the folder of informal feedback compiled, we prepared a comprehensive report on the efforts of the seven months devoted to designing, implementing, and evaluating the agent community of practice. The report included an overview of the project, the first draft of the community development model, a list of insights and reflections, and an outline of recommended next steps.

The recommendations were tabled with the Steering Group and a summary was developed for the sponsors. During this step, a team space was established for the Steering Group within the community site—a private space for the Steering Group to discuss issues pertaining to their community mandate. It provided the group with an opportunity to build a closer working relationship and to test another functional layer in the community software. The key actions at this point included:

- **Evaluate the recommendations**—review the recommendations that the community facilitator had compiled on the basis of evaluation findings.

- **Involve the membership in community expansion**—communicate the findings from the evaluation and propose next steps for feedback.

- **Implement next steps**—establish a work plan to implement community expansion.

- **Recognize participation**—bring closure to Phase I of the pilot project.

- **Review direction with project sponsors**—communicate plans for further community expansion.

Recommendations were formulated on the basis of survey findings from the community members and the opinion of the community facilitator/project manager who was the primary Clarica resource on the project. The recommendations were presented to the Steering Group and next steps were planned based on these recommendations.

Evaluate the Recommendations

The recommendations were distributed to the Steering Group and discussed during a teleconference. At that point, there was concern that the

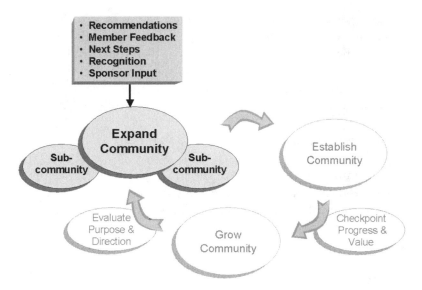

Figure 7.6.
Expand the Community

timbre of the community could become heated as member conversations moved more toward Clarica policy issues than issues directly related to practice or how they do business.

Involve the Membership in Community Expansion

As a pilot, the community membership limit was set at 150. With over 3,000 agents across the country and a desire to provide a community for as many agents as possible, a plan needed to be devised to expand the community. We realized that there are some scalability issues with online communities because they can become too big, too impersonal, and too divergent. But we hoped to be able to double the size of the community membership in the next Phase. A plan was outlined to contact members who were not actively involved (there was a small percentage who had never logged in or who had not been active for the better part of the pilot period) and ascertain their wish to continue.

At the same time, the Knowledge Architect began to work with the community software vendor to put a model in place that would have a mega-community level for all 3,000 agents and then subgroups that would self-select or organize depending on product interest, markets served, and business organizations.

Members were encouraged to invite other agents to join the community—similar to a referral process. A request was sent to the community facilitator by the prospective member who was then contacted by the facilitator to discuss the purpose of the community, a suggested level of commitment, and comfort level with a Web-based application. After the interview, the new member was enrolled and introduced to the community.

Implement Next Steps

The recommendations included specific suggestions for developing process and policy statements—guidelines for participation and liaison with Clarica, contributing materials to the knowledge repository, roles and responsibilities of the steering group, and roles and responsibilities for the facilitator.

Recognize Participation

For the most part, agents are motivated by recognition. One sales force senior manager explained that agents who had significant incomes would still make the extra effort to be recognized in a competition that might have a Clarica jacket or set of luggage as the prize. With the success of the Agent Network, the community facilitator suggested that there be some form of recognition and asked the Steering Group for its advice on how to proceed. To acknowledge their leadership with the community, would the founding members like a framed certificate of achievement, a plaque with the community purpose, or a symbolic *inukshuk* (an Inuit rock formation used as signposts in the Arctic that is a popular symbol of leadership)? Should we have a dinner and give out individual awards, make a donation to a charity in their names, or have special portfolios made with the Agent Network slogan on the cover? What could we do for the founding members to say thank you—to formally recognize their efforts in making the launch of this strategic community such a success.

With little hesitation, the Steering Group was unanimous that it was the community that deserved the recognition—not the individual members. There was no need for individual acknowledgement other than a letter of thanks from the sponsors. The success should be celebrated through a variety of communication activities that highlighted the value of the community to its members and to Clarica. What the members got back from the community was reward enough for their efforts.

Review Direction with Project Sponsors

Because the Agent Network was a pilot project sponsored jointly by the Strategic Capabilities Unit and the Retail Sales Force, expanding the community and moving through next steps would need the approval of the original sponsors.

Reflection

As the expansion efforts got underway, facilitation of the Agent Network was transferred to a new position within the Knowledge Team—a community consultant role that would provide part-time facilitation for the Agent Network and provide support for other communities that wanted to form or were selected by sponsors as community development projects. The former facilitator and project manager stayed with the community to get next steps underway. Two agents were added to the Steering Group.

The key issue that surfaced during this step was the need for guidelines for certain aspects of community participation and development, but an uncertainty persisted about just how comprehensive the guidelines should be.

Draft guidelines on community participation, contributing materials to the knowledge repository, and roles and responsibilities for the Steering Group and the facilitator were prepared by the community facilitator for reaction from the Steering Group. The drafts were very comprehensive, covering the wide range of possibilities for each topic. In the end, the Steering Group found the draft guidelines too overwhelming and felt that the members would not accept this level of direction.

The issue remains—how comprehensive should guidelines be? Must one provide solutions for all anticipated issues, or just deal with them as they arise? Can facilitation keep the membership heading in the right direction without stringent guidelines?

Best Practice

Membership has its own rewards. We learned a great deal from the implementation and growth phase of our project. In particular:

- Focus on the accomplishments of the community, not the individual members.

- Keep the channels of communication open with both formal and informal assessment processes. Communicate findings on a regular basis.

- Turn challenges into learning opportunities.

- Trust the community to know its own needs, set its own directions, monitor its membership's conduct.

- Make the community aware of the organization's continued support. Establish an open line of communication to ensure that needed information flows from the corporation to the community and issues identified in the community are addressed by the corporation in an appropriate manner.

Conclusion

The five C's that we outlined at the end of Chapter 5 form the foundation for the community's growth and development and fuel the members' ability to increase individual and organizational capabilities, the building blocks of the organization's knowledge capital assets. We found that the community provided an extremely dynamic environment, situated in practice—a vibrant place for agents to learn, increase their capabilities, and contribute to building knowledge capital.

In addition, the multigenerational aspect of the membership provided an interesting element of knowledge exchange. Not only were experienced agents helping agents who were new to the business, agents skilled in technology where helping other agents navigate through the Web-based community application and introducing new ways that technology could enhance other agents' businesses.

During the implementation and growth of the community (see Figure 7.7), we saw that:

- **Conversations were the key to learning.** The dialogue section continued to be the most popular part of the community site. The ability to pose a question, make a statement and solicit feedback, or contribute to a discussion formed the core of the community's growth. Productive inquiry that was focused on the immediate needs of an individual soon became a resource to the whole community. The network effect of one to many took conversations in directions that could never have been orchestrated in a face-to-face meeting or an individual conversation.

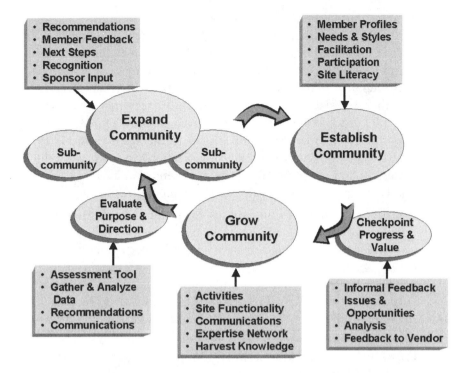

Figure 7.7.
Phase II—Community Implementation and Growth

- **Collaboration between agents occurred beyond the usual patterns.** If two heads are better than one, what's the impact of an additional 148? Sometimes that means too many cooks in the kitchen. But for the most part, it meant that a member had the ability to draw on the expertise of a wide variety of practitioners to collaborate on finding a solution to a problem that would more than likely repeat itself elsewhere in the community. This collaboration laid the groundwork for a new way of doing business. Being an agent was all too often a sales effort. The community now provided a way of dynamically creating a team of experts that could accelerate problem-solving, find a solution for the customer faster than before, and close a sale. Agility and speed to market were greatly enhanced.

- **Commitment to the community from its members and sponsors grew.** In the invitation, we asked agents to commit to checking in on the community once a week. For some that commitment was easily met. For others, it was a challenge to juggle participation with current workload and priorities. But for most members, the commitment to make the community work only grew stronger. Believing that their contribution could make a difference, feeling that they would at some point gain from the reciprocity that was possible, or knowing that they had been directly helped by the community, the member commitment to the agent community showed the importance of an organization's providing time, materials, and attention (to quote a presentation by Larry Prusak, Director of IBM's Knowledge Management Institute).

- **Connectivity enhances our ability to increase capabilities and improve practice.** Connectivity can be addressed on many levels—the ability to contact people via technology (the physical connection), a network that forms as people collaborate (being connected), or the linking of like situations or environment (making a connection). In all instances, connectivity facilitates the interdependence that we need to make a difference in finding solutions, forming relationships, and furthering our practice.

- **Capabilities are the link between our strategy and our performance.** The skills, attitudes, beliefs, mindsets, and knowledge sets that we bring to our practice as the bridge between what is strategically important and how we achieve our successes (what the Special Library Association has coined as "putting our knowledge to work") are best increased in the vessel that a community creates.

A true confession to conclude this chapter on community implementation and growth. It's relatively easy to talk about the applied science (the tangible work) of community development—the part that is guided by a project plan with a project manager cracking a whip. It's more difficult to talk about the art of community building in terms of process because for the most part, community building is dependent on the community itself and its membership, not on a prescribed process. And in attempting to describe what we did, there's a much less clear path for the community development process than what we saw in the logistics phase.

On the other hand, the community implementation and growth phase is far more exciting than putting the foundation in place. Everyone gets caught up in the successes of the community. And emotions run high when actions by members or the facilitator jeopardize the value proposition of the community. While the process of creating a sense of community and establishing value from community participation may be difficult to explain, the rewards are far greater when the community's ability to advance strategic imperatives is recognized by the members, the people involved in supporting the community's efforts, and the most senior levels of the organization.

COMMUNITY BUILDING—WILL IT PLAY IN PEORIA?

Most companies should be able to put a community infrastructure in place—the bricks and mortar, bits and bytes, people and processes, or any combination thereof. With a few resources, a project plan, and a group of interested people, the foundation of a community can readily be constructed. But taking the community the next step—establishing trust, growing the commitments, establishing the value proposition, making a difference to strategic imperatives, and proving results—requires capabilities beyond project management.

Using the five components we identified as key to the success of a community, think about your organization's ability to engender:

1. **Conversation**—Are people encouraged to voice opinions, discuss problems, highlight successes? Does your organization promote productive inquiry, active learning, case-based problem solving? Will a community of people be encouraged to push the envelop, to explore new ideas, to innovate?

2. **Commitment**—Is your senior executive committed to the value of communities? Will they provide the resources, their time, their trust to the creation of a community without direct input or control? Are people committed to finding solutions to problems that might emerge in the course of developing a community?

3. **Collaboration**—Does your organization's culture promote knowledge exchange? Will people work together to collectively solve a problem, or is there a sink or swim attitude. Is knowledge "power" in your organization or is knowledge seen as "growing when it flows?"

4. **Connectivity**—Is there an infrastructure to support collaboration? Can people get together face-to-face or through some other form or communication or collaborative tool?

5. **Capabilities**—Is your organization a learning organization, an organization that values its knowledge assets and provides its employees with opportunities to increase capabilities? Do you know what capabilities are required to meet your strategic imperatives? Is there a plan, process, and resources available to increase both individual and organizational capabilities through a community vessel?

6. What initial steps would you need to launch a community in your organization?

Chapter 8

ESTABLISHING COMMUNITY VALUE: MEASUREMENT AND REFLECTION

Creating the value proposition for the individual, the community, and the organization may be the single most important part of community development. But how do you know if you've succeeded? With a discussion of measurement approaches and a reflection on lessons learned, we look at the value created by the community and the contribution of the community development process to organizational capabilities. Approaches for assessing the community's value include: a formal survey, the personal insights of the community facilitator and project manager, a team review of the process, and recommendations for next steps.

ASSESSING VALUE

We live in an environment where cost justification is a way of life. Whether a for-profit private-sector business, a not-for-profit organization, or an arm of government, we have the responsibility to ensure that resources committed to a project are wisely spent. But a positive return on investment (ROI), a balanced scorecard, or any other more traditional means of measuring the direct effect of an expenditure on an organization's bottom line can be difficult to apply to knowledge capital initiatives.

In the case of a community of practice that is resourced by an organization as part of its plan for achieving strategic imperatives, measuring the value of the investment in community development can't be accomplished with a straightforward mathematical formula. The metrics are a bit more complicated than what this might imply. Support for the measurement approach may need to be sold at the same level at which you originally gained sponsor support for your community development project, if not higher. Equally challenging as the shift from "knowledge is power" to "knowledge grows when it flows" within an organization's culture, valuing the investment in a knowledge capital initiative requires some new ways of thinking about measurement.

Communities of Practice: Measuring the Value Proposition

When the concept of knowledge management began taking shape in the late 1980s and early 1990s, little was said about how to measure a rate of return on knowledge management initiatives. In many cases, we didn't have a clear understanding of what we were doing, let alone a method for measuring its effect on creating shareholder value, reducing costs of operation, or contributing directly to the bottom line on a balance sheet.

While we haven't undertaken a bonafide study, a quick review of the new literature in the field of knowledge management shows that the measurement issue has come front and center. Discussions are heating up on how to best show that expenditures on knowledge initiatives are well worth the investment.

Like the debate on the value of investing in learning, the value of investing in knowledge management can be discussed in terms of increasing capabilities that in turn contribute to achieving organizational goals. These goals may be measured by:

- A positive number on a profit and loss statement
- A high level of customer satisfaction
- Increased share price
- Growing percentage of market penetration

Or, they may be measured by a combination of qualitative and quantitative approaches. At any rate, only in a rare instance would you *not* have to provide some form of information on the community's value proposition.

In other words, you're going to have to think about how you can justify the organization's investment in community development. And depending on the approach currently used in your organization to measure success, you may find that you have a significant challenge on your hands.

As we move from a focus on tangible assets to a focus on intangible assets in the knowledge era, Phillips and Phillips (2002) note, "measuring human capital is part of a bigger issue." They suggest that there are 12 "common and feasible human capital measures" (pp. 4–18):

- **Innovation**—from relatively easy to measure outcomes such as copyright, patents, inventions, and employee suggestions to more difficult measures of employee creativity.

- **Job satisfaction**—linked to employee recruitment and retention, a measure of an employee's overall job satisfaction or satisfaction in a specific area related to his or her employment.

- **Organizational commitment**—building on job satisfaction, the measure of an employee's identification with an organization's goals, mission, values.

- **Turnover**—rate at which employees voluntarily leave an organization.

- **Tenure**—measure of employee longevity.

- **Experience**—measure of number of years' experience in a particular department or functional area.

- **Learning**—a micro-level measure of new skills and knowledge obtained through formal learning or at a more challenging macro-level where knowledge attained through informal channels adds to individual and organizational capabilities.

- **Competencies**—self and management assessment of the competencies held (or needed) in key areas.

- **Education level**—degrees, certification, and other professional designations attained by employees.

- **HR investment**—the amount of investment in a human resources department that is devoted to increasing the organization's human capital.

- **Leadership**—the identification of leadership characteristics in support of increasing human capital.

- **Productivity**—measure of revenue, income, or earnings per employee.

Stewart (2002) takes another look at knowledge capital measurement approaches in his second book on intellectual capital. He provides perspectives at the organizational level on measuring the role of knowledge, taking stock of knowledge assets, rating intellectual capital strategies, measuring the efficiency of knowledge work and knowledge workers, and calculating a dollar value for intellectual capital. While his comments are not specifically directed toward communities of practice, we can find support for a new approach to measurement in his discussion of "the inadequacies of industrial-age accounting" and his illustrations of how companies have used financial and nonfinancial measures to show their productive use of knowledge.

"Measuring and Managing Value Creation" is the title of Wenger et al.'s (2002) discussion of measuring the value of communities of practice. The authors make many important points that we wish we'd had the benefit of knowing BEFORE we began our community development project. We highly recommend that you read their entire chapter before you establish your measurement approach. Here, briefly, are the key points that resonated with us:

- It's important that both the community members and the people responsible for supporting the community (sponsors, stakeholders, facilitators) are aware of the value that the community generates and work to make that value widely known.

- Knowledge is a very difficult thing to measure—it can't be treated in the same way as tangible assets such as property or inventory. But it can be measured in the form of the "knowledge system" that supports the creation and sharing of knowledge.

- Although difficult to execute, measures are worth investing in because they help communities gain visibility and influence, guide community development through the identification of priorities, legitimize their role in the organization, and reinforce participation in the community.

- The measurement process consists of five steps: identify audience and purpose, outline data to be collected and method of collection, raise awareness about the measurement process, identify where and when to gather data, and create an overall picture of the community's activities directly linked to value statements.

- Measurement requirements will change as the community develops, from with ad hoc intuition in early phases to formal measurement systems as the community matures.

CLARICA'S MEASUREMENT APPROACH

The value proposition for the Agent Network was directly tied to Sales Force business objectives and the goals of Clarica's corporate knowledge strategy. In addition to the increased capabilities that were expected to be generated in the community, we were also testing the community development process. Our assessment, then, covered the full range of creating individual, community, and organizational value.

Measurement criteria for the Agent Network pilot project were not based on quantitative measures (e.g., statistics in the form of numerical data). While early discussions with sponsors and the Steering Group suggested that it would be possible to identify some statistics, primarily in the area of use (number of discussions, amount of contribution to dialogues), frequency of participation number of log ins in a specific period of time), and contribution by member profile (member participation), and so forth, the decision was made not to focus on those aspects.

Instead, the measures were qualitative and focused on the perceived value of the community by members and sponsors. This approach parallels Clarica's statements on measuring the effect of the knowledge strategy.

How does one measure the impact of a strategy that is so pervasive in shaping the way things are done across the firm? Not easily! . . . The investment made by the firm to support the Knowledge Strategy will need to be based on the conviction of the senior leadership that the Knowledge Strategy represents a worthwhile investment. Senior management has to look at the logic that links the Knowledge Strategy to: the creation of competitive advantage; the generation of superior customer perceived value; and, finally, the resulting enhancement in financial performance (Clarica, 1999).

By focusing on perceived value, we could make the case that the Agent Network was contributing to achieving specific Sales Force objectives (e.g., to increase agent productivity, retention, and sales growth). And as part of the Knowledge Strategy, the value of communities of practice could be measured as contributing to desired business outcomes:

- Agility
- Collaboration
- Quality and speed of decision making
- Accelerated learning and capability building
- Coherence (making sense)
- Innovation
- Retention of talent

In Chapter 7, we discussed the informal and formal evaluation approaches, the gathering of anecdotal evidence from community participation, and the formal survey of members at the end of Phase I of the pilot project. In this section, we'd like to turn to what we learned in a discussion of the community member survey results and the Knowledge Team's assessment of the community development process. In doing so, we address both the value of the community to the various stakeholders (individual and organizational) and the community development process (the design, launch, implementation, growth, and evaluation of the community).

Survey Results

Has the community of practice increased individual and organizational capabilities at Clarica and contributed to achieving selected strategic imperatives? The results of the Agent Network Phase I evaluation indicated a high level of satisfaction with the opportunities for knowledge creation and exchange within the community. The following points summarize the findings:

- **Rate of return.** Forty-four percent of the 153 members surveyed responded. While somewhat low for such a targeted survey, this rate was actually higher than the level of persistent involvement in the community during Phase I.
- **Profile of survey respondents.** The majority of the responses were from agents who worked within agency offices (Occupant Agents), had been with Clarica for 10 years or more, and accessed

the Agent Network via office Ethernet or home ISPs between one and five times a week. Nineteen percent of the survey respondents never logged into the community site.

- **Experience with the Agent Network.** The majority of the responses regarding various aspects of the Agent Network experience were favorable. Agents either agreed or strongly agreed that:
  — The purpose and objective were clear.
  — The updates (e-mail newsletter) were informative.
  — The site was user friendly.
  — Technical support was sufficient.
  — Learning materials were adequate.
- **Use of the Agent Network site components.** The respondents indicated that they contributed to some areas and only read others. Dialogue, Chat, and Member Profiles were the most frequently used sections of the site.
- **Value of the Agent Network.** The respondents indicated that the Agent Network was valuable. The following points were identified as the "most valuable" aspects:
  — Provided an opportunity to grow personally, professionally, and technically.
  — Introduced new ideas, approaches, and strategies.
  — Created a network of colleagues who understand their issues and challenges.
  — Provided them with links to product and market specialists.
  — Helped clarify something they didn't understand before.
  — Made a difference to a sale.
- **Continuing the Agent Network.** Ninety-three percent of the respondents thought that the Agent Network should be continued. Of that total, 54 percent felt that it was "very important."
- **Limitations.** Respondents identified a number of limitations or problems that they experienced in participating in the community, including:
  — Time constraints.
  — Some site functionality was limited.

— Difficulty in accessing and using site (not on desktop, difficult to navigate, too slow throughout, not user friendly).

— Amount of information available—couldn't get through it all.

— Technology issues (not comfortable with the technology, printing, passwords; didn't have the right kind of access or the dial access was too slow).

— Costs.

— Follow-up on issues by company representatives not completed.

▪ **Reasons for nonuse.** Nineteen percent of the respondents indicated that they had not used the Agent Network for the following reasons:

— Lack of time—too many other things to do in the day.

— Not a priority.

— Didn't know how to do various things such as add an attachment; not Internet confident; couldn't locate the site.

— Needed hands-on instruction.

▪ Agents who didn't use the Network indicated that they share knowledge with their colleagues in other ways:

— Dialogue: e-mail, phone, in person.

— Meetings: branch, various agent gatherings, councils, and advisory boards.

— Mentoring and coaching programs.

Project Manager and Community Facilitator Review of Process

For nine months, the Agent Network facilitator and project manager was involved in every aspect of the community's design, implementation, and evaluation. As part of the evaluation, she included thoughts on the issues, challenges, and successes from a personal perspective. This form of reflection and knowledge exchange is a key component of Clarica's project management approach—insights on a project are recorded in order to inform others who may implement a similar project. These insights help to avoid repeating errors, reduce duplication, leverage synergies, and improve on previous practice. They provide a rich description that ensures that the knowledge capital is made persistent, that it won't be lost should the employee leave the organization.

Due to the length of the material, we've chosen to highlight representative comments for each phase to give you a flavor of the reflective process and the contribution to knowledge creation and exchange. This personal reflection helped to increase our capabilities for building additional communities with a strategic context.

Define Project/Set Context

- Understanding objectives and purpose begins the setting context phase. Why does the organization want to support the development of a community? What is the purpose of bringing the group together? What are the projected benefits? What return might the organization expect on its investment? In the end, who "owns" the community?

- From the very beginning, it is important to discuss the role that head office (HO) representatives will play in the community. How will management and community leaders balance the tensions between grassroots development and HO-provided support? How will HO expectations regarding their "involvement" in the community be managed? HO is footing the bill. Is there an implied presence?

- How will trust be established? Trust from the point of view of the community members that the space provided is a confidential space, devoted to the development of their practice; and trust from the point of view of HO that the community will be used to further business practice, not focus solely on company policy or procedural issues.

- How will value be established? Value from the point of view of the community members who are giving up their time and committing their resources to developing the community without a guarantee of immediate payback; and value from the point of view of HO that the investment in developing and supporting the community will meet their expectations of increased productivity and retention.

- For the project manager and community facilitator, it was extremely important to "get under the skin" of the agent. Although a facilitator can never totally predict the community members' behaviour, it was necessary to at least learn more about their issues, challenges, and opportunities in order to steer the community toward success—to anticipate where discussions might go, what resources would be necessary to support their problem resolution, and what public relations activities might be needed to gain support and increase awareness of the community's value.

- Clarica agents already had a natural affinity to sharing. Even in a competitive environment, there was an overwhelming commitment to making Clarica agents the best they could be and a recognition that knowledge sharing could be the basis for that development. In the end, was it really important that they understood the concept of a community of practice from the literature's point of view, or that they developed an understanding of community through a collaborative effort? It really doesn't matter what it's called. The value is in what the community can generate through its collaboration. We didn't get hung up on terminology. Instead, we focused on the activities and the value that the members generated through their collaborative efforts.

Develop Project Components

- Because the community's development was so tied to a technology solution, the involvement of the vendor's sales and project management staff was key to the launch success. Given that the vendor had experience in developing communities, although not exactly like the one Clarica was developing, their staff provided a valuable resource.

- One suggestion from the vendor that we didn't follow concerned developing guidelines and procedures. The vendor suggested a formal approach to establishing these statements before the community launch. Clarica believed that these guiding statements should be developed as the community itself developed, focusing on what was needed rather than anticipating what might be needed. Is it necessary to develop all aspects of the community ahead of the community launch? What is the balance? Does the community need to be guided by rules and regulations, outlines of roles and responsibilities? Can a general understanding be identified and then further developed should it be necessary?

  Case in point: A few guidelines were identified for submitting materials to the references section. After the community contributed to and used the reference material, a compliance issue was identified—especially in materials where facts and figures are presented for use with clients. The question then became, how do we to incorporate a compliance step without slowing down the process or squelching the agents' enthusiasm/work, yet ensuring that members are protected?

One way to deal with this dilemma might be to identify the values held by individuals and from there to surface the shared values of the community. This would be a move positive and less imposing than defining rules based on compliance requirements.

- Given that the community support tool was new to all of us, we might have benefited from using the tool (in either sandbox form or an initial release of the community) for our own planning purposes. The functionality has since been enhanced to include a "team" feature that is now being used for the Steering Group. Had this access been available, we might have better understood the technical issues and perhaps been able to use the application's functionality to its fullest sooner.

- The planning for the first community was focused on the Agent Network. In the end, we made some decisions that were too narrowly focused. We didn't keep the "enterprise-wide" view that we might have. In some instances, we didn't realize that there were enterprise-wide implications for some features in the application. For example:

  — The URL chosen contained the word "agent." Although access can be obtained through other means (e.g., button on the intranet or inclusion as a "favorite" in the browser) communities developed at a later date might query why "agent" is in the URL. There may be some cause for concern regarding purpose, confidentiality, etc. Cost impact to change the URL (coding, testing, new SSL certificate, changing the intranet page, training current community members) is substantial.

  — In the member profile section of the software (a standard template employed across all communities using the same software), the fields chosen were specific to the agents. The section would need to be adapted as other communities start to use the application.

- In many respects, establishing the agent community of practice broke new ground for Clarica. A few points that were not sufficiently covered in the planning process:

— Because the application would be hosted outside of Clarica's firewall, we needed to undertake a security audit. This process was done at the eleventh hour before launch and nearly delayed rollout because one sponsor was not comfortable with the efforts to protect agent data and agent conversations (which in the end was the more crucial point, as the agent data are available on the public Web site). The legal department became involved in writing a security and privacy statement that addressed these concerns.

Launch Community

■ A decision was made to delay the launch of the community in order to use the latest version of the software. The two-week delay was considered well worth the wait as opposed to training members on one version of the software and then having to upgrade everyone within a month to a significantly different version. However, we hadn't anticipated the extent of problems with the new version. We should have insisted on being part of the beta-testing phase. As a result, facilitation at the point of launch was not as comprehensive inside the community as it could have been had the facilitator not had to spend so much time working with the vendor and trouble-shooting support problems.

Grow Community

■ A concern at launch was the level of activity that should be available to the community. We were advised to outline a full calendar of activities—chats, polls, games, on-line presentations, and other community-building activities. We knew that time was going to be a big challenge for participation. Members were finding it difficult to commit the time necessary to go through the dialogues, let alone participate in a wide range of "activities." In the end, we decided to focus on keeping the dialogues moving, providing resources and further information wherever possible, and lightening up on the number of activities that would be scheduled. Dialogues continue to be the focus of the activities in the community, with real-time sessions about every four to six weeks as the only other facilitated activity. We learned early that any games, contests, or "fun" would not be welcomed by the members who wanted to keep a professional focus for the community.

- A significant challenge for the community resulted when a member who was not in favour of a recent policy was seen as using the Agent Network to "stir up" other agents without first understanding the issue from all sides. The incident raised many issues:

— How and when to escalate items in order to find a solution.

— The responsible use of the Agent Network by its members.

— Breach of confidentiality.

— The role of the facilitator.

— PR efforts with sponsors, executives, and senior management.

The community facilitators worked with the Knowledge Architect to outline a resolution strategy that used the situation as a learning experience for the community. In the end, the PR efforts were effective, several guidelines to address similar situations were drafted for consideration by the Steering Group, and the community and the dialogues in question continued on a normal resolution cycle (i.e., the facilitator didn't delete anything).

Assess Community Progress and Value

- As noted in the process model discussion, the Phase I evaluation was completed by Clarica's Marketing Research Department. The use of a third party to measure success increased the credibility of the findings. A limitation was that the survey was distributed only by e-mail, and the response rate was rather low. There wasn't a critical mass of data in any one demographic group to do more sophisticated analysis that might have revealed correlations between demographics and specific answers. We were very glad to see a relatively high return rate from the members who had never logged in. Their responses supported our understanding of the time and technology constraints on participating in the community.

- For Phase I, the sponsors did not set a series of quantitative measures. There was a general consensus that supporting a community would be wise use of resources. Thus, the evaluation focused on qualitative measures, testing assumptions about value attributed to community participation. Perhaps the most significant measure was an unstated one that was on the minds of those who worked on the design and implementation of the community: Would the agents participate in a community of practice and could that participation be sustained over time? Agents generally have a strong performance focus and would not spend time on something that doesn't bring tangible benefits.

Knowledge Team Review of Process

Clarica's experience with the Agent Network yielded a wealth of new knowledge about building communities of practice and the use of technology to enable a virtual gathering of expertise across the country. To help organize these points, we used Choo's (1999) framework for planning and evaluating knowledge management initiatives.

Vision and Strategy

- **Purpose.** A corporate-sponsored community of practice recognizes that there are multiple purposes at work in the community that differ based on the perspectives of the stakeholders—the individual community members, the community as a collective, and the organization. In order to increase the trust level for everyone involved, it is important to recognize that multiple purposes exist and need to be reconciled into mutually reinforcing objectives.

- **Vulnerability.** Never consider that a corporately supported community is sacrosanct. Unexpected challenges to its value can call into question the organization's support. The community needs to actively engage in communication with stakeholders to ensure that misunderstandings are avoided and that issues and opportunities are escalated through appropriate liaison channels without breaching the confidentiality of the community or its individual members.

Roles and Responsibilities

- **Facilitation.** Facilitation increases the community's ability to innovate. Left on its own, the community would most likely succeed to some degree, but the speed at which it achieves its goals and the extent of the success are increased through facilitation. The facilitator must be aligned with the community, but need not be a content expert. Facilitation competencies (knowledge base, skills, and attitudes) outweigh the need for expertise in the field(s) represented by the community. The facilitation role should be clearly defined, with responsibilities agreed upon by the community.

- **Responsible participation.** Negative incidents within the community (such as breach in confidentiality, misuse of information, unprofessional conduct) may be indicative of the community's growth and should be used as learning experiences to strengthen the sense of community and thus further its development. Guidelines for responsible participation can assist in establishing a code of conduct. But these guidelines should be framed as informing a member's decision regarding how he/she will participate, not as a set of rules to police the membership.

Policies and Processes

- **Process model.** When developing a community of practice, a process model should be situated as a framework, not a cookbook with strict recipes to follow. The process model is there as a guide to identify resources that will be required and point out possible pitfalls. Each community will have unique characteristics that need to be at the center of the development plan. The community purpose is the driver of the process, not an unrelated outcome of a prescribed process.

Tools and Approaches

- **Technology.** Technology is an enabler, not the focus of community development. Is the novelty of using a new technology to communicate the reason for the community's success? Does the tool define the community? If the answer is yes to either of those questions, then it is questionable that the community can be sustained. Set expectations as to what the technology can and can't do as an element of the community infrastructure, and focus on the community, not on the technology that supports it.

RECOMMENDATIONS—NEXT-STEP SUGGESTIONS

As was noted earlier, measurements help identify priorities and plan next steps. As part of the formal evaluation step discussed in Chapter 7, we prepared a report at the end of the pilot phase that outlined the community development process, highlighted key issues, outlined lessons learned, and recommended next steps.

The recommendations were grouped into four sections:

- **Sponsor support:** Recommendations on the continuation of the company's support of the community, expansion of the membership, and continued provision of facilitation resources from the Knowledge Team consultants.

- **Community building:** Recommendations that would support the growth and development of the community, with a focus on strengthening the sense of community, increasing the value of participation, and expanding the depth and breadth of knowledge creation and exchange.

- **Community support:** Recommendations in four key areas (communications, evaluation, governance, and infrastructure) that would increase Clarica's ability to establish and support other communities.

- **Community value creation:** Recommendations that leverage the individual and organizational capabilities that are generated in communities, formalizing the significant role that communities play in the company's success.

The creation of the Agent Network was an experiment to see how communities that are typically grassroots, informal organisms that bring together people to learn or solve problems might be positioned with a support infrastructure, resources, and facilitation to achieve strategic objectives. In the end, the project:

- Created a vibrant community that continues today in its purpose of knowledge creation and exchange to increase capabilities related to a specific practice.

- Identified a process model for community development that has reduced the time and cost of creating virtual communities and continues to be improved upon with each new community launch.

■ Leveraged the company's technology infrastructure.

■ Confirmed an assumption about communities as an effective approach to capability generation and knowledge creation.

CONCLUSION

Stewart (2002) acknowledges that measurements are important because they help us make sense of what we see. "They describe—is it big, fast, good, strong, healthy? They diagnose—is it damaged, overheated, underused? And they evaluate—is it fixed, stronger, better?" (p. 291). And as Wenger et al. (2002) note, measures help the community develop by understanding its priorities and identifying directions for growth.

When dealing with intangible assets, it is more a matter of correlation and direction than absolute weight. While we could represent the community's value with quantitative measures of improved performance at Clarica (e.g., increase in share price, sales volumes, and overall profit), we chose to highlight achievements in terms of the sales forces' goals of increased agent retention and growth of the sales force. We were able to attract new agents at unprecedented levels and retain the size of the sales force beyond expectations. These measures were more meaningful in terms of the intangible assets that the community contributed to the organization.

Analysis and reflection will also generate measurements that you might not have even thought to pursue. For example, when we were discussing how we would present measurement issues and approaches in this chapter, we realized that we had a key benefit from creating the Agent Network that we had never anticipated or set out to measure. This community of practice for Clarica agents had in fact allowed the company to learn directly from the agents in a collaborative learning environment. When Clarica personnel were invited to participate in online sessions with the community members, they participated in a two-way learning conversation. They brought ideas into the community that were then tested, expanded upon, and refined by the members in conversation with the Clarica "expert."

Is Clarica a better organization because of its commitment to communities? We think so. How one measures that value, whether in agent retention, sales force growth and productivity, increased knowledge assets, agility and innovation, or just plain gut-feeling, the bottom line is that communities can contribute to the overall success of an organization. Measures can directly link participation in communities with improved performance based on innovative approaches and processes, increased levels of service and relationship quality, and employee satisfaction.

The anecdotal comment in a dialogue discussion, "It made a difference to my sale," speaks volumes.

Measuring Value—Will It Play in Peoria?

For organizations experienced in knowledge management principles and approaches, where the value of "knowing what you know" has already been acknowledged, measuring the value of a community of practice's contribution may not be as difficult as for organizations where knowledge initiatives have yet to be formally established. Taking the leap of faith to a nontraditional, nonfinancial approach to measurement may have to be carefully managed.

1. How is the value of certain programs (e.g., learning, innovation, leadership development) measured in your organization, especially for programs that may not be easily quantified?

2. If you have identified communities of practice at work in your organization, what is the current method of identifying what they contribute—what their value is? How do members value the community?

3. If you were required to provide a cost benefit analysis of developing a community, what key points would you include to make the case?

References

Choo, C.W. (1999). Presentation and lecture materials from faculty Web-site: http://www.choo.fis.utoronto.ca

Clarica. (1999). *Developing a Knowledge Strategy at Clarica*. Strategic Capabilities Unit.

Phillips, P.P. (2002). "Measuring and Monitoring Intellectual Capital: Progress and Future Challenges," in Phillips, P. (Ed.) *In Action: Measuring Intellectual Capital*. Alexandria, VA: ASTD, pp. 4–18.

Stewart, T.A. (2002). *The Wealth of Knowledge: Intellectual Capital and the Twenty-first Century Organization.* New York: Doubleday.

Wenger, E., R. McDermott, and W. M. Snyder (2002). *Cultivating Communities of Practice: A Guide to Managing Knowledge.* Cambridge, MA: Harvard Business School Press.

Part III

CREATING COMMUNITIES: A COURSE OF ACTION

In Part II, we provided an overview of our tactical approach to creating communities in a strategic context with a process description and reflection of our lessons learned. We now move to the last layer of our framework to look at community building from an operational perspective.

In this part of the book, we continue our discussion on how we designed, implemented, and supported the growth of the Agent Network—a community with a strategic purpose at Clarica. Following the steps of the process model outlined in Chapters 5–7, we bring our experience to an operational level. This is where we "roll up our sleeves" with a description of the nuts and bolts of our activities to get the community up and running and to support it in its early stages of development.

In making use of this part of the book, it will be important to first validate whether or not the situations that we've provided apply in your own organi-

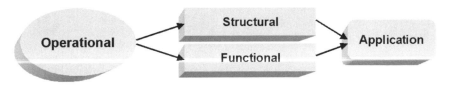

Figure PIII.1.
Operational Framework

zation. You can then use these illustrations of how we created a foundation and encouraged the growth of a community of practice situated in a strategic context.

By understanding what has been our experience, you can use what makes sense for your situation, modify it to your needs, and create new knowledge about what worked in your application of this knowledge creation and exchange structure. We encourage you to share your experience with all of us who are working in the growing practice of building communities by participating in the discussion at our Web site (http://www.knowinc.com).

Chapter 9

COMMUNITY DESIGN
AND LAUNCH:
ILLUSTRATION OF ACTIVITIES

Using the phases of the community development process model as our guide, we provide the operational perspective on how we designed and launched the Agent Network at Clarica. This collection of documents and resources developed during Phase I (define community project, develop community components, launch community) illustrates the types of activities that were undertaken to put the community in place.

PROCESS MODEL TO PRACTICE

In Part II, we discussed the general steps that were used to guide the process of building a community of practice as a strategic resource. To add another level of detail to that process, we turn to the operational perspective—what did we actually *do* to get the community up and running for the members?

It would be impossible to include examples of everything we did—that would mean replicating a discussion database with over 100 topics, a filing cabinet of meeting notes and draft documents, and several bound notebooks of checklists, journal entries, and materials from our community software vendor.

Instead, we've chosen items that represent some of the key actions—resources that should give you an idea of the types of things we did at each step. Some are more developed than others—some could use improve-

231

ment, and we've noted where we might change things as part of our reflective process of lessons learned.

As a summary for each of the main steps in the development process, we've created a table that attempts to gather the majority of the actions that we went through with each step. No doubt, like trying to codify tacit knowledge, we've missed some of the finer points, but it gives you an idea of the amount of activity it takes to put a community in place.

Step 1—Define Community Project

In Step 1, the main goal is to identify the parameters of the community development project. We learned from our earlier failures in establishing communities as a strategic resource that we hadn't put a formal approach in place—we needed to adopt a more rigorous project management approach. Under the guidance of a project manager, we began by defining the community development project: set the context, outline the project approach, identify resource requirements, and define the deliverables.

Set Context—Identify a Purpose

Communities of practice had been identified as a component of Clarica's Knowledge Strategy, and over 30 informal or sponsored communities were well established. However, developing a community as a strategic resource required a different kind of purpose statement—one that recognized the strategic context of the community. What was the reason for building the community? What did we hope to accomplish? What could we leverage from the perspective of individual and organizational capability generation?

Early in the project, the Steering Group was asked to develop a purpose statement. Various versions were drafted in an effort to reflect the clarity of voice that is central to Clarica's brand promise. The following sequence shows the development of the purpose from a Clarica-centric to a member-centric purpose. What should have seemed obvious from the start took us a while to achieve!

- Original draft by Steering Group:

    The purpose of this Agent Network is to support the growth and productivity of Clarica's Retail Sales Force—to help agents grow personally, professionally, and technically, leading to innovation in sales strategies.

- The second iteration that resulted from working on clarity of language:

  The Agent Network supports agents of Clarica's retail sales force to develop personal, professional and technical expertise, leading to innovation in sales strategies and increased productivity.

- A third, more streamlined version:

  To help agents develop their personal, professional and technical expertise, leading to innovative strategies and increased productivity.

- And the final version that more closely reflects an agent focus:

  To develop and share our personal, professional and technical expertise, leading to innovative strategies and growth of our business.

This statement was then taken to the community as a draft statement. It was one of the first activities that the community did together—they discussed the various aspects of the purpose statement and agreed to adopt it as drafted.

Set Context—Define *Communities of Practice*

In Chapter 2, we noted that the field of knowledge management is only about a decade old, so it stands to reason that establishing meaning for the vocabulary is still an issue—the term *communities of practice* is no exception. With so much emphasis on this term, we suggest that you take time at the very beginning to establish a definition for your organization—one that will reflect the general consensus but that is meaningful to your organization.

Let's look at several definitions of communities of practice to see the common threads and the differences. By seeing how other people define communities, you may be able to help shape a definition for your purposes. The following definitions have been accumulated by the Community Intelligence Labs in the Knowledge Garden Website (2000).

. . . a group of professionals, informally bound to one another through exposure to a common class of problems, common pursuit of solutions, and thereby themselves, embodying a store of knowledge. (Peter and Trudy Johnson-Lenz, Awakening Technology)

More than a "community of learners," a community of practice is also a "community that learns." Not merely peers exchanging ideas around the water cooler, sharing and benefiting from each other's expertise, but colleagues committed to jointly develop better practices. (George Pór, Community Intelligence Labs)

A diverse group of people engaged in real work over a significant period of time during which they build things, solve problems, learn and invent . . . in short, they evolve a practice that is highly skilled and highly creative. (Robert Bauer, Xerox PARC)

Groups of people who share similar goals and interests. In pursuit of these goals and interests, they employ common practices, work with the same tools and express themselves in a common language. Through such common activity, they come to hold similar beliefs and value systems. (Collaborative Visualization Project)

They are peers in the execution of "real work." What holds them together is a common sense of purpose and a real need to know what each other knows. There are many communities of practice within a single company, and most people belong to more than one of them. (John Seely Brown, Xerox)

It might help to look at these definitions in terms of their elements. We created Table 9.1 as a synthesis of the ideas expressed in each of the definitions above.

You might think this too academic an exercise, but when the nuances are examined, significant differences can be seen—differences that could create confusion with your stakeholders and limit your abilities to get the level of buy-in you need to help the community succeed. Let's look more closely at the differences:

- **Membership description:** Is the community just a group of people, a select group of people, or a diverse group of people? Are the members professionals or a collection of colleagues and peers who may not have a professional standing?

- **Membership characteristics:** Arc the community members engaged in a project or wanting to learn how to work effectively at whatever they are doing? Does it take a significant amount of time to form a community of practice? Must the members work with the same tools and share a common language? Is this possible in a diverse group?

- **Community characteristics:** Is the community informally bound or brought together? Are they focused on a common set of problems or do they want to better the practice in general?

- **Community purpose:** Will they find solutions to a common set of problems or find solutions to any problem presented? Will they invent and eventually build something?

MEMBERSHIP DESCRIPTION	<ul><li>Group of professionals</li><li>Diverse group of people</li><li>Group of people</li><li>Peers</li><li>Colleagues</li></ul>
MEMBERSHIP CHARACTERISTICS	<ul><li>Desire to work more effectively</li><li>Engaged in real work</li><li>Worked together over a significant period of time</li><li>Similar goals & interests</li><li>Employ common practices</li><li>Work with the same tools</li><li>Have a common language</li><li>Brought together though exposure to common set of problems</li></ul>
COMMUNITY CHARACTERISTICS	<ul><li>Informally bound</li><li>Focused on a common set of problems</li><li>Committed to jointly develop better practice</li><li>More than just an exchange of ideas</li><li>Evolves over time</li></ul>
COMMUNITY PURPOSE	<ul><li>Common pursuit of a solution</li><li>Build things</li><li>Solve problems</li><li>Learn</li><li>Invent</li></ul>
COMMUNITY OUTCOMES	<ul><li>Store of knowledge</li><li>Network of people</li><li>Evolved practice</li><li>Highly skilled and creative members</li><li>Similar beliefs & value systems held by members</li></ul>

Table 9.1.

Communities of Practice Definition Components

The definitions we presented above are just a sampling of what's available in the literature. Before proceeding further with community of practice development, ensure that you have a definition for community clearly stated as part of setting the context.

As you gain more experience with communities in your organization, you may find, as we did, that you need to refine the term. When we developed the Knowledge Strategy Clarica in 1999, we defined a community of practice as:

> *A group of people with common business goals who come together to create and exchange knowledge in order to increase their individual capabilities as practitioners.*

As we learned how to leverage communities in a strategic context, we had to take another look at our definition and make some changes to reflect communities as a strategic resource:

> *A group of self-governing people whose practice is aligned with strategic imperatives and are challenged to create shareholder value by increasing capabilities and improving their practice.*

Chances are that as we continue to gain experience with communities, our definitions will also evolve.

Project Approach—Outline Project Overview

To record our steps and present ideas that could then be discussed by the Steering Group, we began developing what we called *Project Documents* on key issues. These documents provided a purpose for the activity, outlined the content, and identified issues and opportunities that would need to be addressed. One of the first documents that we developed was a high-level outline of the project. We didn't have a process model in place when we started this project, so documents like this one were used to identify key steps and as the basis of our work plan and communications. This high-level overview was also used in creating the project charter, which is outlined in the next section.

The project overview covers what was called "Phase I"—a pilot phase that would see the community launched and operating for approximately three months and then assess whether or not to continue with the project.

Project Plan

To provide a high-level outline of the milestones, key action items, and support strategies required to design and implement the Agent Community.

I.   Design Project Plan
   A.   Develop polices and guidelines
   B.   Establish Phase I participant group
   C.   Develop communication plan
   D.   Implement site application
   Milestone: Finalize Planning Phase

II. Implement Phase I
   A.   Kick-off activities
   B.   Agent participant training
   C.   Community activities and discussions
   Milestone: Launch Community—Phase I

III. Assess Phase I
   A.   Develop assessment tool
   B.   Implement assessment
   C.   Prepare recommendations
   Milestone: Assessment and Recommendations

IV. Implement Phase II
   A.   Review Phase I recommendations
   B.   Implement modifications
   Milestone: Launch Community—Phase II

Project Approach—Develop Project Charter

At Clarica, project charters are required for any project that takes more than 20 days to complete, costs $10,000 or more, or involves multiple stakeholders. The purpose of the charter is to ensure that: the sponsor(s) commitment is reinforced; the project is stated as a priority and aligned with business objectives; resources are committed; and project priorities and impacts are broadly communicated. To prepare for drafting the charter, guidelines suggest that the project manager:

- Define the project objectives.
- Determine stakeholders.
- Produce an initial scope statement.
- Identify assumptions and constraints.
- Outline project approach.
- Define deliverables.
- Identify roles and responsibilities.
- Outline a high level plan.
- Identify costs.
- Determine success criteria.

Before the charter is developed, a significant amount of work is completed on the project design. Due to the confidential nature of some of the charter contents for establishing the Agent Network, we are not able to produce the charter in its entirety. We can highlight some of the statements that help position the community as a strategic resource and give you a flavor of what the charter entails.

Agent Community Development—Project Charter

Executive Summary

Communities are not new to us, yet it is only recently that the value of communities has been recognized in the business environment. Communities suggest a group of people who share a common interest, situation, or goal; who want to talk with others in the community for support or development; or wish to collaborate in order to further the purpose of that community.

The power of communities was recognized after several Clarica agents participated in a Web-based community-building learning opportunity, facilitated by Etienne Wenger (an internationally recognized consultant). In particular, four of the agents further pursued the possibility of forming an agent community at Clarica. This project is the result of their expressed interest and support.

The primary purpose of this Agent Community is to support the growth and productivity of Clarica's sales force. The community is to be a "space" for agents where:

- Developing agents (less than five years' experience) gain support.

- Experienced agents (five or more years' experience) are continually renewed.

- Agents can network to grow personally, professionally, and technically, leading to innovations in sales strategies.

The primary purpose of this project is to design and deliver the socio-technical requirements of the Agent Community, starting with a small group of senior and developing agents in Phase I and continuing with full agent participation in Phase II.

This project is co-sponsored by the Knowledge Team and Retail Sales Force, with accountability lying with the Knowledge Team. Several steps have been taken in this project to ensure success:

- A Project Steering Group has been formed including two agents, two representatives from Retail Sales Force, and two representatives from the Knowledge Team.

- An experienced project leader/facilitator for the community has been secured.

- Software to support simple, effective dialogue on the Web has been identified and will be implemented.

Purpose—"For Agents, By Agents"

The purpose of this project is to create an environment that will facilitate the natural development of an agent community, serving all agents across Canada. This includes:

- Creating a value proposition to merit agents' participation.

- Developing guidelines for a governance structure, membership, and responsibilities of participation (code of ethics).

- Encouraging agent participation: marketing the Community, developing skills (software training), nurturing the Community.

- Selecting collaborative tools that are "agent friendly."

- Providing excellent facilitation of Web-based discussions to encourage and enhance networking opportunities and experiences.

- Developing a communication plan for head office and the field.

- Developing processes and policies that will sustain the community after launch.

- Developing an evaluation method to assess the outcomes of the Community in Phase I and make recommendations for implementing Phase II.

The Community will be dedicated to agents and thus will not serve as a direct tool of the sales force. The purposes of this community (in order of importance) are to:

- Support the career growth of developing agents (less than five years' experience) in order to improve career satisfaction, productivity, and retention.
- Support the renewal and continued professional development of experienced agents (five or more years' experience). The community will be a means to step experienced agents to their next range of professional potential.
- Provide opportunities for agent networking that will lead to greater sales innovation and professional cohesiveness and strength.

Project Objectives

- To support the growth and increased productivity of Clarica's sales force through the formation of an Agent Community.
- To implement Communispace, a Web-based tool that supports a discussion forum, so as to facilitate agent dialogue and relationship building, leading to knowledge exchange.
- To develop processes required to sustain the value of the agent community.

In addition to the primary objectives, Clarica seeks to document the community-building process and assess its success, capturing best practice.

Assumptions and Constraints

Assumptions:

- Agents will be self-governing; discussion content and appropriateness based on a membership charter.
- Membership will be by invitation; list to be developed by and vetted by appropriate Retail Sales Force management. During Phase I, there will be no Head Office management membership. Subsequent inclusion will be by invitation only from the Agent Community.
- Participation in the community is not mandatory—agents can "deal themselves out" at any time.
- A Project Steering Group comprising agents and Head Office staff will guide the development of Phase I.

Constraints:

- Agents' time on the Project Steering Group must be judiciously used.
- Some agents are not internet savvy; keyboarding skills are uneven.
- Technical design must deliver to the lowest common denominator (e.g., phone lines), but not preclude better technologies (e.g., cable connect); 56k modems are required.
- Aiming for an Oct 31 launch.
- The software is currently only available in English; French language capabilities are not expected for one year (estimated).
- Head Office resources—The agent commissions project has been given priority.

Risk Managementt

Risk	Management Strategy
We'll build it and agents will not use—the value proposition is not clear enough in the beginning	Construction of the community is accomplished by partnering with founding agent members
	Vendor provides not only the software, but also consulting based on their community development experience
	A facilitator will be provided to keep discussions alive
Agents will use the community forum inappropriately	A "code of ethics" for community participants will govern discussion content
	Agents will have a self-governing body
Managers and executives will not want agent communities	Communication plans will be developed to show the value proposition for management groups and other audiences

Risk	Management Strategy
The project will become a technical exercise, but development of a community is much more a social exercise	A dedicated facilitator has been appointed Vendor's consultants bring a balanced approach to community design Having agents on the Project Steering Group ensures that their perspective is always present

Quality Management

Quality is probably the most important factor in the balance of time, cost, and quality. If the quality of this community is not high, agents will not participate.

- Quality will be reviewed at major milestones.
- Vendor's consultants will evaluate our community design based on their experience.
- Measures for success will be established early in the project.
- Agent community experience will be monitored closely to ensure there is a valid value proposition.

Communications

A communication plan, recognizing the many distribution channels available, will be developed as one of the first steps in this project. Audiences include:

- Agents.
- Project sponsors and other Clarica senior management.
- Retail Sales Force management.
- Regional Agency Vice Presidents (RAVPs), Branch and regional managers.
- Sales Force Council.
- Clarica employees.

Change Management

A plan for change management will need to be developed, based on the outcomes of Phase I. Issues to consider are:

- Not all agents are Web-literate.
- Access to the Web varies (e.g., line speed).
- The community site is managed by a software package that requires some training for effective use and is "in transition" to more robust software.
- The value of establishing communities is not yet documented.

Roles and Responsibilities

Role	Responsibility
Sponsors	Participate in milestone reviews Clear barriers
Project Manager	Negotiate contract with vendor Develop project plan for successful implementation Coordinate development of communication plan Coordinate development of Change Management Plans (including agent rollout)
Project Steering Group	Design the agent community (social and technical) Guide the development of working documents Provide sales force input Review and confirm
Senior Management	Support development of the community Participate when invited by the Agent Community
Facilitator	Organize community events (in or out of the discussion forum) Ensure agents have necessary skills to participate Monitor discussions in the forum, ensuring issues are resolved, summarizing key conclusions Manage the community's resource library
Vendor Sales Representative	Overall client relationship and satisfaction Participate in appropriate milestone events to provide strategic and objective advice Conduct periodic check in meetings with Clarica Main point of contact for contractual issues

Role	Responsibility
Vendor Account Manager Vendor Project Managers	Main point of contact for the day-to-day work associated with the creation of the community Coordinate and deliver resources from vendor Communicate with Clarica and consult on successful implementation and facilitation of the Agent Network
Vendor Community Designers	Develop and maintain success metrics and community health Consult with Clarica on designing a successful community experience
Vendor End User Support	Adapt user training as appropriate for Clarica Conduct user training sessions Provide end user with telephone and e-mail support Update membership and member data as appropriate
Vendor Technical Support	Partner with Clarica technical staff re security, bandwidth, etc.

Success Criteria

- Agents see the value proposition through the quality of the community.
- Management recognizes the value of an Agent Network.
- Implementation dates are met within specified budget.

Overview of *Define Community Project* Actions

To provide an overview of the types of actions that were taken during this first step of the community development process, we've outlined the key objectives, activities undertaken to meet the objectives, the people required to complete tasks, and the deliverables (see Table 9.2).

STEP	OBJECTIVES	ACTIONS	PERSONNEL REQUIRED	DELIVERABLES
Set Context	Understand Clarica business environment and strategic imperatives	Review Clarica Website, promotional materials, and internal documents Review Knowledge Strategy	Sponsors and executive assistants Senior Executives	Overview of environment—position paper
	Understand community members' and sponsors' environment—opportunities and issues Identify the knowledge sharing environment: cultural aspects—level of trust, existing sharing opportunities, challenges and issues in sharing knowledge	Identify Retail Sales Force objectives Understand Clarica/Agent relationship Identify context of an agent's business: what business are they in, how do they practice, what is the market like, what are the agent's issues/challenges and opportunities? Explore context, objectives, and desired outcomes in Steering Group meetings and meetings with individual Steering Group members Identify key informants for interviews	Sales Force Management Steering Group Senior Agents' Committee Representatives of the community membership and related management Project manager Community facilitator Facilitator(s) of existing Clarica communities of practice	Overview of environment—position paper

Table 9.2.
Phase I—Design and Launch Community

STEP	OBJECTIVES	ACTIONS	PERSONNEL REQUIRED	DELIVERABLES
		Interview agents, Regional Agency Vice Presidents, Head Office staff in agent support roles, branch managers, and agency trainers Attend agent-related meetings (e.g., Senior Agents Committee, Sales Force Council, RAVP meetings)		
	Define community of practice; identify characteristics	Consult literature Participate in and/or review Community of Practice on-line course	Project Manager	Overview of environment— position paper
Design Project	Create Steering Group to guide project development and evaluation	Identify potential Steering Group members (recommended by Sponsors) Invite participation Outline expectations and estimate time commitment	Sponsors Project Manager Knowledge Architect	

Establish project management approach: project manager/facilitator interacting with Steering Group and Sponsors	Establish routines including: working documents, standard presentation core, Steering Group meetings, reporting processes, project management role, Lotus Notes Discussion databases, e-mail discussions	Project Manager	High-level project map
Identify role of Head Office personnel and potential community members in project	Identify how agents and Head Office management involved with Retail Sales Force will participate in the project	Knowledge Architect	
Identify Head Office resource network to support project task completion	Create contact list of people who will provide assistance Create internal teams to address specific issues Work with Head Office Steering Group members		Resource list

Table 9.2. (*continued*)
Phase I—Design and Launch Community

STEP	OBJECTIVES	ACTIONS	PERSONNEL REQUIRED	DELIVERABLES
	Identify tool (software program) to support community development	Negotiate software agreement Establish partnership with vendor	Knowledge Architect Project Manager Vendor personnel	
	Identify Project Strategy and Design	Develop project charter Develop purpose statement	Steering Group Project Manager	Working Documents: Project Overview Governance Documents: Project Charter & Purpose Statement
	Draft Project Action Plan	Identify milestones, actions, resources required—estimate timeframe.	Project Manager	Project Plan Presentations

Table 9.2. (*continued*)
Phase I—Design and Launch Community

Step 2—Develop Community Components

Focused on putting the groundwork in place for launching the community, this step covers a wide range of activities related to establishing structure and infrastructure for the community. Selected materials illustrate the work done to address issues of governance, membership, education and training, and communications.

Governance—Membership Selection Process

Purpose

To establish a process by which the pilot project participants are identified and invited to participate.

Assumptions:

- The Agent Network Steering Group is responsible for outlining the selection process.
- The selection process relies on the Agent Profile—Pilot Project Participation.
- Participant group should include approximately 100 members; in order to achieve this number, approximately 125 nominees should be identified.
- Clarica Sales Force management should be involved in selection process; they can help evaluate attributes of possible participants and their involvement can create buy-in for support and promotion of the project.

Process

- Steering Group Agent Members suggest names of experienced agents.
- List of experienced agents is reviewed by Sales Force Regional Agency Vice Presidents for evaluation against profile criteria.
- Steering Group Members invite experienced agents to participate.
- Based on profile criteria, experienced agent pilot project members and Sales Force Regional Area Vice Presidents suggest developing agent participants.
- Steering Group members invite developing agents to participate.

> **Support Items**
>
> - Sales Force Area Regional Vice Presidents must first be informed of the project and their help solicited in identifying pilot project members.
> - Script for Steering Group members needs to be developed to ensure consistency in message when inviting agents to participate.

Membership—Invitation Letter

> Dear Colleagues,
>
> Enclosed you will find an invitation to join the Agent Network, an innovative project that will link agents to agents in a community of practice via the Web.
>
> As a founding member, you have the opportunity to grow and share your knowledge, while helping to establish a community prototype that will be extended to the entire Clarica sales force in 2001. We don't have all the answers—this is new territory that presents a wealth of possibilities for adding value to our profession. I welcome your participation to help shape the direction.
>
> Please take a few moments to learn about the Agent Network. A checklist is included to help you evaluate whether or not you are able to join this initial phase. You've been selected by your peers and senior management as a person who is a champion of professional growth.
>
> I invite you join the Agent Network and watch your business grow!
>
> Sincerely,
>
>
> Hubert Saint-Onge
> Vice President, Strategic Capabilities

Membership—Call-Back Script

To ensure that all invited members had the same information on which to base their decision to participate in the community, we prepared an outline for the three people who would be calling the invitees to talk to them about the project.

Process

1. Introduce yourself as a member of the Agent Network Steering Group.

2. Did he/she receive the invitation? If not, it's on the way, but here's an outline. Or if they did receive, here's more information about the Network.

3. Give some background on the project:

   ■ Agents involved in online course on community building.

   ■ Clarica commitment to knowledge sharing.

   ■ Agents group helping each other in pockets; want to expand across country.

4. WIIFM (What's in it for me?) Benefits of Participating in the Community.

   ■ Link to product and market specialists.

   ■ Agents to agents—understand your situation.

   ■ Practical experience—lessons learned; examples of best-case scenarios.

   ■ Shorten time in finding innovative ways to approach your business.

   ■ Build a network of colleagues; expand business boundaries in collaboration.

   ■ Opportunity to grow personally, professionally, and technically.

   ■ Opportunity to help move the profession of agents ahead—new ways to "practice."

   ■ Opportunity to find innovative ways to succeed and grow your business.

   ■ There's something for everyone, no matter your years of experience.

5. What is a community?

   "Community" has many meanings:

   ■ A physical location, like a city.

   ■ A feeling of belonging.

   ■ A collection of people with like interests.

   ■ In fact, sociologists say that it is the most difficult and controversial term to try to define.

   We've adopted this definition:

A community is a group of people who are willing and able to help each other.

And we've captured that in our "tag line" or the motto for the community:

FOR AGENTS—BY AGENTS

6. Background on the project:

Our goal is to provide a platform, an arena, basically a "place" for all Clarica agents across the country to come and talk. With over 3000 agents, that's a significant undertaking. So, we're starting with a smaller group of agents—those who:

- Have a variety of product expertise and market experience.

- Are interested in professional excellence and are willing to share their knowledge with other agents.

- Are experienced with computer technology—have their own Internet Service Provider (ISP) and a 56k modem and have used the Web before.

We'll roll out The Agent Network in a pilot phase to this small group (about 100) agents with the support of a Web-based software application called Communispace. It's the "space" where we'll all pose questions, share ideas, and work collectively to develop new strategies.

The pilot phase will last 2–3 months. Then we'll have some experience with community building in this smaller group that we can apply to the larger group, we hope in early 2001.

7. What does it take to participate?

- Your own ISP—that means you can connect to the Internet (if you don't have one, unlimited rates are about $25/month); a 56k modem; and some Web experience.

- A commitment to "check" the Agent Network space at least 3 times a week.

- A willingness to help develop the community, lay the foundation, identify ground rules, try approaches, and evaluate progress. All the responsibilities of being a "FOUNDING MEMBER"—we pave the way for others.

8. How do I get started?

We have a full-time person devoted to facilitating the Network—her name is Deb Wallace, and she'll ensure that you have everything you need to participate. She'll also be facilitating the community—

helping to keep discussions moving along and then capturing the "nuggets" of experience so that other people can learn/benefit from the conversations.

Deb will be in touch shortly to:

- Ensure that your computer can access the community site.
- Give you your log-on information.
- Provide you with some training on the software.
- Outline sample scenarios of how you might work in the community site.
- Answer your questions about participation.
- Get you rolling on the various discussions.

9. Can I sign you up?

- You can make a significant difference in helping both yourself and other agents succeed in this business.
- You can meet colleagues across the country—or in your own backyard!
- You can expand your technical expertise—this is leading-edge software.
- You can be a founding member in a network that is bound to grow beyond our wildest dreams.
- You can vary your level of participation week by week if you have other priorities.
- You can bow out at any point and then join in the network later when we roll it out across the country.

10. Confirm contact information

- E-mail address:
- Use this business number?

Process Note

1. Keep track of their questions so that we can update the script and perhaps produce a FAQ sheet to put up on the Web site.

2. Let Deb know outcome of each call so that she can follow up to get their data selected and their log-on information to them.

Learning—Information Package Introductory Letter

> Dear Founding Members,
>
> On behalf of the Steering Group and Sponsors, I welcome you to the Agent Network, a community of practice for Clarica agents.
>
> We're breaking new ground in the insurance and financial services industry, bringing together agents from across the country with the help of a Web-based application. We're in somewhat uncharted waters, but our purpose is clear:
>
> To develop and share our personal, professional, and technical expertise, leading to innovative strategies and growth of our business.
>
> Enclosed are a number of items for you to review before logging into the Agent Network community site. For security reasons, your member name and temporary password will be e-mailed to you.
>
> I invite you to visit the Agent Network as often as you can, participating in dialogues and other activities and contributing to the agent-generated resource materials. I will be facilitating the community, helping you to maximize the benefits of this dynamic exchange of expertise and ideas.
>
> Thank you for your enthusiastic support of the Agent Network. The response has been overwhelming, with over 150 people ready to roll up their sleeves and lay the foundation for an innovative approach to growing our business. See you online!
>
> Sincerely,
>
> Deb Wallace
> Agent Network Facilitator

Learning—Day-One Guide

The community used a Web-based collaborative tool. Because the members had a wide range of skill and comfort level with Web-based applications, we felt it was necessary to provide them with an introductory-level guide. We didn't want the technology to be the focus of the community. On the other hand, we wanted to ensure that members knew how to use the functionality in order to actively participate in the community conversations.

We include one of the guides we developed as an example of the type of support materials that you may have to provide for your members. While the community collaborative tool had a fairly comprehensive help facility built into the system, the help was based on functionality (i.e., how things work—the system features) rather than on application (i.e., how do I use the functionality to do the things I want to do?).

This guide was distributed in paper form with the introductory package and was available online as a resource in the community's knowledge repository. It was also distributed to the agency trainers who would help members become familiar with the application.

Day One: A Short Tour of the Community Site for People Who Dislike Reading Instructions

Here's a quick introduction to using the Agent Network site. By following these eight simple steps, you'll have an overview of the major features. If you get stuck and need more information, please refer to the *Ready, Set GO! Users' Guide* or the help menu in the site.

1. Log in
   - Access the Internet, connecting via the Clarica Network or your Internet Service Provider (ISP).
   - Access the site through the Sales Force Central home page, clicking on Sales Tools and Advertising or through your browser, typing the URL.
   - Log in to the site with your Membername and Password.

2. Change your password
   - Click the Change password box on the log-in screen.
   - Click the log in button.
   - Type your new password and press Tab.
   - In the Confirm field, type your new password again.
   - Click the log in button.

3. Access and review the home page
   - Scan the Agent Network Home Page and find the sections: What's New—items added to the community since you last logged in like dialogues or comments on references; Latest References—new agent-generated items added to the collection; Announcements—things about the Network; and Events—a schedule of activities and dialogues.

4. Update your member profile

- Select Members in the People section of the navigation panel on the left of your screen.
- The page defaults to the "Online" list. Click on your name to view your profile.
- Select the Edit Your Profile button.
- Review the pre-filled information and edit where necessary, using Tab to move between the text boxes.
- Complete the professional background fields (recommended).
- Add personal information (optional).
- Save the profile changes by clicking on the Update Profile button at the bottom of the page.

5. Look at a dialogue

- Select Dialogue in the Activities section of the navigation panel. A listing of all the dialogues and corresponding comments is displayed.
- Choose a dialogue that you want to read or participate in.
- Add to the dialogue or respond to a particular point of the discussion.
- Submit your comments.

6. Review reference materials

- Select References in the Resources section of the navigation panel.
- Under View, click on Files and Links.
- Scroll through the brief descriptions and select an item to view.
- Click on Reviewers Comment to see what other people have said about the resource.
- Use the Back button on your browser (Internet Explorer) to get back to the listing.
- Click on the title of the item you'd like to review.
- The resource will be displayed by the application it was created in, such as Word or Excel. Once you've read it, you need to get back to the community site by exiting the application (click on the x in the top right hand corner of the screen) or clicking on your browser button displayed at the bottom of the screen in line with your Start button.
- Add your own comment (optional).

7. Engage in a chat

- Select Chat in the People section of the navigation panel.

- Under Current Conversations, click on an existing chat or create a new chat topic by typing it in the text box.

- Pull down the text color drop-down menu at the bottom left corner of the screen and choose a color.

- Type your comment, and then click on Submit.

- Check out the profile of one of the contributors by clicking on their name in the Who's Here list.

- When you've finished your session, click on the "X" in the top right hand corner of the chat screen.

8. Log out

- Exit the Agent Network by clicking on the "X" in the top line of the upper right corner of your screen.

Communication—High-Level Plan

Purpose

To outline a comprehensive communication strategy that informs agents, Clarica management, other stakeholder groups, and the Clarica employee community about the development of the Agent Community. To provide a basis for creating the communication plan as a project plan.

Assumptions

This outline is designed around a communications framework that moves people through a decision-making cycle from awareness, to interest, to decision making, to action.

The desired "action" is to create and maintain active participation in the Agent Community.

Agent Community Project Purpose

The primary purpose of this Agent Community is to support the growth and productivity of Clarica's sales force. The community is to be a "space" for agents where:

- Developing agents (less than 5 years' experience) gain support.

- Experienced agents (5 or more years' experience) are continually renewed.
- Agent can network to grow personally, professionally, and technically, leading to innovation in sales strategies.

(See Purpose Statement—Project Plan Working Documents for further information.)

Communication Plan Objectives

- To inform the many audiences of the Agent Network project.
- To encourage agents to participate in Phase I of the project.
- To create interest among the remainder of the agents so that, when the first phase is completed, they will want to join in as well.
- To gain support from Clarica management so that they will promote the active involvement of agents.
- To tie the Agent Network Project to Clarica's knowledge strategy.

Risks/Critical Success Factors of the Communication Plan

- A critical mass of enthusiastic, supportive agents is required for Phase I success.
- Agents not involved in Phase I must be "chomping at the bit" to be involved with the next phase of the project (early 2001).
- Clarica management must feel comfortable that this community is not a vehicle for discontented discussion.
- French language capabilities of the community site software must be addressed.

Key Benefits of Project

- Agent productivity, retention, and size of sales force are increased.
- Agents are more Web-aware for e-business purposed.
- Agent knowledge is made persistent (tacit to explicit).
- Agent recruitment is enhanced.

Key Messages for Communications

- For agents, by agents.
- The project is a partnership between the agents and Clarica. Agents provide guidance to develop to meet their needs; Clarica provides

the infrastructure that enables the community to function. Both parties participate in the assessment.

- This is a first phase—not a test of whether or not to continue, but a preliminary implementation to see how best to roll out to the entire group of Clarica agents.

Audiences for Communication Plan

- Phase I Agent Participants
- Agents
- Project Sponsors + Selected Head Office Senior Management
- RAVPs and regional teams
- Clarica Senior Management
- Sales Force Managers
- Sales Force Central
- Sales Force Council
- Clarica Employees

Formats/Distribution Channels of Communication

- E-mail messages
- Website for Agent Network; Sales Force Central Link
- Information brochure; FAQ sheet
- Video clip
- Presentations: Deck, Walk around
- Agent meetings: regional, sales and marketing workshops, agent advisories
- Clarica intranet; hotline e-mail
- One-on-one meetings and phone calls

Overview of Phases of a Communication Strategy

1. Setting the Context; Creating Meaning (Information/Awareness)

   This phase helps people understand the Agent Network and answers questions such as:

   - What is a community of practice?
   - Who is involved in creating the Agent Network?
   - How was I identified?
   - Who else is involved?

- What's in it for me?
- What's in it for Clarica?
- What's head office's role?
- What other communities exist at Clarica or for agents?
- How is this different that anything else that I'm already doing?

II. Creating Buy-In; Making a Decision

This phase helps people make a decision about whether or not they want to participate and answers questions such as:

- How will it work; what's the plan and timeframe?
- What are my responsibilities?
- How is the community managed, facilitated; what is the governance structure?
- How much time will it take?
- What do I need to participate?
- Can I discontinue my participation?
- How does it fit with existing Clarica resources?
- What does it cost?

III. Joining the Community; Acting on Decision

- This phase moves people to action.
- How do I sign up?
- What's my next step?
- When will I be trained?

Implementation Priorities for Communication

(Order of implementation—strategies to be developed)

- Information for RAVPs—selected group required to help identify Phase I participants.
- Outline for agents who will be invited to participate in Phase I.
- Information for agents who have confirmed participation.
- Clarica management.
- Clarica employees.

Communication Delivery

Audience	Purpose	Method
Phase I Agents	Action	E-mail, phone calls, newsletters
Agents Project Sponsors +HO Mgmt. RAVPs + regional teams Sales Force Central Sales Force Mgrs.	Decision Making (to support; promote)	Presentations One page summaries News items for regular communication methods One on one meetings
Clarica Sr. Mgmt. Sales Force Council	Interest	One page summary Meetings
Clarica employees	Awareness	News item

Assessment of Communication Plan

The communication plan will be one of the items assessed at the end of the Phase I.

The facilitator will routinely ask any contacts if they've heard about the Agent Community project.

Communication—Fact Sheet

We developed a fact sheet that gave an overview of the community development project. It standardized the key messages that we wanted to present, providing a consistent message for all communication activities.

Background

Communities are not new to us, yet it is only recently that the value of communities has been recognized in the business environment. Communities suggest a group of people who share a common interest, situation, or goal—who want to talk with others in the community for support, development, and/or innovation in order to further the purpose of that community.

The power of communities has been recognized by Clarica's knowledge strategy and was further developed as a possible direction after several Clarica agents participated in a Web-based community-building learning opportunity, facilitated by Etienne. In particular, four of the agents pursued further the possibility of forming an agent community at Clarica.

This project is the result of the expressed interest of a nucleus of agents and the support of Clarica management.

Purpose

For Agents, By Agents

The primary purpose of this Agent Community is to support the growth and productivity of Clarica's sales force. The community is to be a "space" for agents where

- Developing agents (less than 5 years' experience) gain support.
- Experienced agents (5 or more years' experience) are continually renewed.
- Agents can network to grow personally, professionally, and technically leading to innovations in sales strategies.

The community will be dedicated to agents and, as such, will not serve as a direct tool of the sales force. Specifically, the purpose of this community is to:

- Support the career growth of developing agents in order to improve career satisfaction, productivity, and retention.
- Support the renewal and continued professional development of experienced agents. The community will be a means to step experienced agents to their next range of professional potential.
- Provide opportunities for agent networking, which will lead to greater sales innovation and professional cohesiveness and strength.

The primary purpose of this project is to design and deliver the socio-technical requirements of the Agent Community, starting with a small group of senior and developing agents in Phase I and moving to full agent participation in Phase II.

Project Participants

Sponsors

- Senior Vice President, Strategic Capabilities
- Vice President, Sales Force Operations

Steering Group Members

- Experienced agent
- Developing agent
- Knowledge Architect
- Director Sales Force Training and Development
- Manger, Sales Force Business Initiatives
- Community Facilitator and Project Manager

Phase I Agent Participants

150 Experienced and developing agents from across Canada

Implementation Plan Milestones

Mid-Oct.	Finalize community design
Mid-Nov.	Finalize Phase I participants
Early Dec.	Introduce community to participants
Mid-Dec.	Launch Phase I—on-line community
End Feb.	Assess first phase of implementation
Early 2001	Launch Phase II

Overview of *Develop Community Components* Actions

During this second step, the activities were focused on deliverables—getting the community's structure and technology infrastructure in place. Table 9.3 provides an overview of the activities.

	OBJECTIVES	RESOURCES AND PERSONNEL	DELIVERABLES
Governance	Establish membership criteria Develop community purpose statement Identify legal responsibilities Develop French language statement Set up project development infrastructure	Steering Group; Sponsors Legal department Code of Business Practice Code of Business Conduct	Membership: Profile and Selection Process Invitation—Nominee List Purpose statement Statement on security, privacy, and liability issues French language application projection Project Plan (MS Office) Mail-in Database Lotus Notes Discussion Database
Membership	Outline invitation process Finalize participant list Develop invitations Follow-up calls/e-mails Employee termination notification distribution list	Graphic Services Brand Membership Services or Sales Force Admin.	Invitation (print) Confirmation to join (e-mail response) Call back script Participant contact list Log-in process (e-mail)

Infrastructure & Tools	Identify site customization requirements	Vendor Personnel	Customization requirements
	Vendor references consulted	IT	
		Help Desk	
Technical & User Support	Identify technical infrastructure and needs: application, access, agent tools	Help Desk	Technical Implementation Outline—Discussion Document
	Identify firewall, network security issues	IT	Application Security Profile
		Shared Technology Services	Risk Management Outline
	Complete a corporate audit	Corporate Audit Office	Help Desk Workplan
	Identify support needs; identify processes		User Support Outline
	Establish access procedures; button on intranet		Level 1 Technical Outline
Content	Establish criteria for resources	IT	Content Management Discussion Document (criteria for inclusion, content focus, service focus)
	Identify keywords for references	Related Web sites	Keyword list
	Identify content to pre-populate site		
	Select, send and test profile data		

Table 9.3.

Step 2—Develop Community Components

	OBJECTIVES	RESOURCES AND PERSONNEL	DELIVERABLES
Education & Training	Identify training needs Develop materials (day 1 scenario; quick reference guide, users guide) Develop agency trainer as resource	Plain language Other community facilitators Learning Architect Technical writers	Information Packages—Phase I Participants Information Packages—Agency Trainers (guiding principles for use)
Facilitation	Establish role of facilitator Learn site & administration functionality Establish facilitation "style"	Nancy White Full Circle Associates' Facilitation Course Master Facilitators	Working Document: Facilitator—Roles and Responsibilities
Communications	Develop communication plan; stakeholder groups Helpdesk Update Session	Business Unit Group Communication Strategy—Planning Template (Corporate Communications) Corporate Communications Staff	Communications Plan-Discussion Document Executive Summary Clarica staff update breakfast Presentations Communication bulletins Newsletter (e-mail)

Table 9.3. (continued)

Step 2—Develop Community Components

STEP 3—LAUNCH COMMUNITY

The majority of the activities at this step were handled within the community space online. Unfortunately we can't reproduce them here due to the confidentiality agreement with the Agent Network not to represent direct discussion outside of the community's space. But there are a couple of items that we can include that give a flavor of the types of communication we had with the members and support people just in advance of the community launch.

E-mail Message to Members Regarding Log in Information

Welcome to the Agent Network—we're up and running!

Information on how to use the system was sent to you yesterday via Clarica's mail system to agencies. But to speed up your access, we're e-mailing your log in information.

You can access The Agent Network from the new home page of Sales Force Central under the Sales Tools and Advertising button. Or, input the URL . . . in your browser.

We've given you a temporary password, so that you can then choose one of your own. Please change your password the first time that you log in. Instructions are included in the user's guide and the day1 scenario outline—materials in the information package. Or, simply check the Change password box on your log in screen and it will prompt you.

Your new password should be from 6–8 characters and can be either all letters or numbers or a combination of both. (Note: Please avoid symbols like &, %, or $ as they aren't recognized by the system.) For security reasons, we ask that you do not use a password that you have for other Clarica applications.

Here are the pieces that you need to log in:

Member Name: John.Doe

(Don't forget the "dot" between names, just like your Clarica e-mail address.)

Temporary Password: XXXX

The Agent Network "ramp up" period is from Dec. 15–31st, During that time, I suggest that you:

- Change your password
- Familiarize yourself with the site's features and navigation
- Complete your member profile

- Try a dialogue
- Give a chat a go
- Look at some of the reference material

Whew—there will be a lot of new information coming your way.... But I hope we can get you online so that you can start seeing the benefits!

Welcome to the Agent Network and thank you once again for agreeing to participate. I look forward to meeting you online!

Deb

Invitation to Log in for Agency Coach

Dear Agency Coach,

The Agent Network will be ready to roll on Friday, December 15th. Changes to Sales Force Central will allow agents to access the community site from the SFC home page, or they can use their own browser's URL . . ..

Given the level of technical support that you provide to agents, you will probably receive questions about the community site access and functionality. While fairly "intuitive," we recognize that they might need some help, especially if they are not very Web-savy!

Enclosed in this package are several items that we hope will give you some background on the community site and the Agent Network program:

- List of Phase I Participants from your branch
- User's guide
- Quick reference card
- Day I Guide
- Information on privacy and security issues

As with most Web applications, there is no "hot line" support for the site. SFTS Helpdesk will support connectivity questions for agents using the Clarica network. Other support options are outlined in the user's guide. We have a mail-in database for queries under "agent network." Or, please feel free to contact me via e-mail. I'll try to be as responsive as possible.

Although the Agent Network is for agents only, we have several guest passes available for trainers during the first stages of implementation. For security reasons, I'll forward the log in information via e-mail.

> Thank you again for your assistance. I'll stay in touch to better under-
> stand how the agents embrace this new approach!
>
> With thanks,
>
>
> Deb Wallace
> Project Manager and Community Facilitator

Facilitator Action Log

To help understand the role of the facilitator and to ensure that the community was effectively facilitated, we created a simple log to track issues and follow up approaches. This information was used to establish benchmarks and outline the guidelines for facilitation that were developed in Phase II. The log was also useful in seeing patterns of usage concerns that could be addressed in newsletter items, revision of the users' guide materials, and other member support materials.

Date	Member	Issue/Action/Follow-up
01/04	Jeff	Log in doesn't work, reset and send new information
01/06	Sue	Would like to try chat, set up informal chat with three other members
01/14	Gregg	Trying to upload tax information spreadsheet in references, make arrangements to walk him through the process
01/25	Paul	Wants to change profile photo—do we have any statement on this?

Overview of *Launch Community* Actions

The launch period covered a span of approximately three weeks. Although the community online space became available on a specific day, the launch period includes time to obtain final approvals, get trainers up to speed, and a "ramp-up" period for members to enter the community. Table 9.4 outlines the key objectives, actions, personnel required, and deliverables from this final step in Phase I of the community development process.

STEP	OBJECTIVES	ACTIONS	PERSONNEL REQUIRED	DELIVERABLES
Launch Community	Obtain sign-off from Sponsors	"Go ahead" e-mails from sponsors	Sponsors Project Manager	
	Familiarize trainers Provide support materials and guest log-in information in order to support members' use of the community tool	Distribute information packages to agency trainers;	Facilitator	Introductory letter User's guide Reference card Day 1 scenario guide list of members from their agency
	Provide members with the resources necessary to log in and use the site	Send log-in information via e-mail Distribute information package to members:	Facilitator	Introductory letter Statement of security and liability Users' guide, reference card Day 1 scenario
	Begin facilitation activities	Welcome members as they log in Support questions; reinforce use Establish log to monitor log-in numbers; profile changes; site contributions; member participation	Facilitator	Community Activity Log

Table 9.4.
Step 3—Launch the Community

References

Community Intelligence Labs. (2000). "What is a Community of Practice?" http://www.co-I-l.com/coil/knowledge-garden/cop/definitions.shtml.

Chapter 10

COMMUNITY IMPLEMENTATION AND GROWTH: ILLUSTRATION OF ACTIVITIES

We continue the illustration of how a community with a strategic purpose was developed at Clarica after its launch—a time when the community began to move beyond the intrigue of a new structure for sharing knowledge, using a new set of collaborative tools, into a new phase where the focus was shifted from logistics to creating significant value for the individual members, the community as a whole, and the organization at large. We provide examples of documents and resources that were developed during Phase II (steps: establish the community, access progress and value, grow the community, evaluate purpose and direction, and expand the community) in order to create a sustainable community of practice that functions as a strategic resource for an organization.

PROCESS MODEL TO PRACTICE

As in Chapter 9, which focused on the first phase of community development—getting the community up and running, we've collected a variety of examples of actual work we completed at Clarica in order to support the community's implementation and growth. During this second phase, the community works to further the capabilities of its members and create new knowledge that informs the practice. From individual and organizational perspectives, performance is the focus—how do we apply what we

273

know to strengthen our customer relationships and create shareholder value? How do we collaborate to achieve our corporate imperatives?

When talking about the process model in Chapters 6 and 7, we noted that, as we moved from the project management approach of Phase I where logistics for putting the building blocks in place were the focus, we headed into the uncharted waters of community building. We moved from a fairly controlled, technical approach in Phase I to a facilitation and support role in Phase II that left the majority of the responsibility for the community's activities to its members.

We've selected material to illustrate how we facilitated the community members' use of the community structure to increase their own capabilities, based on the steps outlined in the community development process model. Because of the nature of the activities in Phase II, we have not supplied a table summary after each step unless we could identify "discrete" actions in that particular step. For more detail on the types of actions that were accomplished during this phase, consult Chapter 7.

Due to the confidential nature of the Agent Network, the illustrations in this section tend to focus on the organization's roles as facilitator and guide—the materials and resources that we used to support the community's work and the participation of its members. We also include some of the work that the Steering Group accomplished in helping the community mature—to address issues that arose and to put the infrastructure in place that maintained the healthy tensions needed to keep the community moving forward.

STEP 4—ESTABLISH THE COMMUNITY

The early days of the community's implementation were spent just getting to know one another—learning who was in the community and what possible directions the community might take to achieve its purpose. Key to creating a community persona was the guidance of a facilitator. Two examples are included: an outline of the roles and responsibilities of a facilitator and a checklist that is used by a facilitator to put a community activity in place.

Facilitation

It's impossible to highlight the facilitator's role in a community without showing actual interventions that occur within the community, samples of direct contact with individual members, highlights of participation in steering group or sponsor meetings, presentations to stakeholders and other interested parties, or work with various community support teams.

While our community facilitators had a depth of experience in face-to-face facilitation, they lacked experience with translating these capabilities to an online environment. We enrolled our facilitators in an e-learning course on online facilitation so that their new learning would be situated in practice. They also participated in a community of practice for community facilitators that was hosted by our community application vendor.

The community was launched with only a brief outline of responsibilities for the facilitator. However, as the role became better defined through some trial and error in the community, the Steering Group drafted a guideline that was useful in understanding the facilitator's roles and responsibilities—both within the community and as a liaison to the organization.

**Facilitator Guidelines: Roles and Responsibilities—
Draft for Discussion**

Overview

The research literature has identified the central role that a facilitator plays in the success of a community of practice. The purpose of facilitation is to ensure that the goals and objectives of the community are met. A combination of cheerleader, worker bee, camp counselor, and jack-of-all-trades, the facilitator is instrumental in keeping the community focused and moving forward, while maintaining the infrastructure that supports the community's development.

Facilitation is defined as:

. . . a purposeful, systematic intervention into the actions of an individual or group that results in an enhanced, ongoing capability to meet desired objectives. (Kiser, 1998)

Guiding the facilitator are three key principles:

- Purpose—understanding the purpose of the community and keeping that purpose in the forefront of all actions.

- Results—ensuring that stated objectives are met, that the community continues to move toward attaining its goals.

- Intervention—identifying the level at which the facilitator should intervene in the community's actions based on an assessment of behaviors and situations that impact the community's ability to achieve its goals.

These guidelines incorporate ideas from: a Steering Group working document developed early in the Agent Network project, the content of an online facilitation course, literature on facilitation, and materials developed by the community application vendor.

Facilitator's Role

The role of a community facilitator is multifaceted, requiring the competencies of a/an:

- Steward
- Promoter
- Teacher/Coach
- Administrator
- Coordinator
- Researcher, Information provider
- Referee
- Negotiator
- Diplomat
- Role model
- Change agent
- Evaluator

Facilitator's Responsibilities

A facilitator's responsibilities include:

- Develop and implement community development project plan.
- Liaise with community sponsors and stakeholders.
- Liaise with community support tool vendor, acting as a project manager for problem resolution, upgrade implementation, and enhancement requests.
- Chair Community Steering Group: set agenda, arrange facilities, distribute minutes.
- Facilitate technical support and training for community support tool: liaise with technical writers, trainers, Graphic Services, and technical support units.
- Develop and implement assessment activities, communicating results to members and stakeholders.

- Facilitate community discussions, activities, and presentations.
- Guide development of community through community building activities with a focus on knowledge sharing, ensuring that community members can comfortably navigate the community support tool.

Challenges and Issues

A vibrant community of practice can generate a great deal of energy. The dynamic, creative environment, where members work together to identify new strategies for solving issues confronting them, often pushes the envelope of their traditional practice. This innovation is the result of committed, passionate individuals who may contribute to situations that challenge the facilitator's skills. Keeping the community's purpose and desired results in mind, the facilitator should provide impartial, confidential, and speedy intervention.

When the intervention requires identification of resources to help bring resolution to an issue, the facilitator will in strictest confidence:

- Represent an issue to the organization, setting the context and providing a summary of the content in order to obtain information, opinions, and/or directions from management.
- Represent an issue to the community on behalf of the organization, providing a synthesis of the community's ideas and recommendations for the organization to consider.

This dual role may leave the facilitator's credibility in question. However, if an intervention is treated with honesty, clarity, congruence, and speed, the facilitator cannot only keep intact, but increase his or her credibility with community members.

In the end, the facilitator is not a true member of the community of practice unless he or she is accepted as vital to the community—perhaps not exactly as "one of us," but as a key contributor to the community development process. This level of acceptance is earned over time—often at the expense of a few battle scars.

Overview of *Establish the Community* Actions

During this step, the community moves beyond the ramp-up period and begins to establish itself as a viable community. In Table 10.1, we provide an overview of the objectives, actions, resources, requirements, and deliverables covered in this step that immediately followed the community's launch.

STEP	OBJECTIVES	ACTIONS	PERSONNEL REQUIRED	DELIVERABLES
Complete Member Profiles	Profile members	Review member profiles, highlight expertise & interests within the community	Facilitator	
Assess Needs and Identify Styles	Focus on community building: ■ Assess needs ■ Develop community activities ■ Develop network of content expertise	Review dialogue & references for topics of interest Set up online sessions Bring expert opinion, information, resources in to support conversations	Facilitator Steering Group	Informal survey of needs
Identify Styles	Develop community profile	Identify layers of participation; identify "A-list" of members who will take a lead and provide feedback on direction Acknowledge participation in newsletters Communicate with Sponsors	Facilitator	

Introduce Facilitation	Establish role of facilitator	Provide support, guidance; offer suggestions; bounce ideas off members, etc.	Steering Group	Roles and Responsibilities Document
Encourage Participation; Increase Community Site Literacy	Encourage community involvement Facilitate content growth Support member use of application Communicate with the community	Encourage contributions: dialogues, bookstore items, reference items Develop "UpDate" newsletter Move dialogues ahead; contact resources to provide additional information when needed Provide one-on-one support for site functionality; put tips in newsletter and e-mails	Facilitator Steering Group Members	Newsletters Online session outline & checklist

Table 10.1.
Step 4—Establish the Community

STEP 5—CHECKPOINT: PROGRESS AND VALUE

Most of the work at this point was informal—gathering feedback from conversations in the site, e-mails to the facilitator, comments made to Steering Group members. While we didn't complete a formal report on the progress, we did outline a variety of enhancements that would better facilitate community activities. In the spirit of technology vendor partnerships as outlined in Chapter 4, here is an excerpt from a log that we maintained and used as a basis of discussion with our community software vendor.

The items listed are representative of the need to have technology create a space for quality conversations to take place and humanize the vessel in order to create trust within the community.

Community Application Enhancement Tracking

During early use of the community tool, a number of changes have been identified. Priority has been assigned as:

Low—nice to have, but only marginally impacts the value of the community.

Medium—should be addressed within an 8-month time frame; impact not critical to the immediate success of the community, but could have impact as community expands.

High—should be addressed within 3–4 month time frame; impacts the benefit and value of the community and Clarica's investment.

	Description Existing Functionality	Requested Enhancement	Priority
Members	New community implementation—defaulted all members to "New." The user must view each profile to get rid of the icon.	Reserve "New" to identify profiles that have been updated or added to the community.	Medium

	Description Existing Functionality	Requested Enhancement	Priority
	The layout is not graphically pleasing; layout columns are not intuitive if items are only displayed in the first/ right hand column.	Increase space at the top. The sentence describing what is being viewed should be at the top of the screen, or the letter being viewed should be distinguishable.	Medium
Chat	Menu graphic is too large in proportion to the other elements on the page. It's difficult to scroll down to get to what you want to do.	Reduce the size of the graphic, or allow us to personalize.	Medium
	Chat submissions must be submitted with a mouse click. Delays interactions.	A chat submission be triggered by an <enter>	
Dialogue (Menu)	The organization of the menu doesn't reflect the importance of the information available in the menu.	First column lists Dialogue Title; followed by creator, number of items, and expiry date.	Medium
Dialogue (Contribution view and submit pages)	Dialogue text box is too small to accommodate most contributions.	Enlarge size of text box.	High
	Must read a dialogue by opening each individual contribution.	Provide a view transcript—the user can review/read a dialogue by opening only one window.	High

	Description Existing Functionality	Requested Enhancement	Priority
Dialogue *(cont'd)*	Member cannot view their contribution before submitting.	Allow for editing after submission	High
	Submissions are block text without HTML codes. Dialogue contributions are difficult to read.	Allow for more word processing capability—paragraph breaks, line breaks, bullets, bold, italic, underlining, text color, spell check.	High

STEP 6—GROW THE COMMUNITY VALUE

A sense of community has taken hold as seen in the depth of the conversations, the speed at which replies to productive inquires are posted, and the caliber of collaborative efforts to find solutions to challenge in the member's practice. More channels are introduced as options for pursing productive inquiries and sharing knowledge. The following items illustrate three parts of an effort to increase the members' ability to use the synchronous functionality options for presentations and discussions.

Familiarize Members with Community Tool Functionality

One way to encourage members to use the various forms of functionality available to support conversations was to hold an online chat—a synchronous discussion on a topic of interest. Coordinating this event, especially when most members had never participated in an online chat before, required coordination of logistics, preparation of members prior to the online conversation, facilitation of the discussion and support of users during the discussion, and coordination of follow-up activities to extend the learning from the discussion.

The complexity of implementing an online session seemed overwhelming at first. To avoid certain disaster, we created a checklist to guide the online presentation activity and an overview to send to the online presentation participants. We also wanted to ensure that the session was of value to the members, so we devised a brief information form that we distributed the following day to the session participants.

Online Session—Process Overview & Checklist

The online session is an opportunity for members to participate in a focused presentation and discussion on a particular topic, held in real time. The sessions can be either short and informal (30 minutes or less), such as a "chat" on a topic of interest or an information session, or formal (about an hour), such as a course presentation that may qualify for continuing education credits.

The session encompasses a range of activities—not just the "online" time—and can reach community members who were not able to "attend" the session. The range of activities can include:

- Dialogue to identify issues and pose questions in advance to ensure that the presentation meets the participants' needs and guides the presenter's development of the session content.

- Online chat to present/discuss the topic.

- Reference materials to support the presentation: transcript of the session, synthesis/summary of the session content, reference materials to extend session content (files & links).

- Dialogue to continue discussion—presenter answers advance questions that weren't addressed in session or questions arising from session, further questions from participants or community members who read session summary and/or transcript, update information subsequent to presentation.

- Poll to gain feedback on session or specific items discussed in session.

- Informal chat to continue discussion on particular points raised.

An online session works well with a maximum of 15–20 active participants. One way to include more members is to set up a panel of participants who will "interact" with the guest speaker (5–7 members) and designate other participants as "observers" who can instant message a panel member to contribute a point on their behalf.

Planning is key to the success of the session. The following outline provides a planning approach for establishing a formal session. For an informal session, the organizer can choose the degree to which the session needs to be "planned."

This outline is based on materials supplied by the community tool vendor and Clarica experience.

Step 1—Select a Topic and Presenter

Topic:

Topics for the sessions can be identified from a variety of sources, such as:

- Dialogue topics
- Specific dialogue to gather topic ideas
- Reference material submissions
- Current organizational issues
- Steering Group/Advisory Committee
- Members
- Facilitator

To ensure relevance to the community, the facilitator should ask the community membership whether or not the topic is of interest by:

- Seeking advice from the participants in a dialogue that might make a good topic by making a suggestion to organize an online session in the particular dialogue.
- Contacting Steering Group members or a select group of community members via e-mail or phone.
- Setting up a poll in the community.

Presenter:

Identify the guest speakers and resources required to support the topic, seeking recommendations from:

- Community members, especially those participating in the dialogue on the proposed session
- Steering Group members
- Head Office personnel

The presenter should be:

- A credible expert with practical knowledge of the topic.
- Comfortable with the technology and on-line presentation environment.

- Willing to prepare the presentation and required support materials as well as follow up on items identified but not addressed during the online session.

The presenter may not be familiar with the community and might need an introduction to both the community and the on-line presentation approach. (See Session Proposal attached). Prior to the session, the facilitator should familiarize the presenter with the community technology tool, offering to hold a practice session if necessary.

Step II—Pre-Session Activities

Before the session, the facilitator should:

- Advertise the session via: e-mail to membership, announcement on community home page, item in community newsletter.
- Establish a dialogue on the topic, including: topic overview, presenter profile, session sign-up process, request for topic questions or content areas for the presenter to discuss, reference to on-line resources for pre-reading.
- Line-up resource team if required—user technical support, typing assistance for speaker, additional topic resource people.
- Invite observers if appropriate (e.g., PR targets, future guest speakers).
- Prepare session support materials: presenter profile, participant list including location, session overview and procedures, facilitator script, session outline/schedule.
- Review participant list. If a participant is inexperienced, suggest familiarizing themselves with the chat facility and refer to training materials or offer to walk through process if necessary (meet in an informal chat and show how to instant message).
- Orient guest presenter to the process. Hold a practice session if necessary.
- Book facilities and equipment for presentation and support.
- Order refreshments for session team.
- Obtain technical support telephone number.
- Distribute session information to participants (one week before).
- Send reminder to participants, outlining time-zone differences for log-in and support telephone number (day before).

Step III—The Session

Prepare for the session about an hour in advance:

- Set-up equipment
- Profile the guest speaker in the community
- Set-up the session in "chat"
- Open support telephone line (about 15 minutes before log in time)
- Log in to chat

Ensure that the session begins on time:

- Welcome participants as they log in.
- Facilitate session. See script attached.
- Begin to wrap up session about 5 minutes before scheduled conclusion.

Step IV—Post-Session Activities

The post-session activities continue the learning and extend the knowledge sharing that was started in the session. Many of the activities at this step go beyond the actual session participants and make it possible for people who could not attend the session to learn from the experience. At this point, the facilitator should:

- Send an e-mail evaluation to participants. Collect data and outline action items for next session. Post survey summary in session dialogue.
- Summarize the session content and post in references. Place a short summary note in the session dialogue, pointing to the complete summary in references.
- Address follow-up points from session or answers to questions that you didn't "get to" during the session in the session dialogue.
- Provide the speaker with: a thank you for the session, a list of outstanding action items for follow-up, a summary of the evaluation. Involve the speaker as appropriate with subsequent dialogue entries (additional questions, queries on session points)
- Post transcript in references.
- Apply for Continuing Education (CE) credits (supply background information on session, session summary, participant list to agent development manager). Notify participants if CE credits are awarded.
- Include item on the session in newsletter.

Online Session Participant Information E-mail

To: Session Participants

cc:

Subject: Critical Illness Online Session on May 9th
Critical Illness Insurance on the Agent Network
Guest Speaker Session with Laurel Pedersen
Session Outline

Thank you for signing up for this on-line session, scheduled for Wed., May 9th from 11:30 to 12:30 EDT. Here's an overview of the process and some suggestions that will help you get ready for the session. If you have any questions, please e-mail JJ.

If you've never participated in a chat, you may find it a double-barrelled learning experience—in content and in the technology, which sometimes gets a bit frustrating. So, RELAX and enjoy the session. We're here to help the technology work for you!

Get Ready!

If you haven't tried a chat, give it a whirl. You may not find anyone "in" there, but you can work through the functionality and talk to yourself if need be! (Deb and JJ do it all the time....) Usually there is a chat set up, or you can start one of your own from the initial chat screen. Try out using different colors. Refer to the Ready, Set, GO! User's Guide for further information. If you'd like to practice a chat, send JJ an e-mail and she'll make arrangements to "meet" you in chat for a trial run.

Become familiar with INSTANT MESSAGE. Once again if no one is on-line, it will be a bit difficult to "use"—but have a look at the features. You can use this feature during the chat if you experience any technical questions or want to send a "private" message to anyone on-line.

Get Set!

About 11:15 EDT, log into the Agent Network as you would normally do. Choose CHAT in the navigation bar. When the initial CHAT screen appears, click on Critical Illness Session. If you log in a bit earlier than the start time, we'll be ready to roll on time. (That's Newfoundland: 12:45, Atlantic: 12:15, Central: 10:15, Mountain: 9:15, Pacific: 8:15.)

Choose a colour—it helps distinguish you in the conversation. Please don't use Blue, which is reserved for the guest speaker, or Maroon, which is reserved for the facilitator. If people choose the same colours, we can adjust once we get started. You can experiment during the 11:15–11:30 log-in time.

GO!

The session will start at 11:30 EDT with a quick overview of the process.

Laurel will make a brief statement about the session and then we'll jump into the questions.

Contribute your thoughts, questions, or comments by typing in the text box at the bottom of the screen. Click on submit to contribute. (Tip: leave your cursor "over" the submit button—then when you get done typing, you can just click instead of taking the time to both position the mouse and click!)

If you've signed up as an observer... not to worry, you can still participate and join in the discussion. Or if you want to send an Instant Message to one of the participating members, they'll put up a question or comment for you.

Here's a tentative schedule:

11:15   Start to log in to Chat; choose colours—It's our WARM UP period

11:30   Introduction; overview of process: Deb

11:35   Laurel's opening comments

11:45   Discussion in Chat

12:25   Wrap up

12:30   End of session

The discussion will be available in its entirety in the REFERENCES section under View Files and Links. A summary of the presentation will also be available as an MS Word document in REFERENCES under View Files and Links.

"Tricks of the Trade"—How Chat Works

A few points to keep in mind:

There's a bit of lag time between when you submit and when your comments are posted.... so sometimes the conversation may be a bit disjointed. Just pretend you're at a party trying to follow several conversations at once. The facilitator will try to keep the flow going. Using different colours will help us keep "track" of the conversation.

Post questions one at a time, giving the people a chance to respond before you ask another one. This helps keep the conversation focused, finishing a point before moving on to the next.

Use short phrases and sentences. If you have a "long" comment, break it up into several "submits" so that people can start reading. Show that you are continuing your sentence with a " ...." then submit.

Spelellign dsen't coutnnt! Don't worry about typos. It's more important to keep the flow going. Don't worry about correcting spelling in your comments before you submit them! We're all in the same boat.

You can send a comment to anyone participating in the session using INSTANT MESSAGE. This message is seen only by the person whom you sent it to. Just click on INSTANT MESSAGE in the navigation bar and a window will appear. Choose the name of the person you'd like to send an instant message to, type your message, and submit. Remember that there is a delay as the message is sent, responded to, and returned to you.

The facilitator will direct traffic, both within the chat and via instant message. If things get a bit chaotic, TIME OUT might be called to regroup. If someone is monopolizing the conversation, the facilitator will encourage others to participate.

Having Problems?

We have a support team ready to help you with technical or functional problems during the session. You can:

Send an instant message to Deb Wallace, the head of our support team. (Please be patient. The INSTANT MESSAGE function takes a bit of time... Sorry!)

Phone 1-877-xxxxx. The Passcode is xxxxx. It's a toll free number where the support team will help you out.

Profiles

Agent Network Members:

Here's the list of participants as of today. We'll update it so that it's current for your participation on the 9th.

Guest Speaker:

Insert short description of person and his/her experience in the area.

Online Session Evaluation E-mail

To:	Session Participants
cc:	
Subject: Evaluation—Assistant Session	

Thank you for your participation in the Agent Network's first guest speaker session last week. I hope you can find a few minutes and provide us with your feedback. Given that this presentation was a TOTALLY new experience for many of us, your comments will help guide the development of other sessions in the community.

To respond, please click on "Reply with History", choose the Permanent Pen option in the toolbar or text drop-down menu (your answers will display in red for easy analysis), type in your answers below, and return to me at your convenience. If you prefer to be anonymous, print out the questionnaire, fill in your responses and forward to me at Head Office, location 01Q10.

Thanks again! Deb

Feedback on the Assistant Guest Speaker Session

Participant Profile: please answer yes or no

1. Was this your first experience with an "online" session?
2. Was this your first time using a "chat session"?

Pre-Session Information: please rate as 1 (poor) 3 (adequate) 5 (excellent) and add any comments

1. Dialogue entries introducing topic in the Agent Network:
2. Overview in Agent Network references:
3. Session Overview distributed via e-mail:

Session Content and Process: please rate as 1 (poor) 3 (adequate) 5 (excellent) and add any comments

1. Did the content meet your expectations?
2. Did you get some new ideas or references to consult?
3. Was it valuable to identify other agents in your same/similar situation?

Post-Session Information: please rate as 1 (poor) 3 (adequate) 5 (excellent) and add any comments

1. Session transcript in Agent Network references:

2. Session summary e-mailed:

3. Continued dialogue in the Agent Network:

General Comments:

1. What is your general impression of this way of presenting a topic—online with guest speakers and other agents?

2. What could we have done to make the session more valuable to you? Easier to use?

3. Are there other topics that you would like to see presented in this manner?

Communication Activities

The communication plan outlined audiences, key messages, and channels. To keep community development in the forefront of Clarica's knowledge strategy, we continued to promote the value proposition realized by this dynamic community. We developed short pieces to go into newsletters, made presentations to a wide range of groups internally and externally, and continued to promote the value of community participation to the members.

Agent News Item

"For agents; By agents" is the mantra for 150 Clarica agents across the country who are participating in the development of a community of practice, a place where agents can share expertise, experiences, and materials to help build their business.

Using a Web-based application, the founding members have developed discussions on 18 topics ranging from hiring an assistant to workplace marketing approaches to the pros and cons of incorporating. The community site also contains a reference center for agent-generated materials and a "real-time" chat facility for catching up with people online.

Phase I of the Agent Network continues until mid-March—a time to test the application, work out the kinks, identify activities of value, and outline guidelines for participation. Following an evaluation, plans are to extend the membership of the group.

The Agent Network is the only one of its kind in the insurance and financial services industry, breaking new ground not only in the use of web-based technology, but in sharing knowledge to spark innovation.

Community Newsletter

THE AGENT NETWORK UPDATE
FOR AGENTS; BY AGENTS

Welcome!

The Agent Network was "launched" on December 15th, using a Web-based application called Communispace. During the ramp-up period, agents have been logging in to check out the site's functionality, edit their profiles, and contribute ideas to various *Dialogues* and *Chat*.

The Agent Network was designed as a resource network for the Clarica agent community with the purpose:

To develop and share our personal, professional and technical expertise, leading to innovative strategies and growth of our business.

Dialogues

A number of topics are currently being "discussed" in the *Dialogue* section, including:

- approaches to a "tricky" case
- hiring assistants
- overcoming call reluctance
- planning for 2001

Log in to any or all of the discussions and contribute your thoughts!

References

The reference centre houses materials that have been generated by agents. To view these materials, Click on *References* in the navigation bar, then click on *Files and Links,* and choose an item. The reference material will be "displayed" in another window, in the application that it was developed with—like Microsoft Word or Excel. You can copy the file to your hard drive, print it from the site, and use it with your clients! Don't forget to comment on the item—your feedback helps extend our experience!

Check out Paul's piece on *Market Volatility* or Morris's *Product Kit Checklists* —plus others.

Help build the collection of agent generated resources and submit materials that you've found useful in your business!

Did you know . . .

Clarica agents lead the way! No other insurance or financial institution has developed a community of practice like the Agent Network. We're on the leading edge!

The Agent Network has 155 founding members. For a list, click on *Members*.

The launch on Dec. 15th logged many "firsts". Jeff was the first to try the *Instant Message* facility, only 45 minutes after the log-in information was distributed. Ron was the first to give *Chat* a try. Richard contributed the first comment to a *Dialogue*.

Haven't Logged in Yet?

The Agent Network is available whenever you have a few minutes—7 days a week, 24 hours a day. Access through your Internet browser or from Sales Force Central, click on Sales Tools & Advertising.

During your first visit, we suggest that you:

- orient yourself to the *home page* and *navigation panel*
- update your *member profile*
- contribute to a *dialogue*
- check-out *references*

Communispace Version 3.0

The Agent Network uses Communispace, a Web-based community-ware application that has won numerous awards for its innovative design. We've just upgraded to a new version, but there are a few bugs that are being addressed. We'll update you in the *home page announcements*.

Need Help?

Deb Wallace is our community facilitator and she'll help you with any problems that you're having. Can't get connected? Lost your password? Can't figure out how to "do" something in the site? .... whatever! Contact Deb at:

deb.wallace@clarica.com or agent.network@clarica.com

Step 7—Evaluate Purpose and Direction

In order to identify value, we measured activity in the community to gather quantitative data based on use and surveyed the membership using a third party to obtain qualitative data.

Usage Statistics

The following quantitative statistics were gathered three months after the launch to establish a benchmark for use and to provide feedback to the community and sponsors about the level of activity in the community. Due to the confidential nature of the discussions, titles of dialogues and references have been deleted.

Membership & Use by members:

1. Total number of members: 159

2. Frequency of log in:
   - Frequent (over 5 times a week)   5   3%
   - Above Average (3–5 times a week)   3   2%
   - Average (1–2 times a week)   18   11%
   - Infrequent (under once a week)   94   59%
   - Never logged in   39   25%

Dialogues:

1. Current dialogues underway   14
2. Current contributions   106
3. Archived dialogues   45
4. Archived contributions   416
5. Top five dialogues (based on number of contributions):
   - A   35
   - B   26
   - C   25
   - D   23
   - E   21

References:

1. Total number of items: 38
2. Agent Generated   30   79%
3. Facilitator Generated   8   21%
4. Total number of reviewers   263
5. Most frequently rated items and average rating:
    - A   6.9   40 reviewers
    - B   9.2   36 reviewers
    - C   7.5   18 reviewers
    - D   7.8   18 reviewers
    - E   8.5   16 reviewers
6. Top rated items (out of 10):
    - A   10   2 reviewers
    - B   9.5   6 reviewers
    - C   9.2   36 reviewers

Bookstore:

1. Total number of items: 13

Member Survey

The formal assessment was facilitated by our marketing research department, which created the following survey:

To:

cc:

Subject: Agent Network—your input please!

Dear Founding Member:

Phase I of the Agent Network was designed to introduce the concept of a community of practice supported by a facilitated Web-based application. It's now time to assess how far we've come, our approaches, the value you've seen, and where we want to head next. To ensure efficiency in design and confidentiality in tabulating the results, we've solic-

---

ited the help of the Marketing Department to develop and conduct the survey.

Please take a few minutes and complete the following survey. Your responses and recommendations are critical to the development of the Agent Network. "For Agents; By Agents" means that as a Founding Member, you have the opportunity to help shape the community for the benefit of all Clarica agents. A summary of the survey responses will be distributed to all members.

Thank you for your participation,

The Agent Network Steering Group

Please respond no later than Thursday @ 4:00 pm. The survey should take approximately 20 minutes to complete. Please rest assured that your individual answers will be kept completely confidential.

Instructions for completing the survey:

1. From the Lotus Notes toolbar, click on the Reply with History button.
2. Scroll down and complete the survey.

Once you have completed the survey, from the Lotus Notes toolbar, click on the Send button.

PLEASE PLACE AN "X" TO INDICATE YOUR RESPONSE(S):

Tell Us About Yourself

1. What is your current role?
   _____ Occupant Agent
   _____ Non-Occupant Agent
2. Are you a member of a _____ ?
   _____ Multi-Agent Organization (MAO)
   _____ Multi-Agent Corporation (MAC)
   _____ Neither
3. How long have you been an agent with Clarica?
   _____ Less than 1 year
   _____ Between 1 and 5 years
   _____ More than 5 years but less than 10 years
   _____ Ten years or more

4. Which of the following best describes your comfort level in using internet technology?

_____ Very comfortable

_____ Comfortable

_____ Somewhat comfortable

_____ Not at all comfortable

5. How often do you use the Agent Network?

_____ Never (proceed to question #6)

_____ 1–5 times per week (proceed to question #8)

_____ 6–10 times per week (proceed to question #8)

_____ More than 10 times per week (proceed to question #8)

6. Please indicate some reasons why you haven't used the Agent Network (proceed to question #7)

7. Do you use any other ways of sharing personal, professional and technical expertise with other Clarica agents?

_____ Yes, Please specify _____

_____ No

(Thank you for your participation. From the Lotus Notes Toolbar, please click on the SEND button)

8. How do you access the Agent Network? (Check all that apply)

_____ Home—Own ISP

_____ Office via the Ethernet

_____ Office Dial-Up

_____ Other, please specify _____

9. We would like to get an understanding of your experience using the Agent Network. Please place an "X" in the appropriate column to indicate your level of agreement with the following statements.

Statement	Strongly Agree	Agree	Disagree	Strongly Disagree
The purpose and objectives of the Agent Network is clear				
The Agent Network is user friendly				

Statement	Strongly Agree	Agree	Disagree	Strongly Disagree
Navigating around the Agent Network is straight-forward				
Adequate training materials are provided for the Agent Network				
Communication Updates (i.e., e-mails, newsletters) are informative				
Technical help/support for the Agent Network is sufficient				

10. Please indicate your level of participation for each of the following sections in the Agent Network site. Please place an "X" in the appropriate column.

Sections	I Read and Contributed	I Read Only
Dialogue		
References		
Bookstore		
Chat		
Poll		
Gallery		
Member Profiles		

11. We would like to get an understanding of the value/importance of the Agent Network. Please place an "X" in the appropriate column to indicate your level of agreement with the following statements.

Statement	Strongly Agree	Agree	Disagree	Strongly Disagree
The Agent Network provides me with an opportunity to grow personally, professionally, and technically.				
The Agent Network helps me create a network of colleagues who understand my issues and challenges				
The Agent Network provides me with links to product and market specialists				
The Agent Network introduces new ideas, approaches, and strategies				
The Agent Network made a difference to a sale				
The Agent Network helped clarify something I didn't understand before				
I consider my participation in the Agent Network to be a valuable experience				
I would encourage other agents to join				
The Facilitation role adds value to the Agent Network				

12. How important is it to continue having this Agent Network community?

_____ Very important

_____ Somewhat important

_____ Important

_____ Not at all important

13. Please describe any limitations/problems you have experienced using the Agent Network

14. Would you be interested in participating in a more in-depth interview regarding the Agent Network community?

_____ Yes

_____ No

Thank you for taking the time to complete this survey!

From the Lotus Notes toolbar, click on the Send button

Report—End of Phase I

The Agent Network community development project was an experiment into a new approach for building communities in a strategic context. After the formal evaluation, the project manager prepared a report for the sponsors and the Knowledge Team that outlined the assessment findings, identified a community development process model, and proposed a series of recommendations. While it isn't practical to include the entire report, an outline of the table of contents gives an idea of the type of report that should be prepared, especially when the community development project is serving as a pilot or test case.

Part I	Introduction and Project Overview
	Report Introduction
	The Agent Network Project Background
Part II	The Community of Practice Development Model
	Identifying the Model: Process Overview
	Outline of Each Step and Its Components
	Overview
	Objectives
	Actions and Illustrations

             Resources Required

             Deliverables

             Key Issues

             Best Practice

   Part III Insights and Reflections

             Outlined by Step

   Part IV   Recommendations

             Recommendations to Sponsors and Outline of Next Steps

             Recommendations on Community Development Strategy

             Recommendations for Community Administration
             Processes

             Recommendation for Community Coordinating Role

   Appendix

             Sample of Communication Materials

             Sample of Community Activity Guidelines

             Sample of Policy Statements and Guidelines

             Outline of Items in the Community Discussion Database

STEP 8—EXPAND THE COMMUNITY

The founding members had carried the community through its pilot phase and recommended that the membership be expanded. At the same time, the Steering Group recommended that a number of policies and guidelines should be drafted for discussion by the community. These governance items would help orient new members and prepare the community for increasing the depth of their conversations and their sophistication as a forum for generating capabilities. Two illustrations of draft documents are included. These guidelines were prepared by the community facilitator and were situated not as "policing policies" but as guidelines that would help members make decisions about their own participation.

To continue the goodwill between Clarica and the community, the Steering Group and the project sponsors sent letters of recognition to the founding members. In doing so, they strengthened the foundation on which to expand the community.

Guidelines for Agent Network Participation and Liaison with Clarica

Overview

The Agent Network is a community of practice established by Clarica for a selected group of agents from across the country. Community facilitation and a communication infrastructure are supplied by Clarica. The discussion content, community activities, and related knowledge-sharing materials are provided by the agent members, assisted as appropriate by the community facilitator.

As outlined below, the Agent Network is a place where members can trust that their participation is confidential. From a technology perspective, we implemented special measures to ensure the security of the data. From a community development perspective, the Steering Group outlined guidelines of responsible participation for members. And from a facilitation perspective, guidelines govern the roles and responsibilities of the community facilitator.

Upholding confidentiality is a key responsibility for all members. In order to participate fully, members must trust that their comments are exchanged only within the community and have confidence that the community's purpose is not compromised by another member, the community facilitator, or members of the Steering Group.

Guiding Principles

The Agent Network slogan, For Agents; By Agents, sets the tone for the following principles:

1. Invited agents, members of the Agent Network Steering Group, and the community facilitator form the community membership.

2. Access to the Agent Network is for members only.

3. Confidentiality regarding client information, individual contributions of members, or Agent Network discussions and activities is the responsibility of all members.

4. The community is founded as a vehicle for sharing knowledge and expertise, collaboratively developing strategies, and collectively addressing issues confronting agents.

5. The Agent Network's purpose statement provides direction for the community:

To develop and share our personal, professional, and technical expertise, leading to innovative strategies and growth of our business.

Code of Participation

These guidelines form a base from which members can assess their own and other members' contributions and participation. They are not intended to restrict the actions of members, but to provide direction for continuing the community's development. As a community of practice for insurance and financial professionals, the Agent Network is an extension of the agents' commitment to quality practice in the industry and to quality service for their customers.

1. The Code of Business Practice for Clarica Agents (available on Sales Force Central) sets out the minimum standards of ethical conduct and behavior for all agents and serves as the basic guide to participation in the Agent Network.

2. The Agent Network is a confidential knowledge exchange. This confidentiality extends to:

   - Individuals as subjects—Outside of the community, we don't disclose information that would identify people (e.g., clients, staff, other agents) whom we may refer to in discussions or other form of contributions.

   - Individuals as members—Outside of the community, we don't discuss specific dialogue contributions or other items submitted by a member to the community (e.g., identifying an opinion expressed in a dialogue).

   - The Agent Network—Outside of the community, we don't discuss specific topics and activities that form the collaborative knowledge creation and sharing among members of the community.

   From time to time, it may be appropriate to inform people outside of the Agent Network of particular issues and opportunities discussed within the community or to seek additional resources from other agents or Clarica staff. See the following section on Clarica Liaison for further information.

3. Access to the Agent Network is restricted to members. Temporary log-ins are available for specific purposes. Guest speakers and others (e.g., agency trainers) can be profiled as guests upon request to the community facilitator. Member log-in information should be maintained in a secure place. Contact the community facilitator for misplaced log-in information.

4. Reflecting the professional nature of the Agent Network, discussions should be constructive and courteous. Issues should be pre-

sented with the intent of finding solutions, not finding fault or laying blame. Abusive language and other derogatory comments are not permitted.

5. The Agent Network is a peer-regulated group where members ensure that the community's purpose is upheld. The Steering Group acts as the governing body that makes decisions, based on member input and functions as a second layer of regulatory action. Questionable participation can be identified by a member or the community facilitator. The action may be brought to the attention of the member by another member or by the community facilitator. In any instance, the questionable action should be framed as a learning experience, an opportunity to further our collective understanding of community.

6. Membership in the Agent Network brings a certain degree of commitment on the part of each member. While levels of participation will vary over time depending on the members' work and personal commitments and their interest in the current Agent Network activities, members are encouraged to be active members in the community.

7. Addition information on participation can be found in:

   - Guidelines for Contributing Materials to the Agent network: References, Bookstore, and Gallery

   - Facilitator Guidelines: Roles and Responsibilities—provides direction for the community facilitator's conduct

   - Using the Community Application—Security and Privacy Issues

Clarica Liaison Process

Benefits of a liaison process between the Agent Network and Clarica:

- Relay concerns raised in the Agent Network to appropriate Clarica staff;
- Obtain information to clarify and/or assist the development of a resolution to address an issue or opportunity;
- Communicate the value of the Agent Network as a knowledge-sharing resource to sponsors and senior executives;
- Avoid misconceptions that can be the result of exclusivity of membership and nonparticipation of any Clarica staff.

Forms of Liaison:

1. Informal e-mail or telephone conversation
2. Meeting
3. Summary in standard report or presentation

Liaison Process Guiding Principles:

1. Protect the confidentiality of the member/contributor and the Agent Network.
2. Establish the context. Simply lifting dialogue contributions and forwarding sections could result in misrepresenting the nature of the inquiry.
3. Present information in a concise, clear, and objective manner.
4. Facilitate a timely resolution.

Outline of liaison process:

1. Member identifies topic/item that requires further clarification and requests that the community facilitator seeks input from Clarica.
2. Facilitator identifies topic/item that requires further clarification, contacts member/contributor(s), provides notice that additional information is being sought (i.e., posts a comment in the dialogue or sends an e-mail to the appropriate members), contacts appropriate Clarica resource, provides feedback to the community.
3. If warranted, topic/item is referred to the Steering Group for discussion and recommended action

Guidelines for Contributing Materials to the Agent Network: References, Bookstore, and Gallery—Draft for Discussion

Overview

The Agent Network is a place where agents can "share their knowledge." Often this knowledge is in a tangible format, such as a text document, a chart or table, or a photograph. As guidelines, the following points are intended to help each community member make decisions on the item content and the contribution process.

These guidelines focus on 3 key issues:

- Relevance—Is the item something that will help me make a sale? Improve my business organization? Strengthen my relationship with my clients?
- Reliability—Is the content correct? Current? Clear? Compliant?
- Copyright—Is the material under copyright? Did I give credit to the original source?

References

The references section can store items in a variety of material formats. These guidelines are focused on items that are contributed as "reference materials."

Criteria for Contribution

1. Source of item—emphasis is placed on original materials that have been generated by agents or their employees.
2. Availability—in order to avoid duplication of information, materials should not be "found" anyplace else in Clarica resources. Instead, links or directions on where to find existing materials should be contributed.
3. Relevance—materials should be related to growing an agent's business.
4. Reliability—information must be correct and verifiable.

Examples: agent articles, presentations, case studies, conference or course summaries, sales & marketing tools (newsletters, client letters), business support tools.

Responsibility of the Contributor

1. Verify item's authenticity. Check source of the material. Verify with Compliance if you have any concern on impact due to possible use by other agents. A Compliance review can be requested by the author of the item, or the community facilitator can submit it on the author's behalf if requested.
2. Give credit to source if not original to the agent. If modified, include name and date of original source.
3. Provide an overview of the item. (See format below)

4. Assign key word from existing list. (If there is no appropriate key word, contact the community facilitator to establish. Maintaining valid keywords is crucial to accurate searching.)

5. Include introductory information at the beginning of each item (See format below)

6. Include disclaimer statement.

7. Keep information current, or remove item when no longer current.

Reference Format:

Introductory paragraph—(limit 250 characters). In the site, this is the description that will appear in the references section as an overview of the item.

- Title—a concise descriptor of the item
- Brief overview of material with emphasis on application—how the time is used with your clients
- Your name as contributor
- Author's name if different from member submitting the item and date originally created
- File format (Word, Excel, PDF)

Item Header—to be placed at the top of the item to be contributed (within the document).

- Title of item
- Author
- Date submitted
- Original source (if other than agent generated), including author's name and date of creation

Disclaimer—Draft (under review!)

This material has been posted on the Agent Network as a reference. It has been developed with the best of my ability to ensure accuracy and reliability. Neither Clarica nor I assume liability that may result from the use of this material. (Agent name)

Reference Example:

Introductory Paragraph:

Clarica CI / Competitor Comparison

Laurel, Clarica Retail Insurance Product Manager, provides a comparison of two CI products as a reference for her online Critical Illness session. Word document. JJ Smits. May 10/01

Item:

Clarica CI / Competitor Comparison

Laurel

May 10, 2001

Submitted by: JJ Smits

(Body of document)

This material has been posted on the Agent Network as a reference. It has been developed with the best of my ability to ensure accuracy and reliability. Neither Clarica nor I assume liability that may result from the use of this material. (JJ Smits)

Responsibility of the User

1. The majority of the items in references are intended for individual use. They can be copied (especially items such as product checklist, yearly planning guides) for use in an agent's business.

2. Some items are copyrighted by the author (e.g., newspaper items, journal articles, brochure items) and should not be copied in multiples for distribution. These articles are intend for personal use only.

3. If a member has a question or concern about the contents of a reference item, contact the member who contributed the item.

4. If a member has a question on using or distributing an item, please contact the community facilitator.

Bookstore

The bookstore highlights books or other items that agents have found helpful with their businesses.

Criteria for Contribution:

1. Relevance—items should be related to growing an agent's business.

2. Availability—items should be available for purchase (i.e., in print) or loan (i.e., Clarica's Business Information Service, public library, or personal collection).

3. Reviewed—item should have been read in whole or in part by the submitting agent.

Responsibility of the Contributor:

1. Verify that information about the item is correct (e.g., author, title)
2. Provide a descriptive overview of the item. (See format below)
3. Provide a link for online purchasing.

Bookstore Format:

The majority of the "format" is managed by the form that you fill in when submitting the item. In the descriptive paragraph, please include:

1. Brief overview of the item, including your evaluation of its strengths
2. Your name

Example:

"Risk is a Four Letter Word: The Asset Allocation Approach to Investing"

When George Harman first released Risk is a Four Letter Word, it became a classic guide to the world of financial planning, and Hartman won over 50,000 readers with his shrewd investment tips. You'll learn about the advantages and drawbacks of money managers, as well as the importance of not trying to outguess the markets—all through a clear, straightforward text that eschews number-crunching in favour of sound fiscal planning.
Recommended by Jeff Saunders

Gallery

Pictures can say a thousand words, and Gallery is a place to do just that!

Criteria for Contribution

1. Relevance—items should be related to growing an agent's business.
2. Uniqueness—items should not be "available" in other agent resource databases

Responsibility of the Contributor

1. If the photo subject(s) is other than the contributor, permission from the subject(s) to include should be obtained prior to submitting.
2. Provide title and brief overview of exhibit focus.

Gallery Format

1. Title
2. Description of photo collection

Gallery Example:

Online Session on Assistants

Here's what "command central" looked like for the Agent Network's first guest speaker session.

Contribution Process

The technical process for contributing items to References, Bookstore, or Gallery is outlined in:

- The Agent Network—Ready, Set, GO! User's Guide. Consult your paper copy or access an electronic copy in the Agent Network references section.
- The Agent Network site help facility.
- If you need assistance, please contact the Agent Network facilitator.

Letters of Recognition to Founding Members

Letters were sent to founding members from the community sponsors. A general letter was sent to all members, and a special letter was sent to founding members who had made a significant contribution to creating community value.

Dear Founding Member of the Agent Network,

We thought it was a good idea. We thought you might be interested in trying out some new technology. We thought you liked our plan to get the ball rolling. And we thought you could make the industry sit up and take notice as Clarica agents led the way once again. Well, you did all that—AND MORE!

We didn't expect the Agent Network would leap out of the starting gate with the speed it did. We didn't expect you to exceed industry standards so significantly. We didn't expect you to embrace the new technology so easily. And we sure didn't expect to see such amazing benefits so quickly! Our sponsors are thrilled with the success! Other agents are clamouring to join up. Other organizations are asking, "How did they do it?" Other Clarica communities want to get rolling.

As a founding member, you are responsible for taking the idea of a community and giving it more than we could have hoped to receive. You took a leap of faith ("They want us to do what?") and ran with the vision of an agent network.

Thank you for all of your efforts in getting the Agent Network off the ground. Your commitment and dedication made our job easy (Well, relatively easy—you did throw a couple of curve balls!). We look forward to the next phase of the Agent Network's development and to your continued involvement.

With sincere thanks, on behalf of the Agent Network Steering Group,

Jacqueline J. Smits,
The Agent Network Facilitator

Letter to Outstanding Members from the Sponsors

Dear Founding Member of the Agent Network,

Last October when we invited you to participate in creating the Agent Network, we knew the combination of market and product expertise, years of experience, and dedication to excellent customer service found among the Phase I participants would be key to the success of this endeavor. What we didn't expect were such phenomenal results in this short a period of time.

On all accounts, the Agent Network has exceeded our expectations. The level of participation, depth and breadth of the discussions, quality of references, and commitment to sharing your knowledge has been astounding. The recent Phase I evaluation showed you've significantly surpassed industry standards, creating a benchmark that "raises the bar" on what communities of practice within organizations can accomplish.

Your participation in building the Agent Network is a credit to your dedication in creating the best organization possible from which to serve your clients. You've not only helped to build a foundation on which to grow this community, you've paved the way for establishing more communities throughout Clarica.

On behalf of Jack and John [the other sponsors], I would like to thank you for your commitment to establishing this ground-breaking knowledge-sharing community. We look forward to working with you as the Agent Network expands its membership and continues to develop in its next phase.

With continued best wishes and thanks,

Hubert Saint-Onge
Senior Vice President, Strategic Capabilities

References

Kiser, A.G. (1998). *Masterful Facilitation: Becoming a Catalyst for Meaningful Change.* New York: American Management Association.

Chapter 11

COMMUNITIES AS CATALYSTS FOR CHANGE

From conceptual to tactical to operational. In all areas of the economy, we are on a developmental trajectory, moving at rates never witnessed before in our history. With market demands shaping the way organizations interact with their customers and each other and technology innovations driving changes in how organizations function, we indeed live in interesting times. Understanding the value of communities of practice to an organization and identifying ways to support and nurture them are only preliminary steps in the developmental process underway in the knowledge era. We've provided a context for the need and outlined an approach for generating capabilities and applying knowledge, based on our experience of building communities of practice situated in a strategic context. But where are communities going? How will this new way of thinking about an age-old social structure influence the evolution of organizations and spawn new business models?

COMMUNITIES AT WORK

As practitioners, our purpose has been to provide a context for our work and illustrate a course of action from a variety of perspectives based on our experience. Our challenge has been to provide a strong conceptual framework and outline concrete applications while highlighting the contribution of knowledge-focused work to improving the performance of an individual, a practice, and ultimately an organization.

313

In organizations that have turned the corner and embraced the challenges and opportunities of the knowledge era, the "What's in it for ME?" value proposition for supporting communities of practice is not difficult to identify. But we are only seeing the tip of the iceberg of possibility that communities present.

With this last chapter, we'd like to suggest a developmental cycle for communities of practice within an organization—a transition to a new organizational model where communities of practice become a complimentary structure to the traditional accountability hierarchy. We'll begin with a look at a maturity model that presents a path for this transition and then discuss the components of the new structure. We'll also look at the role that communities of practice can play as agents of change in the transition to the new organizational structure. And, finally, we'll look at challenges to successfully complete this transition.

It's highly probable that communities of practice at some point in the range we discussed in Chapter 2 already exist in your organization. You many not be aware of them, but groups of people who have a common interest in collectively meeting challenges in the workplace are getting together on an informal basis to talk about ways of improving their practice. Recognizing their existence and the value they create is the first step toward leveraging this valuable structure that is an inherent part of your organization.

We plot the progression for leveraging communities of practice in Figure 11.1. The vertical axis shows the development of an organization's ability to increase the meta-capabilities of learning and collaboration through a shift in culture. The horizontal axis represents the increased integration of collaborative technologies on an enterprise-wide platform. As an organization's focus and energies are applied to increasing in both directions, the foundation is in place to further develop and leverage communities of practice as a strategic tool.

Sporadic Emergence of Communities

At the earliest stage of development, an organization becomes aware that communities of practice exist. Through the entrepreneurial spirit of individual community members or the keen eye of a business unit manager, the value of these communities that are working under your nose is recognized. A curiosity may spark further discussion about what these communities are "up to." How do they operate to provide capability

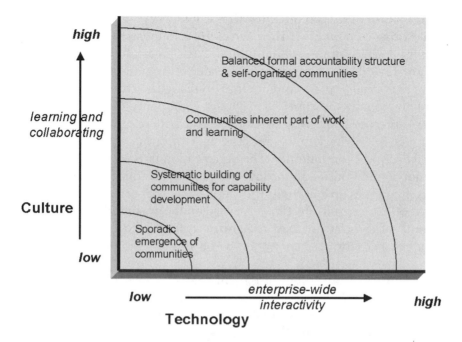

Figure 11.1.
Maturity Model: Communities of Practice within an Organization

generating forums that improve practice? What was the need that brought them together? How do they collaborate to find solutions to their problems? How do they share the new knowledge that they create? What effect do they have on their members? What new approaches have they been able to introduce to their practice?

Systematic Building of Communities

As we progress through the maturity model, the value of communities of practice as vessels for learning and collaboration has been recognized by people at the senior management level. It's unlikely that there will be unilateral acceptance, but a "toe hold" is established, and a champion for sponsoring a systematic approach to community building provides the leadership and resources necessary to develop a strategy.

The organization, existing community members, and other interested people enter into a collaborative learning process of their own—a joint effort to learn about communities of practice. What's the best way to nurture existing communities? How do we put a foundation in place to support the creation of new communities? What pieces do we have in place already? How do we communicate the value of communities to the rest of the organization—to put communities on the radar screen?

At this point, the efforts to support community building take two paths—directions that may be simultaneously developed, but have distinct, yet intertwined, purposes. The first direction is focused on the development of communities. The organization must create the foundation for communities—all the logistics that we identified in Chapter 6 to get communities up and running or to increase support for existing communities. The second direction is focused on the organization—the development of a strategy that recognizes communities as part of the organizational fabric.

Communities as an Inherent Part of the Organization

As capability generation continues to become more ingrained in the organization's culture and the enterprise-wide technology platform integrates more tools for collaboration and communication, the organization begins to rely on communities of practice as a primary source of learning and knowledge creation. The community also facilitates the acquisition and enhancement of meta-capabilities that enable individuals to accelerate their own rate of learning, which in turn builds organizational capabilities. The organization's knowledge base is also increased, growing in value as the community generates new knowledge and adds these objects to repositories for reuse.

Trust has been improved and is operating at a higher level than ever achieved before. The value propositions to the individual, the community, and the organization have increased to the point that customers and shareholders are recognizing performance improvements and strengthening their relationships with the organization. And the speed and agility with which the organization can innovate to find new integrated solutions are contributing at a significant level to realizing the organization's strategic imperatives.

At this stage, the organization has the partnering mindset and capability to successfully participate in the value creation networks that we discussed in Chapter 4—a strategic advantage for succeeding in the knowledge era.

Effective Balance Between Existing and New Organizational Structures

As the organization continues its evolution through the maturity model, it has now implemented a new organizational structure. The traditional hierarchical accountability spine still exists as the bricks of the organization, but the mortar is now made up of a network of communities that come in all shapes and sizes.

This new organizational structure has a high degree of integration of its culture and its technology, has broadly embraced the meta-capabilities of learning and collaboration as the way to generate new knowledge, and relies on communities of practice to innovate at the speed necessary to meet the demands of its marketplace.

Communities of practice have become an integral part of the organization—a strategic tool that has enabled the organization to outperform its goals. Recognized as world-class in its area of expertise, the organization is well positioned to meet the next set of challenges that will fuel its continued evolution.

COMMUNITIES OF PRACTICE INTERTWINE WITH THE ORGANIZATION'S ACCOUNTABILITY SPINE

In order to create organizations that fully realize their potential in the knowledge era, we need to rethink organizational structures. The traditional lines-and-boxes framework of the hierarchical organization is not able to maximize learning and collaboration or effectively participate in value creation networks that provide integrated solutions to customers. It needs to be complemented with a structure that creates a highly effective environment that fosters the development of these meta-capabilities.

Wrapped around the accountability spine and integrated with the existing hierarchical structure of the organization, communities of all shapes and sizes will provide the muscle and flesh needed to perform with a speed and an agility that keep the organization ahead of market demands—to participate in a sense-and-respond model that meets customer needs as opposed to a make-and-sell model that falls short of customer expectations (see Figure 11.2).

We don't believe that there will be a single leap to this new structure. Rather, over time as communities of practice (as well as other types of communities) are appreciated for the value they provide the organization,

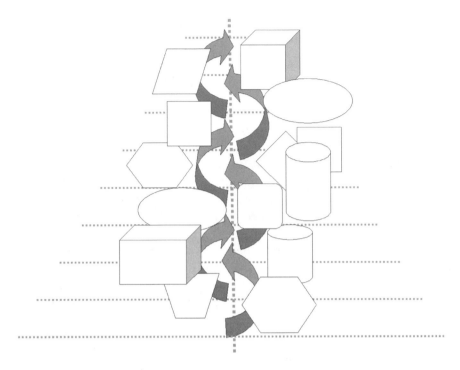

Figure 11.2.
Communities of Practice and the Accountability Spine

they will gain recognition as an essential component of the organizational structure. Communities will function at multiple levels with various purposes and different levels of attachment to the accountability spine of the organization.

Communities will become the focal point for learning, relying on the expertise of their members who have in turn fully embraced a self-initiated learning culture and taken full responsibility for increasing their capabilities.

As networks of communities emerge as an integral structure, organizations will keep an accountability spine that will be flatter and more empowering to ensure that the checks and balances inherent in current accountabilities are effectively addressed throughout the organization. Various communities of practice that represent the many forms of communities in the range we discussed in Chapter 2 will come to complement the traditional organizational structure, filling needs that it was never designed to meet. The combination of the two structures adds up to an entirely new form of organizational design, one that takes advantage of the complementary strengths of both approaches. They co-exist in support of each other, building-in a level of coherence and resilience that would be unattainable by either structure on its own.

COMMUNITIES OF PRACTICE AS CATALYSTS FOR CHANGE

Communities of practice are at the core of the organizational transformation that has already begun. They are one of the primary agents of change that will prepare organizations to more successfully operate in the knowledge era, in which knowledge capital will be readily recognized as a core asset of an organization and strategies will be focused on generating that capital through learning and collaboration.

We'll move beyond thinking of knowledge capital in terms of intellectual property rights, patents, and formulas that currently count toward the financial health of an organization. And organizational capabilities (strategy, systems, structure, culture, and leadership) will complement the value of an employee as an asset rather than as a cost or liability to the organization. As catalysts for change, communities of practice can help the organization evolve in significant ways.

Build Internal Capabilities Parallel to Marketplace Factors

If an organization is going to be able to keep up with its marketplace, staying ahead rather than lagging behind market demands, it must be able to align its capabilities with the fast-changing demands of the market. For example, if the market is demanding an integrated solution, then the organization has to have the capabilities to develop, provide, and support an integrated solution. It needs to develop the capabilities to participate in a multiple partner value creation network. If the market demands Internet options for completing transactions and obtaining support via the Web, then the organization must have Web-enabled capabilities to offer the necessary systems, products, and services.

To create an effective sense-and-respond model, the organization must clearly know what the customer wants, which underscores the importance of building and sustaining high-quality customer relationships—a key element of an organization's knowledge capital.

Whether gathering outside expertise to inform a resolution to a problem in practice or market intelligence to inform strategy development, communities of practice function as conduits into the organization. They channel external information that is then analyzed and used to create new strategies based on customer needs and environmental factors. Communities can directly affect the organization's ability to stay ahead of market demand by practicing internally what is expected externally. In a sense, communities of practice infuse the organization with the same dynamics that have already been adopted by the marketplace. Communities provide the catalyst for creating organizational capability that will enable the organization to put the right strategies and systems in place in order to stay relevant to its customers.

Communities Strengthen Customer Relationships

Communities of practice play a significant role in building an organization's customer capital. The community model need not only include internal members. We've already seen the value of creating customer communities in consumer-driven organizations. Customer communities can act as conduits to an organization. But to have successful customer communities, the organization must have the internal capabilities necessary to create and grow communities.

At Clarica, one of the organization's goals with the Agent Network was to segue to customer communities. By participating in a community of practice, agents could increase their own capabilities—learning how a community functions, how to encourage participation through purposeful facilitation, and how a community creates value. In turn, agents could establish communities of their own customers. Within these communities, agents could interact via multiple channels, strengthen the customer relationship, and create a collaborative learning environment that engages the customer more directly in the organization. The opportunity to learn with the customer is a significant strategic advantage for any organization.

Communities Build Meta-Capabilities Needed to Increase Individual and Organizational Capabilities

We can't emphasize strongly enough the need to build the meta-capabilities of collaboration and learning within the organization—the generative capabilities that enable the organization to gain the required capabilities and increase its knowledge capital. Effective communities are highly functioning platforms for learning and collaborating. These meta-capabilities are strengthened each time a productive inquiry leads the community on a journey to find an appropriate answer, situated in past experience, informed by new insights, and guided by tacit knowledge that has never been articulated.

More and more we are convinced that an organization's performance is based on the quality of its conversations—internally with employees and externally with customers, potential customers, and partners. Through conversations we learn what customers want, where the marketplace is heading, what expertise is held by other organizations—the collective knowledge of the economy. Without quality conversations, we are not able to challenge assumptions, make decisions, or innovate in a meaningful way. Conversations are central to community building. The value isn't in mining existing data, but in talking with experts to learn from experience, extend ideas, and create new knowledge.

A vibrant organization must continue to challenge its assumptions, creating the healthy tension that encourages individuals to "sharpen their saws" and collaborate on the development of new integrated solutions that contribute to the growth of the organization.

Communities of practice provide their members and ultimately their organizations with the meta-capabilities they need to manage the demands for the continuous generation of capabilities.

Communities Increase the Capabilities an Organization Needs to Participate in a Value Creation Network

In a networked economy, organizations that do not participate in a value creation network will quickly fall behind their competitors. Customers are demanding complex, integrated solutions that few organizations could produce in isolation.

The value chains that organizations are most familiar with consist of linking internal capabilities to provide a single solution. With the emergence of knowledge-driven business networks, the costs associated with transacting across organizations have gone down dramatically. As a result, it is now more cost effective to partner across organizations that excel in particular aspects of the value chain than it is to have to develop all the capabilities required within one organization. The integrated solutions that will satisfy customer needs will be generated through partnerships of organizations that bring to the table a world-class advantage in their respective area(s).

Communities of practice create and enhance the capabilities needed to fully participate in a value creation network. The art of productive inquiry that stimulates collaborative problem solving by accessing existing knowledge, validating that knowledge in the experience of its members, and creating new knowledge for effective action is at the center of a community's ability to advance organizational capabilities to partner and jointly innovate.

Communities Leverage the Next Stage of Technology Capability

In Chapter 4 we discussed the maturation process of technology, showing how technology has developed from data management to information management to knowledge management. With communities, technology advances another step in the support of collaboration, which requires the reconciliation of the culture with emerging collaborative technologies.

The key challenge to technology is to move people to the next level of virtual work. The tools that exist today still fall short of supporting the social needs of human interactions. The socio-technical integration required hasn't developed to the level that can support the richness of human encounters. However, organizations can't afford to wait until this integration is achieved. Organizations have to enter the technology arena and evolve with the advances. Otherwise, they will be so far behind in incorporating technology into their work processes and culture that they will never be able to catch up.

As agents of change, communities of practice introduce new methods for collaborating. Blended with other channels of communication, technology provides an opportunity for collaboration at a different level—in instances where geography, physical handicaps, or work demands make face-to-face and other forms of communication impossible. Communities using virtual spaces will help us better understand ways to address the challenges of building trust, supporting spontaneity and serendipity, and leveraging the dynamics of human interchange within a virtual environment.

Not only do communities provide an opportunity for organizations to leverage their investment in a technology platform, they advance the capabilities of the organization to take full advantage of the next stages of technology development.

Communities Represent a New Value Proposition

Participation in communities of practice represents a new value proposition to the individual. As a resource, a learning space, a place to test ideas and innovate with colleagues outside a work-focused team, communities serve to enhance the attachment of the individual to the organization. The community meets personal needs that cannot be fulfilled in what has become the standard organizational form. Rather than finding themselves as anonymous parts of a performance machine, members of a community of practice find that they share commitment for the realization of their collective purpose and for enhancing one another's capabilities. The commitment of communities to their members is at a significantly higher level than that of cross-functional work groups who come together to complete a project and regroup for the next task at hand.

Communities make a commitment to steward the knowledge base of the practice and engage the participants in value-added activities that increase individual capabilities. This new value proposition extends to the long term; it doesn't stop at short-term needs.

Communities Shape a New Organizational Structure

We've come full circle to our opening point—communities of practice have the potential to form an integral part of a new organizational structure where a network of communities complements the existing accountability structure. The transformative potential of communities has a relatively low threshold of entrance. Communities of some form exist in all organizations. The building blocks to support further community development are also more than likely available to some degree in an organization.

What may be missing is the recognition of the value of communities—though not from the point of view of members. They already know the value, otherwise they wouldn't be participating at the level that they do. The recognition of potential value more than likely needs to be realized at the management level and then engendered across the organization in a systematic way through a developmental approach similar to the maturity model we outlined at the beginning of this chapter.

Community Maturity Model

At the early stage of community development for the organization, we noted that, in order to incorporate a systematic approach for building communities, the organization not only needs to put the logistics in place to build communities, it has to develop a strategy that situated community development as a strategic tool—part of the organizational structure.

While we've spent the majority of this chapter outlining the value of leveraging communities as change agents in the transformation of the organization to a new structure, we need to take a step back and look at the maturity model of communities themselves. The organization's evolution to a new organizational model with a highly integrated accountability spine and complementary network of communities is totally dependent on the development of the communities that create that network.

As Figure 11.2 shows, the network is made-up of all different communities from the full range of community types we discussed in Chapter 2. However, to achieve the highest level of integration of community and accountability models, a significant number of communities of practice will need to be functioning at the structured level. And within these structured communities, a high degree of effective performance will be needed to support the balance of the complementary components of a new integrated organizational structure.

To maximize the value of communities, we have to proceed in a systematic manner, building communities through the steps we outlined in the community development process. We also need a strategic context in the organization that will foster the development of these communities (see Chapters 3 and 4).

For the structured communities of practice to contribute at this level of organizational development, roles of people working in and supporting communities need to evolve:

- **Leadership:**

    The exercise of leadership will evolve from a "command and control" to a partnering culture, where leadership is focused on actively engaging the employee through stewardship and appreciation in order to elicit commitment and ownership from employees. New leadership capabilities will be needed to replace the traditional model, where the dominance style of leadership has produced a passive following characterized by an attitude of compliance and entitlement in employees—cultural norms that are still well entrenched in many organizations.

    With the new integrated organizational structure, leadership capabilities are not reserved for executives and managers—they will be needed by all individuals in the organization. A leadership culture of self-initiation, interdependence, and shared success through the achievement of others will be required.

- **Individual:**

  In a network of communities structure, employees will belong to multiple communities and subcommunities. They will need to develop their interpersonal skills, learn to effectively collaborate and participate in the community, and increase their abilities to multitask and innovate. The demands on time and attention will require self-management of schedules and energies. A new feeling of self-satisfaction from the success of the community as well as individual achievement will strengthen an individual's commitment to participate.

  The community will be the employees' focus for learning. Their responsibility to contribute to the community's knowledge will require a knowledge-sharing rather than knowledge-hoarding mindset. This will be in large part fostered by a leadership culture that engenders high levels of trust and shared ownership for the success of the organization.

- **Managerial:**

  Managers will need to learn to manage without direct control. The resource management process will need to evolve to a different level where resources are allocated to projects and/or communities. The management of resources will have to be monitored from the perspective of the whole rather than focused on a segment, as in a traditional department or business unit. A single manager may not control or even have accountability for the outcomes. As a result, it will become even more important for managers to find the right people with the right capabilities to be able to function in a context where success depends on personal responsibility and self-initiation.

As the organization gradually becomes more and more networked through communities, an added challenge will be to facilitate a robust interchange internally and externally with customers and partners. This will require that managers give up direct control, remain fluid, and yet maintain coherence. In optimizing performance, the key managerial contribution becomes that of creating the right organizational context and ensuring that interdependencies are effectively managed through partnering.

As an agent of change, communities of practice prepare an organization to not only survive in the knowledge era, but to thrive and continue to grow. Just as the industrial revolution left behind companies that couldn't successfully automate their processes, organizations that can't collectively share and create new knowledge won't survive the change that is fuelled by increasing societal and market demands.

With an ability to realize the benefits of being a knowledge-driven organization, to span the knowing-doing gap, to effectively use knowledge assets, and to maximize advances in technology, communities provide a vehicle for leveraging expertise through quality conversations that increase individual and organizational capabilities and affect performance.

Challenges to Communities as Change Agents

The evolution to a new organizational structure is not without its challenges. As practitioners involved in numerous changes, we rely on history and our own experience to show us that any organizational change has challenges at multiple levels. Clarica is at the beginning of the maturity model we discussed earlier in this chapter. We're currently building momentum for a systematic approach to community building at the enterprise-wide level. Identifying the challenges helps inform the process and build on the precursors for success that we discussed in Chapter 4.

We can look at challenges to communities as agents of change from the many perspectives that exist within the community structure.

Challenges to the Individual

As we transition to communities of practice as a key organizational structure, individuals will face challenges, especially people who have not developed their interpersonal skills nor have an affinity for collaborating. Within a community structure, individuals will need to learn how to distribute their attention and energy across multiple communities as part of their time-management approach. Self-organizing skills that manage priorities and ensure that commitments are met may need to be further developed.

New mindsets will be necessary to manage a network of relationships that may have blurred lines of responsibility and accountability. Individuals will also need to honestly recognize their own capability gaps and initiate learning that is aligned with accountability and performance. The commitment required to actively take part in communities will need to stem from an experientially based conviction that working collaboratively through communities brings higher levels of capability and performance than not participating.

Challenges to the Community

The organization is not responsible for the community—the community is responsible for itself. With this responsibility comes the key challenge of maintaining relevance to its membership. Just as organizations need to strengthen their relationships with their customers in order to understand their needs, the community must stay in tune with its members. Above all else, the community must remain relevant to members by providing them with a high-trust environment in which they can increase their capabilities and solve the challenges to their practice. As communities become a more integral part of the organization, they must also be relevant to the strategic imperatives of the organization.

The creative tensions that challenge the community to continue in its development are managed by the community through facilitation and guided by evolving community conventions. These tensions may also need the implementation of a liaison process between the community and the organization. Issues that affect the community's or a member's ability to perform will need to be resolved through a process that brings the issue to the attention of the appropriate leadership and facilitates a resolution to the problem. In doing so, the community fulfills its role as a strategic tool to the organization—a tool that can be used to address differences of opinion and challenges to the collective mindset that forms the organization's culture.

Challenges to the Organization

Perhaps the challenges to the organization are the most daunting. The organization is challenged to assess its core—its organizational structure. Does it have the necessary culture and capabilities to enter the value creation network that will position it for success in the knowledge era? Does it have the capabilities to identify a knowledge strategy that encompasses a comprehensive commitment to understanding and leveraging the true value of its knowledge capital? Does it have the energy and resources to embrace a new way of thinking that challenges some of the fundamental beliefs that have until recently held it in good stead with its customers and shareholders?

Recognizing the value of self-governed structures may be a significant challenge for organizations. Giving up the traditional leadership model that exercised command and control as the primary strategy for managing human capital and processes will not be something that can be achieved overnight. Leadership mindsets will change as the value of communities is made clearer, but this is a developmental process that will require significant efforts of a champion with highly developed change management capabilities.

Strategies and the Challenges to Culture

Culture has a great deal of effect on the organization's ability to realize a strategy because it forms the context that shapes how people behave and exercise their leadership in the organization. In fact, a strategy will only have the desired result if it affects the actions of everyone in the organization.

The collective mindset imposed by the organization's culture will in large part shape how people will react to a new strategy. If these strategies do not fit the preconceived notions fed by the this mindset, it will be difficult for individuals to understand the rationale for the strategy, let alone commit to the change it represents. When a strategy is not aligned with the culture, it can't achieve its main purpose—to unify and mobilize employees.

A certain amount of tension is desirable for the organization—it can bring a great deal of focus and momentum to accelerate change. When a strategy is creating considerable tension, it's important for the leadership of the organization to play an active role in spelling out the business imperative for change. Leadership must also be exercised in helping employees understand how the new strategy will fulfill their goals to have a vibrant and successful organization. All this must be done in a credible manner and requires an environment where there is enough trust to openly discuss the pros and cons of the rationale. A closed environment, distrust, and low morale will give leadership limited room to maneuver.

COMMUNITIES—THE NEW FRONTIER?

Are communities of practice just a passing phenomenon that will soon be discarded for yet another trendy management approach? Is the interest in communities primarily a ruse for piloting new technology that holds some promise? Like the field of knowledge management itself, are we looking at old wine—new bottle, a recycled approach for business process re-engineering, or a spate of quick fixes for an ailing economy?

Well, maybe. While we may look at communities of practice as a new frontier, they are in fact situated in everything we know about how people learn, work, and live together—how people interact, look for support, and value experience. So from that perspective, communities of practice aren't anything new. However, communities are being placed in a new context and have the opportunity to play a significant role in evolving organizational structure.

Communities of practice may seem unfamiliar now, but in five or ten years they may be as common to discussions of organizational structure as business units and cross-functional teams are today. Communities will take a more prominent role in the creation of an organizational structure that is able to respond effectively. If managers unlock the value of communities, the boxes and lines of a traditional organizational chart will be altered to become more effective in dealing with a rapidly evolving marketplace.

Most organizations are facing market pressures that require a level of speed and agility that the traditional organization can't muster. Addressing current inadequacies requires that we take a more comprehensive view of organizational architecture that encompasses values, systems, and processes. Moving beyond a single-minded view of the organization as a structure, we must create the processes and approaches that develop the meta-capabilities of collaboration and learning. Although developing and nurturing communities present definite challenges to organizations, the potential benefits far outweigh the costs.

The Internet has only started to affect the economy. It will continue to be a primary catalyst for the foreseeable future. As bandwidth continues to increase, its effect will continue to increase on marketplaces and organizations. The same technological changes that are shaping the forces of global competition can be harnessed within the organization to increase speed and accelerate capability development.

Ironically, these technology-driven changes are placing the need to build meaningful human relationships at the forefront of the strategic agenda. As the internal value chain is subsumed by external value creation networks, the ability to collaborate across boundaries becomes essential both internally and externally.

It's important that organizations start taking steps that will enhance their readiness for these new market conditions. We're not advocating a big bang approach with communities of practice. Rather, we see leveraging communities as one step, albeit a key step, in an evolutionary process that has more likelihood of success than a radical shift.

Communities of practice represent one of the steps that an organization can take without causing excessive disturbance. Supporting the development of communities of practice will have implications for the way people work, and it will be necessary to carefully manage the changes involved in this transition to a new organizational structure.

Once communities are a more pervasive feature, they will transform organizations at a very fundamental level. Cross-functional pursuits, enterprise-wide initiatives, and client-service teams will become the norm, an integral part of the organizational fabric. As this happens, the architecture of the whole organization will shift gradually. An increasing number of employees will experience one or more of these self-governed entities that enhance collaboration, learning, capability acquisition, strategic coherence, and ultimately the performance of the organization.

As communities multiply across the organization, this collaborative experience based on high-trust relationships is reinforced and generalized. In the end, communities of practice will have fundamentally altered the DNA of the organization. This change will affect the leadership mindsets in the organization, the processes by which work is accomplished, and the systems that enable the organization's efforts.

And as we develop in our own organizational maturity model, we should challenge people not just to build a community, but to set the organization on a trajectory that sees communities as a key component of its total structure.

Conclusion

Communities of practice need to be leveraged to enhance the collaborative and learning quotient. As organizations move from the predominant logic of make-and-sell to a sense-and-respond organizational logic, they are striving to make a parallel shift from a mechanical and bureaucratic organizational structure to one that is more collaborative and boundaryless. While the accountability spine of the organization will need to remain in the form of a hierarchy of responsibilities on a vertical axis, there is a key need to complement this structure with a vibrant horizontal axis of cross-enterprise collaboration. Communities of practice are the primary tool we have at our disposal to enhance the collaborative dimension of the organization. The need to move faster and to provide customers with integrated solutions make it imperative for organizations to reinforce their ability to work collaboratively.

The competitive, fast-moving marketplaces where most organizations operate make the ability to generate new capability at an accelerated rate the ultimate strategic imperative for any organization. This is a competitive context where an organization that learns more slowly than the other players in its industry will disappear. Knowledge and learning are closely integrated. Learning comes from working with existing knowledge and generating new knowledge on the basis of understanding and insight. Communities of practice build on the ability to collaborate and to accelerate learning within the organization. By their very dynamics, communities of practice provide solutions to real business issues. But more important, they infuse the organization with an on-going ability to learn.

By increasing an organization's meta-capabilities to collaborate and learn, the culture is gradually transformed. In the end, this is the most important effect and lasting legacy of communities of practice in the organization. They become the catalyst for a shift to a sense-and-respond culture, challenging the organization to incorporate internal capabilities parallel to the external changes taking place in the market. We believe that this new complementary configuration of the organization will enhance its ability to realize its strategic intent.

Communities as Agents of Change— Will It Play in Peoria?

To further the exchange of ideas about situating communities of practice in a strategic context, we invite you to join a dedicated discussion hosted by Know Inc. Access "Communities of Practice as a Strategic Tool" at http://www.knowinc.com. Through continued dialogue, we can help organizations flourish in the knowledge economy.

Appendix

Community Development: Quick-Start Toolkit

Introduction

On the basis of the Agent Network community development experience, a new group called the Knowledge Exchange Team was established at Clarica to spearhead work in building communities of practice throughout the organization. An architect was appointed to outline the knowledge exchange foundation based on communities of practice. A community consultant assumed the facilitation role for the Agent Network and began working with other interested groups to establish new communities at Clarica.

An early project of the Knowledge Exchange Team, which is part of the larger Knowledge Team, was to create a guide for building the foundation of new communities. This series of exercises help community initiators put the building blocks in place, ensuring that the community infrastructure, technology, and sponsorship support are positioned as precursors to a successful launch.

Using these exercises in conjunction with a community consultant has reduced the time needed to launch a community and provided a consistent approach to community development. The speed and efficiency with which the Knowledge Exchange Team can meet the needs of new communities has made a significant contribution to Clarica's ability to move closer to its vision of an organizational structure that will lead the industry in the networked knowledge economy.

For people who are developing their first structured community, the toolkit will help guide the first phase of designing and implementing a community project. For organizations that have experience in building communities, the toolkit approach may be useful in providing support for creating additional communities.

The toolkit components include:

- Identify Steering Committee Members
- Identify Project Coordinator
- Establish Purpose
- Outline Project Work Plan
- Determine Community Membership
- Identify Facilitator(s)
- Identify Community Administrator(s)
- Outline Governance Components
- Identify Technical and Learning Support
- Communicate with Sponsors and Stakeholders

These tools were developed to spawn communities at Clarica and include some Clarica-specific resources. Generic titles are supplied in brackets to guide use in other organizations.

Special thanks to Bob Forrester, Knowledge Exchange Architect, and JJ Smits, Community Consultant, for their work in preparing this toolkit for starting the community development process.

IDENTIFY STEERING COMMITTEE MEMBERS

Community Development Step:

Define Community Project—Outline Project Approach

Objective:

Determine steering committee members

Process:

- Steering committee members are important because they provide input and guidance on the preparations for the launch of a community.

Once the community is launched, they encourage members to join and participate.

- Inform the sponsor that steering committee members will need to spend 1–2 hours a week until the community is launched, then 1 hour a week for the next 4 months. Ask the sponsor, "Whom would you recommend as steering committee members?"

- Invitations have more weight if they come from a sponsor. Draft a letter or e-mail message for the sponsor to modify and send, inviting people to become steering committee members. Invitations to join can also come from the project coordinator.

Tips:

Identify the steering committee members after project sponsorship is gained.

Example:

The Agent Network Steering Committee invitation:

To: Gord K.

cc:

Subject: The Agent Network—Moving forward and growing!

Hi Gord!

I'm writing you today with a request. Well, actually an offer of sorts.

The Steering Committee for the Agent Network met again last week. No doubt you've seen the discussion and the update in our recent newsletter about the completion of Phase One.

Included in the next steps of the Agent Network is an expansion of membership. We plan on increasing the number of agents with access to the Agent Network to 300.

With an increased membership group, we also plan to expand the Steering Committee. Here's where you fit in...we hope! On behalf of the Steering Committee, I invite you to join us and formalize your contribution to the Agent Network and its success.

Your role on the Steering Committee will include:

- Providing guidance and input into the governance of the Agent Network

- Attending (teleconferencing if necessary) Steering Committee meetings—monthly at the most

- Reviewing additional e-mails regarding the Agent Network

Your contribution to the Agent Network in its infancy and your ongoing support have been incredible and very much appreciated. I look forward to hearing from you, Gord.

Thanks again!

. . . JJ

JJ Smits
Community Facilitator
The Agent Network

IDENTIFY PROJECT COORDINATOR

Community Development Step:

Define Community Project—Outline Project Approach

Objective:

Determine who will coordinate the community development process.

Process:

- The project coordinator role is important to the success of a structured community. A structured community should not proceed without identifying who will provide dedicated project coordination.
- If a sponsor has committed to providing a project coordinator, review the coordinator's responsibilities, including:
  - Identify the project scope, business objectives, and stakeholders
  - Develop a project plan that outlines the project objectives and actions, broken down to show tasks and task dependencies at a sufficient level of detail to assign resources and track progress. Key milestones should also be clearly indicated on the project plan
  - Identify the resources required to successfully accomplish the project and secure the commitment of resources from the sponsor
  - Identify project risks, communicate as necessary, and ensure that the risks are appropriately managed
  - Design and implement a project status reporting process to communicate the overall plan status to the sponsor
  - Design and implement a process for tracking progress against the plan

— Manage the scope of the project and communicate the agreement to and the implications of all approved scope changes

— Escalate any situations that could result in the project's falling behind schedule or jeopardize meeting target dates to sponsor as quickly as possible

— Provide post-project assessment to evaluate the success of the project and ensure any lessons learned are captured

- Review recommended characteristics of the coordinator with the sponsor:

— Commitment/passion for work of community

— Sponsor's (if one exists) endorsement

— Project management skills

— Facilitation skills (listening, clarifying, paraphrasing, summarizing)

— Computer literacy if online, e.g., basic business applications, browsers, e-mail

- Tell the sponsor that a coordinator will need to commit 1–2 days a week until the community is launched, then hold follow-up meetings for 1 hour every 2 weeks for 4 months. Ask, "Whom would you like to have as the project coordinator?"

- Involve the sponsor in confirming the role. Have the sponsor explain the importance of the community, outline the role expectations, and confirm with that person whether he/she will coordinate the project.

Tips:

Identify the steering committee members after project sponsorship is gained.

DETERMINE COMMUNITY PURPOSE

Community Development Step:

Define the Community Project—State Purpose

Objective:

Create statement on why this community should exist.

Process:

- Before holding a meeting of people interested in starting a community, send out an e-mail that outlines the discussion for the first meeting—

for example, "We have agreed to meet to determine whether we should start a community. A critical issue is our community's purpose. A clear purpose is essential for making other decisions about our community. Please reflect on these questions before the meeting:

1. Why does this community exist?
2. What are we trying to achieve by having a community?
3. What business problem(s)/issue(s) will the community help address?
4. What makes our community unique from all others?
5. What does our community stand for?"

- In the meeting, ask the questions one at a time, recording the information so others can see it (e.g., use a flip chart/whiteboard, electronic whiteboard).
- Draw everyone's response out, so all perspectives are aired. If people repeat what others have said, put a check beside the comment.
- After all comments are recorded, summarize the similarities indicating a growing consensus. Then draft a purpose statement.
- Ask whether everyone can live with the purpose for now, acknowledging it may change as the community grows and evolves.
- Post the purpose so it is visible and can be referred to easily (e.g., minutes of meeting, on an online community site face page)

Tips:

- Defining purpose is the first issue to decide for a community.
- When facilitating the discussion, clarify responses when unclear. Paraphrase occasionally to make sure everyone understands. This reinforcement makes people feel you are listening and aids in their willingness to proceed toward consensus.
- If there are some aspects not agreed to, ask one person who has one opinion and one who has another to take the comments away and develop a draft of the purpose statement, then distribute to the committee members in an e-mail within a week.

Examples:

View purpose statements of other communities.

Outline Project Work Plan

Community Development Step:

Define the Community Project—Outline Project Approach

Objective:

Develop a project plan that will meet the target date for launching the community.

Process:

- A comprehensive project plan managed by a project coordinator ensures that a community will be launched according to commitments made to sponsors, steering committee, and members.

- Choose a project charter template and timeline or choose an authorized project management tool (e.g., Microsoft Project).

- Establish 1-hour weekly meetings with the Steering Committee, but alert members that work will be done online via a project database between face-to-face or teleconference meetings.

Tips:

Community administrator(s) should be identified after sponsorship is gained but before the first steering committee meeting.

Examples:

- Following is an example of a workplan template aimed at the creation of a new community

Community Work Plan			
Task	**Date Due**	**Who**	**Done**
Demo community site and gain approval to proceed from sponsor			
Identify project coordinator and online facilitator			

Community Work Plan			
Task	**Date Due**	**Who**	**Done**
Discuss specifics on new community			
Meet with facilitator to orient her to project and notify her of Nancy White's upcoming online facilitation course			
Book time in management team session to introduce community in "lab" environment and notify people to bring their laptops			
Enroll facilitator in Nancy White's online facilitation course			
Meet with sponsor and project coordinator to determine directional purpose, key success measures, sub-communities, steering committee members, and cultural readiness			
Send out email inviting steering committee members			
Notify knowledge exchange architect of steering committee member acceptance			
Discuss implications of URL for this new community with vendor			
Meet with help desk to orient project and outline support required			
Book digital photos of sponsor			
Request first and last names of members and send to project coordinator			
Book weekly 1 hr. steering committee meetings forward			
Meet with community consultant to review new community configuration			
Notify vendor to have facilitator given access to Facilitators' Forum			

Community Work Plan			
Task	**Date Due**	**Who**	**Done**
Send project coordinator changes to binder for coaching on community development and online facilitation			
Prelaunch site for preview			
Co-design session for sponsor and members to review site functionality			
Adapt Getting Started and User Guides			
Order 50 copies of above for full launch			
Deliver binders with materials for coaching on initial community development and online facilitation skills			
Put sub-communities members in site			
Coach facilitator on initial community development and online facilitation skills, and showing Facilitator Forum			
Steering committee meeting-orient to project, review purpose, membership, name, key success measures, sub-communities, cultural readiness and demonstrate how to use team space on vendor site			
Insert names of members and steering committee members on site			
Deliver 8 copies of Getting Started & User Guides			
Materials for lab prepared (Getting Started and User Guides, personal cards with ID/passwords, security and privacy issues, packaged in folder)			
Update facilitator on design of sponsor session			

Community Work Plan			
Task	**Date Due**	**Who**	**Done**
Digital photos taken, orientation and "lab" and announcing launch for sponsor and members			
Digital photos sent to community administrator			
Load digital photos			
Steering committee meeting—learn site application.			
Obtain standard photos of all members			
Publish purpose in Announcements and insert initial keywords in Dialogue and References			
Steering committee meeting—review drafts of materials to be sent to members, determine content to "seed" the site with			
Pick up of Getting Started and Users Guides Mail-out to members			
Send draft email announcement that online community is being formed and launched on to sponsor			
E-mail announcement that an online community is being formed and launched to members			
Enroll members on site			
Mail package announcing launch with ID and password, and "Quick Start Guide" and "User Guide"			
Post relevant items in Dialogue and References			

Community Work Plan			
Task	Date Due	Who	Done
Post a welcome message in "Announcements"			
Test site is working as planned			
E-mail announcing launch with ID and password, and "Quick Start Guide" and "User Guide" documents, sent to mebers			

OUTLINE GOVERNANCE COMPONENTS

Community Development Step:

Establish Community Components—Governance

Objective:

Determine the policies and processes by which the community will operate.

Process:

- Before a Steering Committee meeting, send out an e-mail to announce the discussion: "An important issue to determine for the community is our governance. Governance ensures there are clear, agreed-upon boundaries on the participation and conduct of people in the community. Governance can be broken into:

  — protocols (legalities, compliance, brand; processes for sharing, storing, capturing knowledge)

  — ground rules (how we'll treat each other)

  Please reflect on these questions before the meeting:

  1. What legal and compliance issues do we need to address to govern the behavior of our members and reduce our liability that are not covered by Clarica's Code of Business Conduct?

  2. What brand issues do we need to ensure members abide by?

  3. What processes for sharing, capturing, and storing our knowledge make sense?

  4. How would you like to be treated by others in the community?

- In the meeting, ask the questions one at a time, recording the information so others can see it, e.g., on flip chart/whiteboard, electronic whiteboard

- Draw everyone's response out, so all perspectives are aired. If people repeat what others have said, put a check beside the previous comment.

- After all comments are recorded, summarize the similarities indicating a growing consensus. Then draft the protocols and ground rules.

- Ask the people whether they can live with the governance for now, acknowledging it may change as the community grows and evolves.

- Post the protocols and ground rules so they are visible and can be referred to easily (e.g., minutes of meeting, in an online community reference document).

Tips:

- Governance should be defined after community purpose and membership criteria have been determined.

- Legalities generally will not be an issue, since they will be governed by the Clarica Code of Conduct. However, if third parties (e.g., vendors, consultants, or clients) are involved, you may wish to obtain legal advice on whether to establish a separate agreement.

- When facilitating the discussion, clarify responses that are unclear. Paraphrase occasionally to make sure everyone understands. This reinforcement makes people feel you are listening and aids in their willingness to proceed toward consensus.

- If there are some aspects not agreed to, ask one person who has one opinion and one who has another to take the comments away and develop a draft of the community purpose statement, then distribute to the committee members in an e-mail within a week.

Examples:

- Review other community governance documents
- Visit reference sites:

  Nancy White's site: http://www.fullcirc.com/community/sampleguidelines.htm

  multicity: http://www.multicity.com/about/policy/conduct.htm

  blueline-2000: http://www.blueline-2000.com/coptalk.html

  wfm online: http://www.wfmonline.co.uk/communities/code.htm.

Determine Community Membership

Community Development Step:

Establish Community Components—Membership

Objective:

Outline criteria for membership in the community.

Process:

- Before a Steering Group meeting, send out an e-mail, "We have been meeting to establish a community. A critical issue is to determine who will be part of our community—what are the criteria for membership? Clear membership criteria help people know whether they should or should not be part of the community. A diffuse community makes it difficult for members to develop an affinity with the community. Outlining membership criteria also makes recruiting to the community easier.

  1. What are the criteria for gaining membership in the community?
  2. If someone approached you about joining this community, how would you describe who is eligible?
  3. What distinguishes people in this community from others who would never join (i.e., who's in and who's out?)?
  4. What do members have in common?
  5. How would you profile an ideal member?"

- In the meeting, ask the questions one at a time, recording the information so others can see it on a flip chart/whiteboard or electronic whiteboard.

- Draw everyone's response out, so all perspectives are aired. If people repeat what others have said, put a check beside the previous comment.

- After all comments are recorded, summarize the similarities indicating a growing consensus. Then draft the membership criteria.

- Ask the people if they can live with the membership criteria for now, acknowledging it could change as the community grows and evolves.

- Post the membership criteria so that it is visible and can be referred to easily (e.g., minutes of meeting, on an online community site face page).

Tips:

- Membership should be defined after the purpose statement is identified.

- When facilitating the discussion, clarify responses that are unclear. Paraphrase occasionally to make sure everyone understands. This reinforcement makes people feel you are listening and aids in their willingness to proceed toward consensus.

- If there are some aspects not agreed to, ask one person who has one opinion and one who has another to take the comments away and develop a draft of the purpose statement. Then distribute to the committee members in an e-mail within a week

Examples:

Characteristics of people sought for Innovation For Growth Network:

Individual characteristics:

- Knowledgeable about a wide range of topics
- Committed to sharing information, ideas, and expertise, and willing to receive the same
- Forward thinker—constantly looking for opportunities "outside the 9 dots"
- Tenacious and a risk taker—persistence to hang in and move a good idea forward
- Willing to jump in and help develop the community
- Willing to participate in the community site at least 3 times a week.

Demographic considerations:

- Across office locations
- Across levels of management and employees
- From existing areas focusing on innovation.

Identify Community Facilitator

Community Development Step:

Establish Community Components—Facilitation

Objective:

Determine who will be the community's facilitator(s).

Process:

- The facilitator role is crucial to the success of a structured community. A structured community should not proceed without identifying who will provide dedicated facilitation.

- If a sponsor has committed to providing a facilitator, review the facilitator's typical tasks with him/her:
  — Planning and creating activities that continue to build the sense of community
  — Promoting and cheerleading members to continually participate
  — Guiding members through a smooth exchange of ideas
  — Coaching members who have questions about using an online community tool
  — Acting as a liaison between the community and other people in the organization
  — Seeding an online site with content prior to launch.

  Review recommended characteristics:
  — Commitment/passion for work of community
  — Credibility within the community
  — Sponsor's endorsement
  — Facilitation skills (listening, clarifying, paraphrasing, summarizing)
  — A feel for the community's and organization's dynamics (informal leaders, networks, how things get done)
  — Can work in ambiguous situations
  — Good written communication skills
  — Computer literacy if online, e.g., basic business applications, browsers, e-mail

- Tell the sponsor a facilitator will need to commit 2 days a week for the first 2 months and 1 day a week thereafter. Ask, "Whom would you like to have as the project facilitator?"

- Involve the sponsor in confirming the role. Have the sponsor explain the importance of the community, outline the role expectations, and confirm with that person whether he/she will facilitate the project.

- If a community is not structured, informal leaders will often emerge to assume the facilitation role. Some communities may wish to explicitly assign the role as a rotating responsibility (e.g., every 2 months).

Tips:

- Facilitator(s) should be appointed after the purpose and membership criteria have been determined.

- Facilitator(s) need to know support will be available if they assume the role.

Examples:

Refer to course materials on facilitation in the Knowledge Depot (Clarica's corporate intranet).

Identify Community Administrator

Community Development Step:

Establish Community Components—Administration

Objective:

Determine who will provide administrative support to the community.

Process:

- Administrators are important because they do a lot of behind the scenes work to facilitate members' use of the community tool. In an online community, they register new members (e.g., names, e-mail address, photos), coach members on the features of the community tool, and notify the project manager of technical problems. When communities have a face-to-face presence, they book meetings, reproduce materials, and coordinate other logistics.

- Administrators typically spend 1–2 hours a week until an online community is launched, then 1 hour a week for the 4 months thereafter.

- A sponsor or the project coordinator can identify the administrator. Ask, "Whom would you recommend as an administrator?"

- Ask the sponsor or the project coordinator to invite the administrator to support the new community.

Tips:

Administrators should identified after sponsorship is gained but before the first steering committee meeting

Determine Technical and Learning Support

Community Development Step:

Establish Community Components—User Support and Training

Objective:

Determine the nature and location of the technical and learning support.

Process:

- Before the steering committee meeting, send out an e-mail: "A critical issue to determine is our community's technical and learning support. Please reflect on these questions before the meeting:
    1. What user documentation (e.g., Getting Started Guide, Help, User Guide) will community members require to log on and use the community site?
    2. Where can we obtain the documentation, or who can develop it?
    3. Who will act as our "help desk" to ensure that members' questions on using the community tool are answered quickly?
    4. What documentation of tool support is required? Where can we obtain it, or who can develop it?"
- In the meeting, ask the questions one at a time, recording the information so others can see it, e.g., on flip chart/whiteboard, electronic whiteboard.
- Draw everyone's response out, so all perspectives are aired. If people repeat what others have said, put a check beside the previous comment.
- After all comments are recorded, summarize the similarities indicating a growing consensus.
- Ask the people if they can live with the documentation for now, acknowledging it could change as the community grows and evolves.
- Post the technical and learning support decisions so that they are visible and can be referred to easily (e.g., minutes of meeting, on an online community site face page).

Tips:

- Do this exercise after deciding on purpose and choosing a community tool

- If the vendor doesn't have appropriate materials, consult the examples already developed in 3 areas:
  1. Getting Started Guide
  2. Help or User Guide
  3. Overall technical support
- When adapting the training documentation to fit your members' needs, follow plain language principles. (Refer to organization's plain language resources.)
- If choosing the Clarica community template, ask a Knowledge Exchange Team member to post the Help/Getting Started files on the new community site
- Notify or work with other stakeholders, such as Techelp, SFTS, and the Knowledge Exchange Team, to ensure that technical and learning support is comprehensive. (Refer to internal user support and documentation development resources.)

Examples:

- Refer to internal resources on technical writing
- Technical Support Chart
- Community Technical Support

  Most Web applications do not provide the same level of technical support that you would normally receive from your corporate technology help desk or call center or from an Internet Service Provider. Create a chart similar to the one below that outlines support options for your community software.

Problem	Agent/Staff Environment	Resource
Connect to vendor site	Clarica's Internet Explorer Sales Force Central	SFTS Hotline: Agent Service Centre @ 1.877.xxxx option 4, then 1 for "technology support"
Connect to vendor site	Internet Service Provider	Call your ISP

Problem	Agent/Staff Environment	Resource
Log in information: Member name and Password	Clarica's Internet Explorer or Agent's ISP	Send an e-mail to one of: • agent.network@clarica.com • the.manager.network@clarica.com • Innovation for Growth Network in Lotus Notes
Membership inquiries		Send an e-mail to one of: • agent.network@clarica.com • the.manager.network@clarica.com • Innovation for Growth Network in Lotus Notes
Vendor site navigation and functionality	Clarica's Internet Explorer	Check the user's guide for one of: • The Agent Network • The Manager Network • Innovation for Growth Community Use the Help function in vendor site Send an e-mail to one of: • agent.network • the.manager.networkInnovation for Growth Network in Lotus Notes
Log in to vendor site		• Agents—from Sales Force Central > Sales Tools and Advertising > The Agent Network • Sales Managers—from Sales Force Central > Learning Center > The Manager Network • Any member can use the URL address

Communicate with Sponsors
and Stakeholders

Community Development Step:

Establish Community Components—Communications

Objective:

Ensure support for a community remains strong by keeping the sponsor up-to-date.

Process:

- If your sponsor is part of the steering committee, summarize the progress of the committee in meetings and document this periodically.

- If your sponsor is not part of the steering committee, include him/her in the distribution of communication items that are also sent to stakeholders:

  1. Use the communication plan template in the Examples section (below)

  2. Draft a communication piece that reflects the progress to date of your steering committee's work

  3. Send communication piece to the steering committee and invite them to critique it either online or at the next meeting

  4. Create a final copy and e-mail it to the sponsor(s) and stakeholders, inviting them to contact you if they want to discuss anything about the planning process in forming the community.

Examples:

Communication Plan Template (e.g., Clarica Internal Corporate Communications)

This template will help you define the scope of your communication strategy.

1. Communication Objectives
   - What do you want to achieve as a result of this communication?
2. Audience
   - Who is the target audience?

- Whom are you trying to reach in this target audience (breakdown into sub-audiences: decision makers, managers, associates)?

- What is the size of the audience you are trying to reach?

- What are the audience's wants and needs?

- Is the audience active (already interested) or passive (unaware/ uninterested)? Active audience requires feature-oriented approach; Passive audience requires relationship-building and benefit-oriented approach.

3. Product/Services

- What products (e.g. new tools) and services are you communicating about?

- What is the audience going to get or see?

- What is unique about this product/service?

- What's different from the audience's current world?

- What barriers or challenges might we face in communicating about this product/service?

- Is there a potential media relations' issue (positive or negative) with the communication?

4. Key Messages

- What is the most important key message you are trying to communicate?

- What are the secondary messages you are trying to communicate?

- Who is the sender of the messages?

- Who will be the contact for any questions or comments?

- What is the overall tone of your message and why (e.g., friendly, familiar, business-like, professional, firm, light, informational, technical)? For instance, if your message is about the inappropriate use of e-mail, it may require a firm tone.

- What other critical information should be included in the communication plans (e.g., special instructions)?

- What documents support the messages (e.g., policies, guidelines, booklets)?

5. Call for Action

- What do you want the audience to do after receiving the communication?

- What action(s) should they be prepared to take?

6. Communication Vehicles

   ■ What communication vehicles are required (e.g., intranet site on Clarica Connects, Hotlines, power point presentation, hardcopy materials, face-to-face meetings)?

7. Approval Process

   ■ Who needs to be involved in the approval process?

   ■ Who needs to have final approval on the communication (1–3 people max.)?

8. Measurement

   ■ How will you know if your communication is successful?

   ■ What measures will you use to determine success?

9. Other Issues

   ■ What is the timing or deadline for this communication?

   ■ What is the budget for the communication tactics (brochures, etc.)?

INDEX

Access. *See* Knowledge access
Accountability, 39
  assessing, 25
  characteristics, 37
  cross-functional, 62
  expanded, 61–63
  spine, 317–19
Actions, 65
  communication, 291
  community establishment,
    277–79
  component development,
    263–66
  launch, 269–70
  member needs and, 190–91
  project definition, 244–48
Administrator identification, 348
Agility, 19
Allee, Verna, 49
Architecture, community. *See*
    Community architecture

Architecture, knowledge. *See*
    Knowledge architecture
Assessment. *See* Community
    assessment
Assets
  intangible, 4, 5
  tangible, 3, 4

Best practices
  assessment, 187–88, 199
  design, 164–65
  establishment, 183
  expansion, 203–4
  growth, 195–96
  launch, 169–70
  project definition, 152–53
Branding
  process model and, 125
  site, 157
  team, 22
  values and, 86

Building communities. *See*
    Community building
Business case, 68–70
Business rules, 4

Capabilities
    assessing, 24–26
    competitive advantage and,
        6–8, 59, 60–61
    customer demands for,
        8–9
    defined, 4–5
    five C's and, 141, 208
    generative, 80, 82–83
    implementation/growth and,
        206, 208
    increasing, 4–8, 20
    individual, 5–6, 23
    knowledge management
        and, 28
    marketplace factors and, 6–8,
        319–20
    organizational, 4–8, 23, 24–26,
        319–21, 331
    strategic, 21–24
    strategy/performance and,
        59–60, 206
    value networks and, 55–59,
        321–22
    in your organization, 208
    See also Meta-capabilities
Capital, knowledge. *See* Knowledge
    capital
Catalysts. *See* Change agents
Challenges
    community, 327
    individual, 326
    organization, 327–28
    strategies for, 328
Champions, 43

Change agents, 319–23
    capabilities/marketplace and,
        6–8, 319–20
    challenges to, 326–28
    customer relationship, 320
    roles and, 324–26
Change management, 242–43
Charter, project, 237–44
Checkpoints, 183–88, 280–82
Choo, Chun Wei, 29
Clarica, 9
    alignment tool, 70, 71
    communities of practice, 39–40
    Knowledge Capital Initiative,
        13–23
    knowledge strategy, 14–19
    Learning Community, 78–79
    learning/knowledge creation,
        72–73
    measurement approach, 213–23
    organization, 73–74
    overview, 121–22
    problem-solving forum, 71–72
    Strategic Capabilities Unit,
        21–24, 77
    technology infrastructure, 46–47
    value propositions, 213–23
    Web site, 230
    See also Community
        development
Coalescing stage, 48
Codes of conduct, 155
Coherence, 20
Collaboration
    approaches to, 39, 89–90
    architectural components, 84–89
    connectivity and, 141, 206, 207
    external, 63
    factors driving, 62–63
    five C's and, 140, 207

as fundamental, 60–61
as goal, 19–20
implementation/growth and,
        205, 207
internal, 63
organization structure and, 5
processes, 156
synchronous vs. asynchronous,
        89–90
technology and, 99–100, 322
tools, 19
virtual vs. face-to-face, 89–90
in your organization, 116–17,
        207
Commitment
    five C's and, 141, 207
    implementation/growth and,
        205–6, 207
    as measure, 211
Communications
    activities, 291
    best practice, 188
    charter sample, 242
    of data/recommendations,
        197–98
    fact sheets, 261–63
    high-level plan, 257–61
    newsletters, 292
    plan, 154, 161–62
    recognition letters, 309–11
    as structural capital, 25
    toolkit guidelines, 352–54
    value proposition and, 189,
        191–92
Communities, in your organization
    architecture for, 116–17
    capabilities and, 208
    collaboration and, 116–17, 207
    conversations and, 207
    design for, 171–72

development of, 141–42
discussion site, 331
existing, 51–52, 314
human capital and, 24–25
knowledge capital and, 24–26
launching, 171–72
learning and, 116–17
strategic context, 74–75
technology infrastructure for,
        116–17, 171–72
trust and, 117, 316
value proposition and, 52, 226
Communities, strategic context,
        40–47, 55–75
    business case for, 68–70
    at Clarica, 70–74
    competitive advantage and, 55,
        59, 60–63
    components, 91–105
    member roles, 43
    patterns, 74
    policies/procedures, 98–99
    process/practice, 44–45
    roles/responsibilities, 42–44,
        94–98
    strategy and, 59–61
    support roles, 44
    technology infrastructure,
        99–105
    vendor partnerships and, 101–5
    vision/strategy, 41, 91–94
    in your organization, 74–75
    See also Community
        development
Communities of practice
    action and, 64–65
    applying, 24–26, 51–52, 74–75,
        116–17, 171–72, 226
    benefits of, 49–50
    business case for, 68–70

Communities of practice *(cont'd.)*
  characteristics, 34–40, 235
  communities within, 32–33,
    50–51
  competitive advantage and, 55,
    59, 60–63
  conceptual framework, 1
  conventions, 80, 82, 86, 96, 97
  defined, 2, 27–28, 32–34,
    50–51
  elements of, 35
  emergence of, 314–15
  existing, 51–52, 314
  future of, 328–30
  governance of, 39, 154, 155–56,
    249–50, 343–44
  informal, 35, 36–37
  infrastructure, 46–47, 73–74
  knowledge management and,
    13–14, 27–32
  leadership endorsement of,
    108–10
  lifecycles, 47–49
  as new strategy, 12–13
  organizational structure and,
    61–68
  overview of, 1–2
  process/practice of, 206–7
  purpose, common, 39–40
  range of, 34–38
  structured, 36–37, 38
  supported, 36–37, 38
  term origin, 12
Community architecture, 78–91
  components, 79–80
  conventions of, 80, 82
  generative capabilities and, 80,
    82–83
  illustrated, 79
  integrated approach, 89–90

productive inquiry and, 17,
    38–39, 79, 80–81, 84–85
  roles/responsibilities, 90
  technology infrastructure, 80,
    83–89
  in your organization, 116–17
Community assessment
  best practice, 187–88, 199
  communication and, 196, 198
  data collection/analysis and, 196,
    197
  illustrated, 185, 197
  informal feedback, 184, 185, 280
  process review, 221–22
  progress/value, 183–88, 280–82
  purpose/direction, 196–99
  recommendations from, 197–98
  reflections on, 186–87, 198
  stakeholder, 184, 185
  statistics, 186
Community building
  collaboration and, 82–83
  components of, 91–105
  conventions, 80, 82
  environment creation, 77–78
  evolution of, 114, 115–16
  expectations, 110–11
  leadership endorsement, 108–10
  learning and, 82–83, 106–7
  partnering mindset and, 108
  policies/procedures, 98–99
  precursors for, 105–11
  productive inquiry and, 38–39,
    79, 80–81, 84–85
  recommendations, 224
  roles/responsibilities, 90, 94–98
  shared purpose/ownership, 106
  success criteria, 111–14
  systematic, 315–16
  toolkit guidelines, 333–54

trust and, 107
vision/strategy, 91–94
See also Community
    architecture; Technology
    infrastructure
Community definition. *See* Project
    definition
Community design
  best practice, 152–53, 164–65
  components, 153–65
  illustrated, 144, 171
  overview, 143–45
  personnel, 245–48
  project definition, 145–53
  reflections on, 150–51, 162–64
  in your organization, 171–72
  See also Community launch
Community development, 121–42
  agent network, 128–30
  branding and, 125
  capabilities focus, 124 25, 141,
    206, 208
  collaboration and, 140, 205, 207
  commitment, 126, 141, 205–6,
    207
  connectivity and, 141, 206, 207
  conversations and, 140, 204, 207
  exclusive sales force and, 126–28
  guiding principles, 123–24
  knowledge-sharing and, 123–28
  milestones, 130
  objectives of, 135
  outline, 156
  phases, 137, 138–40
  process review, 216–23
  project management approach,
    133–36
  strategic context, 136–40
  strategic imperatives, 124
  subject of, 128–30

technology infrastructure, 126
tools for, 135–36
in your organization, 141–42
Community establishment,
    176–83, 274–80
  actions, example, 277–79
  best practice, 183
  facilitators and, 177, 179–80,
    274–77
  illustrated, 177
  membership and, 177, 178–79
  participation, 177, 180–81
  personnel, 278–79
  reflections on, 182
  Web site and, 177, 181
Community expansion, 199–204
  best practice, 203–4
  contribution guidelines,
    304–9
  example, 300–311
  illustrated, 201
  membership and, 200, 201–2
  next steps, 200, 202
  participation guidelines, 301–4
  recognition and, 200, 202
  recommendations and, 200–201
  reflections on, 203
  sponsor review, 200, 203
Community growth, 188–96
  activities for, 189, 190–91
  best practice, 195–96
  communication and, 189,
    191–92
  expertise network, 189, 192–93
  illustrated, 190
  knowledge harvest and, 189, 193
  process review, 220–21
  reflections on, 193–95
  site expectations/limitations,
    189, 191

Community growth *(cont'd.)*
  value proposition and, 189,
    191–92, 282–92
Community implementation,
    173–88
  assessing, 183–88
  establish community for, 176–83
  illustrated, 176
Community launch, 165–70
  actions, example, 269–70
  best practice, 169–70
  example, 267–70
  illustrated, 144, 165, 171
  member readiness, 166–67
  overview, 143–45
  personnel, 245–48
  process review, 220
  ramping up, 167–68
  reflections on, 168–69
  site readiness, 166
  sponsor sign-off, 166
  in your organization, 171–72
  See also Community design
Community site
  branding, 157
  expectations/limitations, 189,
    191
  literacy, 177, 181
  membership and, 189, 191
  readiness, 166
  as tool, 149
  training, 254–57, 282–92
  See also Web tool
Competencies
  core, 93
  as measure, 211
Competitive advantage
  capabilities and, 6–8, 59, 60–61
  communities of practice and, 55,
    59, 60–63

knowledge strategy and, 4, 9
  strategy for, 55, 59, 60–63
Components, community, 44–45,
    91–105, 153–65
  actions, example, 263–66
  core competencies, 93
  cross-generation exchanges,
    93–94
  deliverables, 264–66
  development example,
    249–66
  development needs, 93
  establishing, 153–65
  functional expertise, 93
  illustrated, 92, 153
  objectives, 264–66
  personnel, 264–66
  process review, 218–20
  strategic theme, 91–93
  vision/strategy, 91–94
Conceptual framework, 1
Confidentiality, 193–95
Connectivity, 141, 206, 207
Connectors, 42
Content, 158–59
  establishing, 154
  identifying, 159
  selection criteria, 158
  soliciting, 159
  submission format, 158
Context
  defining communities and,
    233–36
  process review and, 217–18
  purpose identification, 232–33
  setting, 146–48, 232–36
  See also Communities, strategic
    context
Contribution guidelines, 304–9
Conventions, community, 86

community architecture and, 80, 82
community role and, 96
individual role and, 97
Conversations, 84–85, 88
five C's and, 140, 207
implementation/growth and, 204, 207
individual role in, 97
productive inquiry and, 84–85
in your organization, 207
Core competency, 93
Culture
assessing, 25
capabilities and, 5–6
context and, 147
knowledge-sharing, 142
knowledge strategy and, 17–18
leadership, 14, 15, 17–18, 324
as structural capital, 25
technology infrastructure and, 89
Customer capital, 10–12
assessing, 25
defined, 10
Customers
capabilities, increasing, 9
knowledgeable workforces and, 8–9
relationships, 320

Data
analysis, 196, 197
collection, 187, 196, 197
knowledge exchange and, 65–66
knowledge measurement and, 212–13
recommendations from, 196, 197–98
Davenport, Tom, 28

Decision-making, 20
Defining projects. See Project definition
Deliverables
community establishment, 278–79
component development, 264–66
design/launch, 245–48
project definition, 150
Design, community. See Community design
Development
collaborative, 103
phases, 137, 138–39
See also Community development
Dewey, John, 141
Direction evaluation, 196–99, 293–300
data analysis for, 196–97
member survey, 294–99
recommendations, 197–98
report, 299–300
usage statistics, 293–94

Education. See Online training
Education level, 211
Environmental factors, 62, 63, 147–48
Establishment. See Community establishment
Evaluation. See Community assessment; Direction evaluation
Evolution, community, 114, 115–16
Exchange. See Knowledge exchange
Expansion. See Community expansion

Expectations
    realistic, 110–11
    stakeholder, 187
Experience, employee, 211
Explicit knowledge, 16–17, 44, 65,
        66–67
External collaboration, 63

Face-to-face meetings, 89–90
Facilitators
    action log, 269
    community establishment and,
        177, 179–80, 274–77
    defined, 44
    identifying, 346–48
    introducing, 177, 179–80
    process review, 216–23
    roles/responsibilities, 154,
        160–61, 179–80, 274–77
    toolkit guidelines, 346–48
Feedback
    constant, 188
    informal, 184, 185, 280
    mechanisms, 86
    membership, 185
    sponsor, 185
    survey, 214–16, 294–99
    vendor, 186
Firewalls, 88, 157
Five C's, 140–41, 204–7

Generative capabilities, 80,
        82–83
Governance, 39
    establishing, 154, 155–56
    example, 249–50
    toolkit guidelines, 343–44
Growth. See Community growth

HR investment, 211

Human capital, 10–12
    defined, 10
    measuring, 211–13
    in your organization, 24–25
Hurdles, 172

Implementation. See Community
        implementation
Individual capabilities
    domain, 23
    illustrated, 6
    organizational vs., 5–6
    purpose, 23
    roles, 23
Individual Capability Team, 22
Individuals
    challenges, 326
    learning by, 106–7
    roles of, 96–98, 325
    shared ownership, 106
Informal community of practice,
        35, 36–37
Information
    access, 14, 98–99
    defined, 64
    productive inquiry and, 17,
        38–39, 79, 80–81, 84–85
    See also Knowledge; Knowledge
        exchange
Infrastructure characteristics, 37
Innovation, 20, 69, 211
Inquiry. See Productive inquiry
Intangible assets, 5
    defined, 4
    managing, 9–12
    See also Knowledge capital
Internal collaboration, 63
Internet tools. See Web tools
Interpersonal skills, 108
Invitation letter, 250

Involvement, sustainable, 86
Isolation, 68–69

Job satisfaction, 211

Key words, 158
Know Inc., 331
Knowing cycle, 132
Knowledge
   defined, 64
   harvesting, 189, 193
   information and, 64, 66, 98–99,
     132
   tacit/explicit, 16–17, 44, 65,
     66–67
Knowledgeable workforces, 8–9
Knowledge access, 67–68
   as community component, 44,
     45
   exchange and, 63–65, 67–68
   existing, 44, 45
   productive inquiry and, 17,
     38–39, 79, 80–81, 86–87
   purpose of, 64
   as responsibility, 96
   technology infrastructure and,
     16, 81, 86–87
Knowledge architecture
   illustrated, 16, 64
   Knowledge Capital Initiative
     and, 15–17
   productive inquiry and, 17,
     38–39, 80–81, 84–85
   strategic capabilities and, 23
Knowledge Architecture Team, 22
Knowledge capital
   assessing, 24–26
   assumptions, 10–11
   defined, 4
   generation of, 8

   illustrated, 12
   intangible assets and, 9–12
   measuring, 210–13
   model, 9–12
   strategies, 12–13, 17–18
   in your organization, 24–26
Knowledge Capital Initiative
   core components, 13
   development of, 9–10
   goals of, 19–21
   information access and, 14
   knowledge architecture and, 14,
     15–17
   knowledge strategy, 14–19
   management strategy, 13–14
Knowledge Capital Model, 9–12
Knowledge creation
   center, 72–73
   as community component, 44,
     45, 92
   learning organizations and,
     132–33
   productive inquiry and, 17,
     38–39, 79, 80–81, 84–85
   as responsibility, 96
Knowledge era, 3–4
Knowledge exchange
   access and, 63–65, 67–68
   as community component, 44,
     45
   cross-generational, 93–94
   data and, 65–66
   defined, 64
   diverse applications of, 4
   information access vs., 98–99
   measuring, 210–13
   methods, 44, 45
   need for, 80
   productive inquiry and, 17,
     38–39, 79, 80–81, 84–85

Knowledge exchange *(cont'd.)*
    tacit/explicit, 16–17, 44, 65,
        66–67
    types of, 65
Knowledge management
    communities and, 31–32
    defined, 28–29
    framework, 29–30
    illustrated, 29
    overview, 27–32
    strategy overview, 13–14
    value of, 30–31
Knowledge sharing
    as community component, 92
    cultures, 142
    organizations, 123–28, 142

Language statement, 156
Launch. *See* Community launch
Lave, Jean, 12, 33
Leadership
    culture, 14, 15, 17–18, 324
    endorsement, 108–10
    as measure, 211
Learning
    architectural components, 84–89
    center for, 72–73
    as community component, 154,
        159–60
    conversations and, 204
    as goal, 20
    individual role and, 97
    knowledge/information and,
        66–67
    as measure, 211
    as norm, 4
    productive inquiry and, 17,
        38–39, 79, 81, 82–83,
        84–85
    self-initiated, 106–7

technology infrastructure, 154,
    159–60
in your organization, 116–17
See also Online training
Learning Community, 78–79
Learning organizations, 130–33,
    141
    activities of, 131
    knowing cycle and, 132
Letters of recognition, 309–11
Lifecycles, community, 47–49
Lurkers, 43

Management roles, 325
Management supporters, 44
Mandates, 36
Market influences
    on capabilities, 6–8, 319–20
    value networks and, 57–58
Maturing stage, 48
Maturity model, 323–26
    accountability spine and, 317–19
    community building and,
        315–16
    illustrated, 315
    individual roles and, 325
    inherent communities in, 316
    leadership roles and, 324
    management roles and, 325
    organizational structure and,
        317
Mavens, 42
Measures, 209–26
    Clarica approach to, 213–23
    human capital, 211–13
    organization goals and, 210–11
    survey, 214–16
    value proposition, 210–13
Membership, 174–75
    call-back script, 250–53

characteristics, 36, 234–35
commitment, 141, 205–6, 207
criteria, 155
description, 234, 235
establishing, 154, 156, 173
expansion and, 200, 201–2
expectations, 187
feedback, 185
invitation, 156, 250
needs, activities for, 190–91
needs assessment, 177, 179
profiles of, 177, 178–79
readiness, 166–67
roles, 43
selection process example,
    249–50
styles, 177, 179
survey, 294–99
toolkit guidelines, 345–46
value and, 212–13
Web site and, 189, 191
Membership directory, 86
Meta-capabilities
defined, 60–61
increasing, 331
individual/organization and,
    320–21
Milestones, 130
Mindsets, 5
Multitasking, 86

Networking
connectivity and, 141, 206,
    207
multiple communities, 88
strengthening, 192–93
technology and, 57, 58
Network partnerships, 70
Networks, value, 55–59, 321–22
Newsletter, 292

Objectives
community establishment,
    278–79
component development,
    264–66
design/launch, 245–48
Obstacles, 172
Online training, 282–92
checklist, 283–86
communication activities, 291
evaluating, 289–91
introductory letter, 254
newsletter, 292
one-day guide, 254–57
participant e-mail, 287–88
toolkit guidelines, 349–51
Web tool, 135–36, 154, 159–60,
    254–57, 282–92, 349–51
Operational framework, 229–30
Organizational capabilities
assessing, 24–26
chart, 23
competitive advantage and, 6–8
culture and, 5–6
defined, 5
growth and, 6
illustrated, 6
increasing, 4–8
individual vs., 5–6
market demands and, 8
market influences on, 6–8,
    319–20
meta-capabilities and, 60–61,
    320–21, 331
Organizational Capability Team, 22
Organizational learning, 131
Organizational structure, 5, 61–68
accountability spine and, 317–19
alignment tool, 71
collaboration and, 5

Organizational structure *(cont'd.)*
  competitive advantage and,
    61–63
  existing vs. new, 317
  flexible, 87–88
  infrastructure, 73–74
  knowledge strategies and, 21–24
Organizations
  assets of, 3–4, 5, 9–12
  challenges to, 327–28
  core competencies, 93
  customer capabilities and, 9
  existing communities in, 51–52,
    314
  goals of, 210–11
  inherent communities in, 316
  knowing, 132–33
  knowledge-intensive, 9–10
  knowledge-sharing, 123–28, 142
  knowledgeable workforces and,
    8–9
  learning, 130–33
  roles of, 81, 94–95
  strategic issues, 4
  support from, 37, 39
  value proposition and, 9, 14, 22,
    55–59, 210–13
Outcomes, 36
Ownership, 106

Participation, 85–86
  encouraging, 177, 180–81
  guidelines, 155, 301–4
  process review, 223
Partnerships
  mindset/skills, 108
  network, 70
  with technology vendors, 101–5
Performance, 206
Performance limits, 4

Personnel
  community establishment,
    278–79
  component development,
    264–66
  design/launch, 245–48
Phases, development, 137,
    138–40
Platforms. *See* Technology
Policies, 98–99
  need for, 182
  process review, 223
Potential stage, 47, 48
Problem solving forum, 71–72
Procedures, 98–99
Process review, 216–23
  assessment, 221–22
  community launch, 220
  components, 218–20
  context setting and, 217–18
  facilitator/project manager,
    216–22
  growth, 220–21
  policies/procedures, 223
  project definition, 217–18
  recommendations, 224–25
  roles/responsibilities, 222–23
  technology infrastructure, 223
  vision/strategy, 222
Product evolution, 103
Productive inquiry, 38–39, 79,
    80–81
  conventions, 82
  conversations and, 84–85, 88
  defined, 17, 79
  individual role and, 97
  information and, 80–81
  knowledge access and, 81, 86–87
  knowledge and, 80–81
  learning from, 82–83

tacit/explicit knowledge and, 16–17, 44, 65, 66–67
Productivity, 211
Project charter, 237–44
    overview, 237–38
    sample, 238–44
Project coordinator, 336–37
Project definition, 145–53, 232–48
    actions, example, 245–48
    approach design, 148–49
    best practice, 152–53
    charter sample, 238–44
    components, 235
    context, 146–48, 232–33
    defining communities and, 147, 148, 233–36
    deliverables, 150
    illustrated, 146
    objectives, example, 245–48
    overview, 143–45
    process review, 217–18
    project overview, 236–37
    reflection, 150–51
    resource requirements, 149–50
Project management, 133–36, 142, 174, 216–22
Prusak, Larry, 28
Purpose
    alignment of, 104
    characteristics, 36
    charter sample, 239–40
    common, 39–40
    context and, 147
    evaluating, 196–99, 293–300
    identifying, 232–33, 235
    process review, 222
    shared, 106
    statement of, 155
    strategic, 41

strategic capabilities community, 23
    toolkit guidelines, 337–38

Quality management, 242
Quick-start toolkit, 333–54

Recognition, 202, 309–11
Recommendations
    data and, 196, 197–98
    evaluating, 200–201
    process review, 224–25
Reference card, 159
Reflections
    assessment, 186–87, 198
    community design, 150–51, 162–64
    component, 162–64
    development, 141–42
    establishment, 182
    expansion, 203
    growth, 193–95
    launch, 168–69
    project definition, 150–51
Report, 299–300
Resource requirements, 149–50
Responsibilities
    charter sample, 243–44
    community architecture, 90, 94–98
    defining, 149
    facilitator, 154, 160–61, 179–80, 274–77
    knowledge creation/access, 96
    process review, 222–23
    steering group, 44, 149
Return on investment, 110–11, 209
Risk management, 241–42

Roles
    charter sample, 243–44
    communities of practice, 42–44
    community, 95–96
    community architecture, 90,
        94–98
    connector, 42
    defining, 149
    facilitator, 154, 160–61, 179–80,
        274–77
    individual, 96–98, 325
    leadership, 324
    management, 325
    maven, 42
    member, 43
    organizational, 81, 94–95
    process review, 222–23
    salesman, 42
    steering group, 44, 149
    strategic capabilities community,
        23
    support, 44

Salesmen, 42
Scalability, 88
Schon, Donald, 142
Security, 88
    audit, 157
    firewalls, 88, 157
    statement, 156
Self-service mentality, 86
Sole contributors, 43
Sparkers, 43
Speed, 69–70
Sponsors, 44
    characteristics, 36
    commitment and, 141, 205–6,
        207
    communication with, 352–54
    expansion and, 200, 203

    expectations, 187
    feedback, 185
    recognition from, 309–11
    sign-off from, 166
    support, 174, 224
Stakeholders
    communication with, 174,
        352–54
    expectations, 187
    feedback, 185
Statistics
    baseline, 188
    community assessment, 186
    data for, 187
    usage, 293–94
    See also Measures
Steering group
    feedback, 185
    identifying, 334–36
    roles/responsibilities, 44, 149
Stewardship stage, 48
Strategic Capabilities Unit, 21–24,
        77
Strategic issues
    capabilities and, 4, 5–7
    knowledge capital, 12–13
    old, 4
Strategic theme, 91–93
Strategies
    capability/performance and,
        59–60, 206
    challenge, 328
    charter sample, 241–42
    knowledge, 14–19, 25–26
    knowledge management,
        13–14
    as patterns, 74
Structural capital, 10–12, 25
Structured community of practice,
        36–37, 38, 87–89

Success criteria, 111–14
  acceptance/support, 113
  community building, 111–13
  mechanics, 113–14
Supported community of practice,
      36–37, 38, 87–89
Surveys, 214–16, 294–99
Synthesizers, 43

Tacit knowledge, 16–17, 44, 65,
      66–67
Tactical framework, 119
Tangible assets, 3, 4
Technology
  connectivity and, 141, 206, 207
  development cycle, 99–100
  evolution, 322
  impact, 55–59
  leveraging, 101
  platforms, 46, 99–101, 108
  travel and, 101
Technology infrastructure, 46–47
  blending, 89–90
  choosing, 149
  components, 84–89
  conversations and, 84–85, 88
  customized, 157
  effective, 108
  establishing, 154, 156–57
  flexibility, 87–89
  key challenge, 84
  knowledge access and, 16, 81,
      86–87
  knowledge strategy and, 14, 15,
      18–19
  participation and, 85 86
  process model, 126
  process review, 223
  qualities of, 88–89
  service agreement, 157

vendors, partnering with, 101–5
in your organization, 116–17,
      171–72
  See also Web tools
Tenure, 211
Toolkit, quick-start, 333–54
Tools. See Web tools
Training. See Online training
Transformation stage, 48
Travel, 101
Trust, 85, 107
  confidentiality and, 193–95
  project definition and, 151
  in your organization, 117, 316
Turnover, 211

User support
  determining, 349–51
  establishing, 154
  guide, 159
  technical issues, 157
  See also Online training

Value
  assessing, 25, 183–88, 199,
      209–10, 280–82
  creating, 151, 224
  knowledge management, 30–31
  networks, 55–59
  as structural capital, 25
Value proposition, 9
  capabilities and, 22
  Clarica's measurement of,
      213–23
  communication and, 189,
      191–92
  enhancing, 14
  example, 213–23
  measuring, 210–13
  networks and, 55–59

Value proposition *(cont'd.)*
  new, 322–23
  organization goals and, 210–11
  in your organization, 52, 226
Vendors
  feedback, 186
  partnering with, 101–5
  relationships, 172
Virtual meetings, 89–90
Vulnerability, 222

Web tools
  branding, 157
  components, 83–89

development cycle, 99–101
expectations, 191
limitations, 191
literacy, 177, 181
membership and, 189, 191
project approach and, 149
readiness, 166
training, 135–36, 154, 159–60,
    254–57, 282–92, 349–51
See also Technology
    infrastructure
Wenger, Etienne, 12, 34
Witnesses, 43
Workforces, knowledgeable, 8–9

ABOUT THE AUTHORS

HUBERT SAINT-ONGE
STRATEGIC CAPABILITIES
PRACTITIONER

Hubert Saint-Onge is the Chief Executive Officer of Konverge Digital Solutions Corp., a Toronto-based firm of practitioners that implements fully integrated knowledge strategies based on optimized business processes and custom technology solutions. He is cross-appointed to the role of Executive Vice-President at the parent company S.A. Armstrong Limited, a global manufacturer of fluid engineered products, where he oversees the activities of developing the strategic capabilities of the firm as well as overall e-business strategy.

For over a decade, Hubert has been refining a model known as the Knowledge Assets Framework for the strategic integration of business plans with people management systems, using technology architecture and organizational infrastructure. Hubert is a respected advisor to Fortune 500 companies and is widely recognized as a leading practitioner in the field of knowledge management. Formerly Senior Vice-President of Strategic Capabilities at Clarica Life Insurance Company and Vice-President, Learning Organization and Leadership Development for the Canadian Imperial Bank of Commerce (CIBC), Hubert has been lauded in the international community for his innovative thinking and leadership skills. Hubert is currently Executive in Residence in the Centre for Business, Entrepreneurship and Technology (CBET) at the University of Waterloo.

In his previous role at Clarica, one of the key elements of his mandate was to facilitate the leveraging of the firm's business through the systematic application of knowledge management and learning organization principles. The success of this initiative has been proven. He was instrumental in developing the Clarica brand, which contributed directly to Clarica's three-fold market capitalization prior to its recent merger with Sun Life Financial.

Hubert has developed a comprehensive strategy for building capability through knowledge. This has lead to the implementation of a socio-technical approach where people and technology are brought together in a new organizational configuration. In addition, he has led corporate-wide exercises to define the values and the vision of the firm with the purpose of renewing the development of the organizational culture. This is achieved in complete alignment with the firm's strategic framework.

A decade earlier, his role at CIBC was to support the accelerated development of the capabilities the organization required to achieve its business strategies. To achieve this, Hubert developed the CIBC Leadership Centre from concept to reality and ran it for five years. Hubert and his team at the Centre created an integrated set of programs and tools aimed at changing the culture of the organization and at building the strategic focus, commitment and capabilities of people at CIBC. The Centre's approach was designed based on the principles of the learning organization and the practice of knowledge management for innovation. This work was originally featured in a *Fortune* article as a prime example of how to accelerate organizational learning.

Hubert holds an Honours BA in Political Science from York University and an MA in Political Science with specialization in international economic integration. He was on the Board of the Canadian Centre for Management Development from 1995–1999. Although first and foremost an in-company practitioner, Hubert has given presentations across North America and Europe on organization learning, leadership development, and knowledge value creation. He has published a number of articles on these subjects.

DEBRA WALLACE
CONSULTANT
KNOWLEDGE AND LEARNING
STRATEGY DEVELOPMENT
SUN LIFE FINANCIAL CANADA

Debra is responsible for developing a knowledge and learning strategy for the newly combined Sun Life Financial and Clarica Life Insurance organizations. She manages the process of creating a knowledge and learning blueprint based on foundation elements of strategic imperatives, culture and values, and technology. Working at the enterprise level, she consults with business units to ensure alignment with corporate imperatives, technology directions, and industry standards to provide state-of-the-art knowledge sharing and learning solutions that increase individual and organizational capabilities.

Prior to her current role, Debra was the Project Manager and Community Facilitator for the Agent Network, a community of practice for Clarica agents Canada-wide. She was responsible for the community project design and implementation, the evaluation of the initial phase of the project, the facilitation of the online discussion forum, and the development of a process model and best practice case study.

Debra arrived at Clarica's Knowledge Team with a wide range of experience in libraries, public education (K–post secondary), and the private sector. As Assistant to the Dean for Knowledge Management Initiatives at the Faculty of Information Studies, University of Toronto, Debra developed and implemented new programs that linked information and knowledge management with creating competitive advantages for government and private sector organizations. It was in that capacity that she met Hubert Saint-Onge and began applying her research background to practice at Clarica.

A frequent speaker and lecturer on the benefits of "knowing what you know," Debra co-authored a chapter on communities of practice in *In Action: Measuring Intellectual Capital* (ASTD 2002) and continues the writing partnership with Hubert Saint-Onge in this book.

Debra holds a Bachelor of Science (cum laude) from Moorhead State University, a Masters in Education from the University of Manitoba, and a Ph.D. from the University of Toronto. Her dissertation research focused on the creation of a curriculum development model for professional schools in higher education.